£7.99

Elizabethan Poetry: Lyrical and Narrative

A CASEBOOK

EDITED BY

GERALD HAMMOND

M

MACMILLAN

First published 1984 by
Higher and Further Education Division
MACMILLAN PUBLISHERS LTD
London and Basingstoke
Companies and representatives throughout the world

Typeset by Wessex Typesetters Ltd, Frome, Somerset

Printed in Hong Kong

British Library Cataloguing in Publication Data
Elizabethan poetry.—(Casebook series)
  1. English poetry—Early modern, 1500–1700—
History and criticism
  I. Hammond, Gerald, *1945–* II. Series
821'.3'09   PR531
ISBN 0–333–28971–4
ISBN 0–333–28972–2 Pbk

FOR
FAYAZ AND MARYAM

CONTENTS

GENERAL EDITOR'S PREFACE

The Casebook series, launched in 1968, has become a well-regarded library of critical studies. The central concern of the series remains the 'single-author' volume, but suggestions from the academic community have led to an extension of the original plan, to include occasional volumes on such general themes as literary 'schools' and genres.

Each volume in the central category deals either with one well-known and influential work by an individual author, or with closely related works by one writer. The main section consists of critical readings, mostly modern, collected from books and journals. A selection of reviews and comments by the author's contemporaries is also included, and sometimes comment from the author himself. The Editor's Introduction charts the reputation of the work or works from the first appearance to the present time.

Volumes in the 'general themes' category are variable in structure but follow the basic purpose of the series in presenting an integrated selection of readings, with an Introduction which explores the theme and discusses the literary and critical issues involved.

A single volume can represent no more than a small selection of critical opinions. Some critics are excluded for reasons of space, and it is hoped that readers will pursue the suggestions for further reading in the Select Bibliography. Other contributions are severed from their original context, to which some readers may wish to turn. Indeed, if they take a hint from the critics represented here, they certainly will.

A. E. DYSON

INTRODUCTION

In the final essay in this book, Philip Hobsbaum begins by lamenting the cloud which has hung over Elizabethan poetry for generations. I do not entirely agree with him, and one purpose of the modern part of the collection is to show how lively and varied twentieth-century critical writing on Elizabethan poetry has been. But his next point is surely right: that for too long students have been taught to believe that Elizabethan poetry is a waste land, transformed into a blooming garden only by the daring innovations of John Donne and his Metaphysical followers. This assertion is seldom questioned, with the consequence that two generations of some of the finest poetry written in English is left unread, and dismissed with the epithet 'Petrarchan'.

Unread perhaps, but not unheard. The Elizabethan lyric lives in a way denied to the poetry of other ages, in the songs of the dramatists. From the song of Winter in *Love's Labour's Lost*, with greasy Joan and Marion's red, raw nose, to Ariel's 'Where the Bee Sucks', we do not need an acute critical perception to sense that Shakespeare's songs are elements of a vast body of verse, for which 'Petrarchan' would clearly be a most inappropriate word. How one should describe Elizabethan verse is a matter much in the minds of the critics in the selection of modern essays here, not from the mere desire to classify, but in order to help us understand the paradox of much Elizabethan lyric and narrative poetry: that its most powerful effects come from its being, at the same time, simple and contrived.

'Simple and contrived' is my formulation of the two poles between which Elizabethan poetry moves; but if it were so easy to describe, then there would scarcely have been a need for the subtlety and precision which modern criticism has brought to its treatment of the period's poetry. The basic lines of approach were laid down by Yvor Winters and C. S. Lewis. In a series of essays in the periodical *Poetry* in 1939 Winters gave the Elizabethan lyric a complete revaluation. He saw two distinct schools of sixteenth-century poetry. One, 'almost wholly neglected and forgotten', was a kind whose theme was 'usually broad, simple, and obvious' but 'of some importance', with feeling and rhetoric 'restrained to the minimum required by the subject'. Opposed to these 'plain' poets – and the adversarial sense does not misrepresent the tone of Winters's essay – were the Petrarchan poets, those immersed in 'the pleasures of rhetoric for its own sake', and, furthermore, those who, through the perverse standards of literary history, have come to be the only Elizabethan poets known and read. The essay is a polemic for a change of critical emphasis, so that we might rediscover those poets who, in their plainness, contributed most to the native English tradition, and drew most strongly from it.

Equally influential was C. S. Lewis's division of sixteenth-century poetry into 'drab' and 'golden', in his *English Literature in the Sixteenth Century Excluding Drama*, in the 'Oxford History of English Literature' series. Not published until 1953, but based on his 1944 Clark Lectures, Lewis's book was a restatement and strengthening of the traditional way of looking at sixteenth-century poetry. 'Drab' and 'golden' were principally neutral, chronological terms, but it is clear from the development of Lewis's account that their qualitative implications are unavoidable. 'Drab' describes the poetry of the first three-quarters of the century: flat, plain, tedious hackwork, with no development, but rather a decline from the poets of Henry VIII's court. 'Golden' describes the miraculous upsurge led by Sidney and Spenser in the 1570s and 80s: a poetry of essential innocence, melodic, and rich in its vocabulary.

These opposing views of Winters and Lewis have proved to be powerful determinants of the criticism of the last three decades, and a number of essays in this collection show the effect, implicit or explicit, which they have had. (See, in particular, the pieces by Southall, Nathan and Hobsbaum in Part Three, below.) Something of their usefulness and limitations will appear if we look at a poem probably by Sir Edward Dyer, first published in *A Poetical Rhapsody* in 1602, but probably written shortly after 1580[1]:

> The lowest trees haue topps, the ante her gall,
> The flie her spleene, the little sparke his heat:
> The slender hears cast shadows, though but small,
> And bees haue stinges, although they be not great;
> > Seas haue their sourse, and soe haue shallow springes:
> > And Loue is Loue, in beggers and in Kinges.
>
> Wher waters smothest ronne, ther deepest are the foords,
> The diall stirrs, yet none perceiues it moue;
> The firmest fayth is fownd in fewest woordes;
> The turtles doe not singe, and yet they loue;
> > True heartes haue ears and eyes, no tongues to speake:
> > They heare and see, and sigh, and then they breake.

Winters would probably call this a plain poem, and Lewis a drab one, the first in praise, the second in censure. Certainly Lewis's brief comments on Dyer are damning. He describes him as 'an almost purely Drab writer . . . best when least gnomic . . . most of his poetry may have been old when the great age began' (p. 468). For Winters, however, this is surely the kind of poem which does what the best sixteenth-century lyrics do: combine 'matter-of-factness with passion'. Through ten lines of transparently plain fact it develops to an unexpectedly passionate final couplet, whose syntax, with its four 'ands', leads inexorably to the broken heart. And yet this is an highly rhetorical poem; indeed, uncharitable readers could be forgiven for describing it as a mere exercise in rhetoric as they get into the second stanza. Its forms are those we might associate with the excessive rhetoric of euphuistic prose: repetition, accumulation and sententiousness[2] – so much so, that it seems at the beginning to be the very stuff of parody. Without much difficulty one could imagine an alternative poem which began 'The tallest trees have tops', and whose sentious aim was to chide earthly ambition. Winters holds up for admiration the proverbial nature of 'plain' poetry, but he tends to divorce it from the arts of rhetoric. Lewis scorns Dyer at his most gnomic, yet this, his most gnomic poem, is also his most passionate.

This is not to say that Winters and Lewis are wrong, only that it is in the nature of Elizabethan poetry to demand and then defy critical polarisations. If we remember that Dyer's poem was written principally as a song, then we get a further example of this complexity, for, in both the sweetness of its sound and its developing theme, it promises to be an embodiment of, and argument for, the right of everything, no matter how little, to be perceived and recognised. But it ends in praise of silence – or the nearest thing to silence, the sigh which precedes the heart's breaking. Here the poles are the articulacy of everything in the universe, and the complete inarticulation of the firmest faith. It is, at the same time, advocation for the need to write and a statement of the futility of writing – a theme taken up, and developed notably in Shakespeare's sonnets.[3] One implication of Dyer's and Shakespeare's poems is that the simplicity of silence is truer than the contrivance of poetry, for all organised expression is a form of indirection, if not the actual telling of lies.

Hence arose the great theoretical interest in the nature and purpose of poetry, as exemplified in the various defences and apologies published in the last quarter of the sixteenth century, the most

notable of which are represented in the contemporary comment
section (Part One) of this Casebook.

My selection begins with two revealing pieces written at the very
beginning of Elizabeth's reign, from what were probably the most
widely read of all sixteenth-century books of poetry. The first is
Richard Tottel's preface to his *Miscellany* (also entitled *Songes and
Sonnettes*, at its first appearance in 1557); the second is an extract from
the *Mirror for Magistrates* (1563). The vital importance of Tottel's
Miscellany to the development of Elizabethan poetry lay in its making
public what had hitherto been private. This is the gist of Tottel's brief
preface, whose tone is aggressively defensive as he celebrates his
volume's unlocking of the long hoarded treasure, but anticipates the
opposition this might meet from the swinelike multitude. This 'stigma
of print', as one writer has termed it, lasted through Elizabeth's reign.
It explains, for instance, the 'probablys' which I had to use in
introducing Dyer's poem, for like many Elizabethan courtiers and
men of the world who happened to be poets, Dyer had virtually
nothing he wrote published in his lifetime. It is as if the setting of the
poem in print gave it an existence which it did not deserve. As a song,
or ink on a manuscript, it remained ephemeral, with no claim to
substance. But once it had become public property the poem made
the poet vulnerable, not least to the charge of untruth, the stink of lies
which not all the marjoram in the world could remove.

The other danger of print was that it exposed one to the charge of
sedition. The *Mirror for Magistrates*, compiled in the reigns of Henry
VIII and Bloody Mary, was published in the year after Mary's death
(1559), with an enlarged edition in 1563. It set the pattern for much of
the politico-historical verse and drama of the sixteenth century. It was
as one might expect, determinedly supportive of Tudor concepts of
authority – it could hardly have seen the light of day otherwise – but in
the narrative of the poet Collingbourne, from which my brief extract
is taken, its writers show how aware they are of the dangers of writing
poetry in a police state. Collingbourne, a poet in the reign of Richard
III, wrote a riddle to which everyone knew the answer:

> The Cat, the Rat, and Lovel our Dog,
> Do rule al England, vnder a Hog.[4]

The cat was Catesby, the rat Ratcliffe, the dog Lord Lovell, and the
hog Richard himself. For this Collingbourne was hanged up,

disembowelled while alive, and then had his heart ripped out, leaving lessons to be absorbed about the need for indirectness in poetry.

The later sixteenth-century extracts are more refined as the poet-theorists consider increasingly sophisticated defences of poetic contrivance. George Gascoigne, in the first of his *Notes of Instruction* (1575), emphasises the importance of 'invention' – the passage I have excerpted is described by C. S. Lewis as one 'which should be constantly borne in mind as a prophylactic against that continual slight misinterpretation of the Elizabethans to which our own austerer tastes incessantly tempt us' (p. 271), for it shows a poetic commitment, shared by drab, golden, and Metaphysical poets alike, 'which is the direct opposite of Wordsworthianism, naturalism, or expressionism'. Sidney's *Apologie* (c. 1583) asserts the greater claim to truth which poetic contrivance has over history, philosophy, and even nature itself; and by the end of the century Campion and Daniel are involved in a debate on the need for rhyme in poetry. But even such an apparently rarefied matter has its roots in the idea of being truthful and being false. For Campion, rhyme forces the poet into barbarisms, stretching or contracting what he needs to say so that it is no longer true. For Daniel, however, to attack rhyme is to attack the whole poetic achievement of the century, and to deny its obvious claim to have created something of great substance.

In the next two centuries the taste for Elizabethan poetry became an increasingly antiquarian phenomenon. (This, and the later Romantic revival of approbation, are outlined in Part Two, below.) Through the first half of the seventeenth century the extreme development of the Metaphysical conceit meant that the surviving Elizabethans – poets as different as Michael Drayton and Robert Herrick – appeared increasingly old-fashioned. Where Elizabethan poetry did survive, gloriously, was in the poetry of the young Milton, in 'L'Allegro', 'Il Penseroso', 'Arcades' and *Comus*. But by the second half of the century critics needed to make special pleading for their readers to keep in touch with Elizabethan achievement; and the extract from Edward Phillips, Milton's nephew, is revealing in its argument that readers should make an effort to overcome the barriers in taste and refinement between them and the Elizabethans. The nadir in appreciation of Elizabethan poetry came in the early eighteenth century, in Addison's sneering at Sidney's *Apologie*. Where Sidney had argued that the barbarousness of the old ballad made it difficult to appreciate in the new refinement of the sixteenth century, Addison turned this round, and in a presentiment of the growing taste for the medieval and gothic, he found in the old ballad a majesty and sonority which Elizabethan poetry lacked.

Still, not all eighteenth-century critics were so disdainful. The number of quotations from Elizabethan poets in Samuel Johnson's Dictionary shows him to have read widely among them; and Thomas Warton's *History of English Poetry* (1781) treated their poetry with scrupulous care. The extract from the *History* given here shows Warton first moving tentatively towards an appreciation of the freedom and individuality of Elizabethan poets, and then explaining to his readers the context of the love poetry of the period. His judgement that this was an age 'propitious to the operations of original and true poetry . . . when genius was rather directed than governed by judgement' held a tacit recognition of what was missing in eighteenth-century poetry, but had been present in Elizabethan times.

This recognition, as we would expect, was made explicit by the Romantic poets: and one can see here Coleridge and Keats responding to the strengths of Elizabethan poetry. The rest of the nineteenth century was a time of consolidation, as editors like Alexander Grosart and Edward Arber, and critics like George Saintsbury, gradually recovered the texts of Elizabethan poetry and made them accessible to a general readership. By the end of the nineteenth century there were in print editions not only of the better known, but hitherto neglected poets – such as Campion, Chapman, Daniel, Drayton, Gascoigne, Greville and Ralegh – but also of a host of lesser known poets, including Richard Barfield, Nicholas Breton, Thomas Churchyard, Henry Constable, Sir John Davies, Giles Fletcher, Barnaby Googe, Joseph Hall, Thomas Howell, Thomas Lodge, John Marston, the Earl of Oxford, George Peele, Robert Southwell, Richard Stanyhurst, George Turberville and Thomas Watson. These editions may not be noted for their accuracy, but in many cases they remain the standard texts from which the modern anthologies are compiled, and by which modern readers approach Elizabethan poetry.

Twentieth-century criticism has built on the insights of the Romantics by attempting to describe and define the peculiarly powerful effect Elizabethan poetry has on us. In the case of the songs in Shakespeare's plays this seems not too difficult, because we can fall back on the argument from their dramatic context: that even when read and heard outside the play, it is the memory of their performance in it which makes them so moving. But when modern criticism turns away from the play songs to, say, the poem by Dyer which I looked at earlier, then it meets its greatest challenge. It needs to show how and why a man who was only incidentally a poet could produce a line like 'They heare and see, and sigh, and then they breake'; and how such a line could so easily be written then, but would be impossible in a poem of today. In the first extracts in the modern section (Part Three), from T. S. Eliot, William Empson, Ezra Pound and Yvor Winters, we can see the greatest of the twentieth-century poet-critics reaching for ways of describing what they perceive as a quality of individual poets and of the whole culture. For Eliot, it is 'a quality of sensuous thought . . . thinking through the senses'; for Empson, it is the strength of the language which will bring to life apparently dead metaphors; while for Pound, it lies in a capacity to be 'careless as to which profound and fundamental idea you, at that moment, utter'; and for Winters, it is that 'combination of matter-of-factness with passion'.

The later pieces are chosen to illustrate the variety of ways in which the best criticism engages with Elizabethan poetry. As I have said, the challenges are great. To take one example, the modern critic has to grapple with problems of authorship more complex than those which face critics of later periods. That poem by Dyer may not, after all, be by him. Only one of its manuscript versions assigns it to him, and at least one other gives it to Sir Walter Ralegh. And even then, to gain any sense of Dyer's poetic personality is nearly impossible. His editor attributes a total of only fourteen poems to him, acknowledging that the evidence for his authorship is in many cases slight; while an Elizabethan collection like *England's Helicon* (1600) attributes to Dyer four poems which are certainly not his. In the case of a minor poet like this, one might say that it does not matter too much, but the problem is greater and the matter more important when we try to construct a poetic corpus for a figure like Ralegh. It is impossible to say for certain that any more than a handful of poems are definitely his; and it is quite defensible, and often attempted, to question his authorship of 'The Passionate Man's Pilgrimage', 'The Lie', 'The Nymph's Reply to the Shepherd', and 'As You Came from the Holy Land'. The hoard which

Tottel began to reveal is open to our eyes, but we have the same difficulty he had in knowing whom it belongs to.

It is partly for this reason that modern criticism of Elizabethan poetry concentrates less on authors and more on such matters as genre, style and structure; and most of the essays excerpted here reflect this. James McPeek traces the way a variety of poems translate and adapt a classical original, in this case Catullus's Carmen v. Rosemond Tuve shows how Elizabethan poets shared a common rhetoric which influenced the way they framed argument and image: an approach whose influence can be seen strongly at work in Leonard Nathan's essay on George Gascoigne and the Elizabethan lyric, and in Alastair Fowler's examination of Elizabethan conceits. The need to consider the musical context of much Elizabethan poetry is reflected in two of the pieces here, as first Hallett Smith and then John Hollander consider the poetry of Thomas Campion. Then the relation of the poetry to Renaissance artistic and architectural movements is represented by Wylie Sypher's study of artistic effects in Spenser's poetry.

Historical contextualising is important too. One way in which much Elizabethan poetry may be seen as a form of decline, a falling off from the great achievements of the early Tudor poets, is shown in Raymond Southall's essay. Like many of the pieces here, it suffers a little from being wrenched from its context as part of a carefully developed argument – in this case it is from the final chapter of a study of early Tudor court poetry. In contrast, Arthur E. Barker looks at Renaissance poetry through the other end of the telescope, by considering the importance of its historical study for readers and students in the second half of this century. Then, the essays of G. K. Hunter and Philip Hobsbaum continue the tradition of Winters and C. S. Lewis, of critics intent, in Hunter's words, on showing 'the relation of good poems of a period to one another'.

Finally, we should recognise that Elizabethan poetry has played a major part in the more general movements of literary theory: Coleridge's piece on Shakespeare's narrative poems in the *Biographia* (Part Two, below) is an early example of this. Three pieces in Part Three come from outstanding theoretical critics of this century, and show them using Elizabethan poems to explore poetic structure. I. A. Richards (Coleridge's successor as practical critic[5]), gives a close reading of Shakespeare's 'The Phoenix and the Turtle'; Donald

Davie's study of Sackville's contribution to the *Mirror for Magistrates* comes from his fascinating study of poetic syntax; and Barbara Herrnstein Smith, as part of her analysis of the way poems end, uses a poem which first appeared in Tottel's *Miscellany*.

NOTES

1. From *The Life and Lyrics of Sir Edward Dyer*, by Ralph M. Sargent (Oxford, 1968: originally published in 1935, under the title *At the Court of Queen Elizabeth*), p. 197.

2. Indeed its opening lines occur, virtually word for word, in Lyly's *Euphues and his England*: 'Low trees haue their tops, small sparkes their heat, the Fly his splene, the Ant his gall . . .'; and later in *Euphues* we find 'Nor haire so slender, which hath not his shadowe'.

3. E.g. Sonnets 76, 79, 82, 83, 84, 85, 95, 103 and 115.

4. From Lily B. Campbell (ed.), *The Mirror for Magistrates* (Cambridge, 1938), p. 349.

5. Coleridge uses the phrase 'practical criticism' in the opening sentence of his chapter on *Venus and Adonis* and *The Rape of Lucrece* (see excerpt in Part Two, below).

PART ONE

Contemporary Comment

Richard Tottel (1557)

The Printer to the Reader

That to haue wel written in verse, yea & in small parcelles,[1] deserueth great praise, the workes of diuers Latines, Italians, and other, doe proue sufficiently. That our tong is able in that kynde to do as praiseworthely as the rest, the honorable stile of the noble earle of Surrey, and the weightinesse of the depewitted sir Thomas Wyat the elders verse, with seuerall graces in sondry good Englishe writers, doe show abundantly. It resteth nowe (gentle reder) that thou thinke it not euill doon, to publish, to the honor of the Englishe tong, and for profit of the studious of Englishe eloquence, those workes which the vngentle horders vp of such treasure haue heretofore enuied thee. And for this point (good reder) thine own profit and pleasure, in these presently, and in moe[2] hereafter, shal answere for my defence. If parhappes some mislike the statelinesse of stile remoued from the rude skill of common eares: I aske help of the learned to defend their learned frendes, the authors of this work: And I exhort the vnlearned, by reding to learne to be more skilfull, and to purge that swinelike grossenesse, that maketh the sweet maierome[3] not to smell to their delight.

SOURCE: Preface to *Songes and Sonettes written by the ryght honorable Lorde Henry Haward late Earle of Surrey, and other* (1557) – commonly known as *Tottel's Miscellany*.

EDITOR'S NOTES

1. 'parcelles': i.e. lyric poems.   3. 'maierome': marjoram.
2. 'moe': more.

William Baldwin (?)   (1563)

For he that shal a perfect Poete be,
Must fyrst be bred out of Medusaes blud:
He must be chaste and vertuous as was she,
Who to her power the Ocean god wythstoode.
To thende also his doome be iust and good,
He must (as she had) have one onlye iye,
Regarde of truth, that nought maye leade awrye.

In courage eke[1] he must be like a horse,
He maye not feare to register the ryght.
And that no power or fansie do him force,
No byt nor reyne his tender Iawes may twight.[2]
He must be armed wyth strength of wyt and spryght[3]
To dashe the rockes, darke causes and obscure,
Tyll he attayne the sprynges of truth most pure.

His hooves must also plyant be and strong,
To ryve[4] the rockes of lust and errors blynde,
In brayneles heades, that alway wander wrong:
These must he bryse[5] wyth reasons playne and kinde,
Tyll sprynges of grace do gushe out of the minde.
For tyl affections[6] from the fond[7] be dryven,
In vayne is truth tolde, or good counsayle geuen.

Like Pegasus a Poet must have wynges,
To flye to heaven, thereto to feede and rest:
He must have knoweledge of eternal thynges,
Almighty Ioue must harber in his brest.
With worldly cares he may not be opprest,
The wynges of skyll and hope must heave him hyer,
Than al the ioyes which worldly wyts desyre.

He must be also nymble, free, and swyft
To trauayle farre to viewe the trades of men,
Great knowledge oft is gotten by the shyft:

Thynges notable he must be quicke to pen,
Reprouyng vyces sharpely now and then.
He must be swyft when touched tyrants chafe,
To gallop thence to kepe his carkas safe.

SOURCE: extracts from 'Howe Collingbourne was cruelly executed for making a foolishe rime' (lines 155–89), from *The seconde parte of the Mirrour for Magistrates* (enlarged edition, 1563).

EDITOR'S NOTES

1. 'eke': also.
2. 'twight': pull.
3. 'spryght': spirit.
4. 'ryve': split.

5. 'bryse': bruise.
6. 'affections': irrationality.
7. 'fond': foolish.

George Gascoigne (1575)

. . . The first and most necessarie poynt that euer I founde meete to be considered in making of a delectable poeme is this, to grounde it vpon some fine inuention. For it is not inough to roll in pleasant woordes, not yet to thunder in *Rym, Ram, Ruff* by letter (quoth my master *Chaucer*), nor yet to abounde in apt vocables or epythetes, vnlesse the Inuention haue in it also *aliquid salis.*[1] By this *aliquid salis* I meane some good and fine deuise, shewing the quicke capacitie of a writer: and where I say some *good and fine inuention* I meane that I would haue it both fine and good. For many inuentions are so superfine that they are *Vix good.*[2] And, againe, many Inuentions are good, and yet not finely handled. And for a general forwarning: what Theame soeuer you do take in hande, if you do handle it but *tanquam in oratione perpetua,*[3] and neuer studie for some depth of deuise in the Inuention, and some figures also in the handlyng thereof, it will appeare to the skilfull Reader but a tale of a tubbe. To deliuer vnto you generall examples it were almoste vnpossible, sithence the occasions of Inuentions are (as it were) infinite; neuerthelesse, take in worth mine opinion, and perceyue my furder meanyng in these few poynts. If I should vndertake to wryte in prayse of a gentlewoman, I would neither praise hir christal eye, nor hir cherrie lippe, etc. For these things are *trita et obuia*.[4] But I would either finde some supernaturall cause wherby my penne might walke in the superlatiue degree, or els I would vndertake to aunswere for any imperfection that shee hath, and therevpon rayse the prayse of hir commendacion. Likewise, if I should disclose my pretence in loue, I would eyther make a strange discourse of some intollerable passion, or finde occasion to pleade by the example of some historie, or discouer my disquiet in shadowes *per Allegoriam*, or vse the couertest meane that I could to auoyde the vncomely customes of common writers. Thus much I aduenture to deliuer vnto you (my freend) vpon the rule of Inuention, which of all other rules is most to be marked, and hardest to be prescribed in certayne and infallible rules; neuerthelesse, to conclude therein, I would haue you stand most vpon the excellencie of your Inuention, and sticke not to studie deepely for some fine deuise. For, that beyng founde, pleasant woordes will follow well inough and fast inough.

SOURCE: extract from *Certain Notes of Instruction Concerning the Making of Verse or Rhyme in English* (1575).

EDITOR'S NOTES

1. *'aliquid salis'*: something salty.   only as a continued narration.
2. *'Vix good'*: hardly good.   4. *'trita et obuia'*: clichéd.
3. *'tanquam in oratione perpetua'*:

Sir Philip Sidney   (c. 1583)

. . . Nature neuer set forth the earth in so rich tapistry as diuers Poets haue done, neither with plesant riuers, fruitful trees, sweet smelling flowers, nor whatsoeuer els may make the too much loued earth more louely. Her world is brasen, the Poets only deliuer a golden. But let those things alone and goe to man, for whom as the other things are, so it seemeth in him her vttermost cunning is imployed, and knowe whether shee haue brought foorth so true a louer as *Theagines*, so

constant a friende as *Pilades*, so valiant a man as *Orlando*, so right a
Prince as *Xenophons Cyrus*, so excellent a man euery way as *Virgils
Aeneas*: neither let this be iestingly conceiued, because the works of the
one be essentiall, the other, in imitation or fiction; for any vnderstanding knoweth the skil of the Artificer standeth in that *Idea* or
fore-conceite of the work, and not in the work it selfe. And that the
Poet hath that *Idea* is manifest, by deliuering them forth in such
excellencie as hee hath imagined them. Which deliuering forth also is
not wholie imaginatiue, as we are wont to say by them that build
Castles in the ayre: but so farre substantially it worketh, not onely to
make a *Cyrus*, which had been but a particuler excellencie, as Nature
might haue done, but to bestow a *Cyrus* vpon the worlde, to make
many *Cyrus's*, if they wil learne aright why and how that Maker made
him. . . .

The Philosopher therfore and the Historian are they which would
win the gole, the one by precept, the other by example. But both not
hauing both, doe both halte.[1] For the Philosopher, setting downe with
thorny arguments the bare rule, is so hard of vtterance, and so mistie
to bee conceiued, that one that hath no other guide but him shall wade
in him til hee be olde before he shall finde sufficient cause to bee
honest: for his knowledge standeth so vpon the abstract and generall,
that happie is that man who may vnderstande him, and more happie
that can applye what hee dooth vnderstand. On the other side, the
Historian, wanting the precept, is so tyed, not to what shoulde bee but
to what is, to the particuler truth of things and not to the general
reason of things, that hys example draweth no necessary consequence, and therefore a lesse fruitfull doctrine.

Nowe dooth the peerelesse Poet performe both: for whatsoeuer the
Philosopher sayth shoulde be doone, hee giueth a perfect picture of it in
some one, by whom hee presupposeth it was doone. So as hee
coupleth the generall notion with the particuler example. A perfect
picture I say, for hee yeeldeth to the powers of the minde an image of
that whereof the Philosopher bestoweth but a woordish description:
which dooth neyther strike, pierce, nor possesse the sight of the soule
so much as that other dooth.

For as in outward things, to a man that had neuer seene an
Elephant or a Rinoceros, who should tell him most exquisitely all
theyr shapes, cullour, bignesse, and perticular markes, or of a

gorgeous Pallace the Architecture, with declaring the full beauties, might well make the hearer able to repeate, as it were by rote, all hee had heard, yet should neuer satisfie his inward conceits with being witnes to it selfe of a true liuely knowledge: but the same man, as soone as hee might see those beasts well painted, or the house wel in moddel, should straightwaies grow, without need of any description, to a iudicial comprehending of them: so no doubt the Philosopher with his learned definitions, bee it of vertue, vices, matters of publick policie or priuat gouernment, replenisheth the memory with many infallible grounds of wisdom, which, notwithstanding, lye darke before the imaginatiue and iudging powre, if they bee not illuminated or figured foorth by the speaking picture of Poesie. . . .

. . . That Poesie, thus embraced in all other places, should onely finde in our time a hard welcome in England, I thinke the very earth lamenteth it, and therfore decketh our Soyle with fewer Laurels then it was accustomed. For heertofore Poets haue in England also florished; and, which is to be noted, euen in those times when the trumpet of *Mars* did sounde loudest. And now that an ouer-faint quietnes should seeme to strew the house for Poets, they are almost in as good reputation as the *Mountibancks* at *Venice*. Truly euen that, as of the one side it giueth great praise to Poesie, which like *Venus* (but to better purpose) hath rather be troubled in the net with *Mars* then enioy the homelie quiet of *Vulcan*; so serues it for a peece of a reason why they are lesse gratefull to idle England, which nowe can scarce endure the payne of a pen. Vpon this necessarily followeth, that base men with seruile wits vndertake it: who think it inough if they can be rewarded of the Printer. And so as *Epaminondas* is sayd, with the honor of his vertue, to haue made an office, by his exercising it, which before was contemptible, to become highly respected; so these, no more but setting their names to it, by their owne disgracefulnes disgrace the most gracefull Poesie. . . .

Other sorts of Poetry almost haue we none, but that Lyricall kind of Songs and Sonnets: which, Lord, if he gaue vs so good mindes, how well it might be imployed, and with howe heauenly fruite, both priuate and publique, in singing the prayses of the immortall beauty, the immortall goodnes of that God who gyueth vs hands to write and wits to conceiue; of which we might well want words, but neuer matter; of which we could turne our eies to nothing, but we should euer haue new budding occasions. But truely many of such writings as come vnder the banner of vnresistable loue, if I were a Mistres, would neuer perswade mee they were in loue; so coldely they apply fiery speeches, as men that had rather red Louers writings, and so caught vp certaine swelling phrases, which hang together like a man which once tolde mee the winde was at North West, and by South, because he would be sure to name windes enowe,[2] – then that in truth they feele those passions, which easily (as I think) may be bewrayed by that same forciblenes, or *Energia* (as the Greekes cal it), of the writer. But let this bee a sufficient though short note, that wee misse the right vse of the materiall point of Poesie. . . .

SOURCE: extracts from *An Apologie for Poetrie* (written c. 1583; printed 1595) – also published with the title *The Defence of Poesie*.

EDITOR'S NOTES

1. 'halte': limp.   2. 'enowe': enough.

George Puttenham   (1589)

The subiect or matter of Poesie.

Hauing sufficiently sayd of the dignitie of Poets and Poesie, now it is tyme to speake of the matter or subiect of Poesie, which to myne intent is, what soeuer wittie and delicate conceit of man meet or worthy to be put in written verse, for any necessary vse of the present time, or good instruction of the posteritie. But the chief and principall is: the laud honour & glory of the immortall gods (I speake now in phrase of the Gentiles.) Secondly the worthy gests[1] of noble Princes: the memoriall and registry of all great fortunes, the praise of vertue & reproofe of vice, the instruction of morall doctrines, the reuealing of sciences naturall & other profitable Arts, the redresse of boistrous & sturdie courages by perswasion, the consolation and repose of temperate myndes, finally the common solace of mankind in all his trauails and cares of this transitorie life. And in this last sort being vsed for recreation onely, may allowably beare matter not alwayes of the grauest, or of any great commoditie or profit, but rather in some sort, vaine, dissolute, or wanton, so it be not very scandalous & of euill example. . . .

How if all maner of sodaine innouations were not very
scandalous, specially in the lawes of any langage or
arte, the vse of the Greeke and Latine feete
might be brought into our vulgar Poesie,
and with good grace inough.[2]

Now neuerthelesse albeit we haue before alledged that our vulgar *Saxon English* standing most vpon wordes *monosillable*, and little vpon *polysillables* doth hardly admit the vse of those fine inuented feete of the Greeks & Latines, and that for the most part wise and graue men doe naturally mislike with all sodaine innouations specially of lawes (and this the law of our auncient English Poesie) and therefore lately before we imputed it to a nice[3] & scholasticall curiositie in such makers as haue sought to bring into our vulgar Poesie some of the auncient feete, to wit the *Dactile* into verses *exameters*, as he that translated certaine bookes of *Virgils Eneydos* in such measures & not vncommendably:[4] if I should now say otherwise it would make me seeme contradictorie to my selfe, yet for the information of our yong makers, and pleasure of all others who be delighted in noueltie, and to th'intent we may not seeme by ignorance or ouersight to omit any point of subtillitie, materiall or necessarie to our vulgar arte, we will in this present chapter & by our own idle obseruations shew how one may easily and commodiously lead all those feete of the auncients into our vulgar langage. And if mens eares were not perchaunce to daintie, or their iudgementes ouer partiall, would peraduenture nothing at all misbecome our arte, but make in our meetres a more pleasant numerositie then now is. Thus farre therefore we will aduenture and not beyond, to th'intent to shew some singularitie in our arte that euery man hath not heretofore obserued, and (her maiesties good liking always had) whether we make the common readers to laugh or to lowre, all is a matter, since our intent is not so exactlie to prosecute the purpose, nor so earnestly, as to thinke it should by authority of our owne iudgement be generally applauded at to the discredit of our forefathers maner of vulgar Poesie, or to the alteration or peraduenture totall destruction of the same, which could not stand with any good discretion or curtesie in vs to attempt, but thus much I say, that by some leasurable trauell it were no hard matter to induce all their auncient feete into vse with vs, and that it should proue very agreable to the eare and well according with our ordinary times and pronunciation, which no man could then iustly mislike, and that is to allow euery word *polisillable* one long time of necessitie, which should be where his sharpe accent falls in our owne *ydiome* moft aptly and naturally, wherein we would not follow the licence of the Greeks and Latines, who made not their sharpe accent any necessary prolongation of their times, but vsed such sillable sometimes long sometimes short at their pleasure. . . .

Of Ornament Poeticall.

As no doubt the good proportion of any thing doth greatly adorne and commend it and right so our late remembred proportions doe to our vulgar Poesie: so is there yet requisite to the perfection of this arte, another maner of exornation, which resteth in the fashioning of our makers language and stile, to such purpose as it may delight and allure as well the mynde as the eare of the hearers with a certaine noueltie and strange maner of conueyance, disguising it no litle from the ordinary and accustomed: neuerthelesse making it nothing the more vnseemely or misbecomming, but rather decenter and more agreable to any ciuill eare and vnderstanding. And as we see in these great Madames of honour, be they for personage or otherwise neuer so comely and bewtifull, yet if they want their courtly habillements or at leastwise such other apparell as custome and ciuilitie haue ordained to couer their naked bodies, would be halfe ashamed or greatly out of countenaunce to be seen in that sort, and perchance do then thinke themselues more amiable in euery mans eye, when they be in their richest attire, suppose of silkes or tyssewes & costly embroideries, then when they go in cloth or in any other plaine and simple apparell. Euen so cannot our vulgar Poesie shew it selfe either gallant or gorgious, if any lymme be left naked and bare and not clad in his kindly clothes and coulours, such as may conuey them somwhat out of sight, that is from the common course of ordinary speach and capacitie of the vulgar iudgement, and yet being artificially handled must needes yeld it much more bewtie and commendation. This ornament we speake of is giuen to it by figures and figuratiue speaches, which be the flowers as it were and coulours that a Poet setteth vpon his language by arte, as the embroderer doth his stone and perle, or passements[5] of gold vpon the stuffe of a Princely garment, or as th'excellent painter bestoweth the rich Orient coulours vpon his table of pourtraite: so neuerthelesse as if the same coulours in our arte of Poesie (as well as in those other mechanicall artes) be not well tempered, or not well layd, or be vsed in excesse, or neuer so litle disordered or misplaced, they not onely giue it no maner of grace at all, but rather do disfigure the stuffe and spill the whole workmanship taking away all bewtie and good liking from it, no lesse then if the crimson tainte, which should be laid vpon a Ladies lips, or right in the center of her cheekes should by some ouersight or mishap be applied to her forhead or chinne, it would make (ye would say) but a very ridiculous bewtie, wherfore the chief prayse and cunning of our Poet is in the discreet vsing of his figures, as the skilfull painters is in the good conueyance of his coulours and shadowing traits of his pensill, with a delectable varietie, by all measure and iust proportion, and in places most aptly to be bestowed. . . .

Of Figures and figuratiue speaches.

As figures be the instruments of ornament in euery language, so be they also in a sorte abuses or rather trespasses in speach, because they passe the ordinary limits of common vtterance, and be occupied of purpose to deceiue the eare and also the minde, drawing it from plainnesse and simplicitie to a certaine doublenesse, whereby our talke is the more guilefull & abusing, for what els is your *Metaphor* but an inuersion of sence by transport; your *allegorie* by a duplicitie of meaning or dissimulation vnder couert and darke intendments: one while speaking obscurely and in riddle called *Ænigma*: another while by common prouerbe or Adage called *Paremia*: then by merry skoffe called *Ironia*: then by bitter tawnt called *Sarcasmus*: then by periphrase or circumlocution when all might be said in a word or two: then by incredible comparison giuing credit, as by your *Hyperbole*, and many other waies seeking to inueigle and appassionate the mind: which thing made the graue iudges *Areopagites* (as I find written) to forbid all manner of figuratiue speaches to be vsed before them in their consistorie of Iustice, as meere illusions to the minde, and wresters of vpright iudgement, saying that to allow such manner of forraine & coulored talke to make the iudges affectioned, were all one as if the carpenter before he began to square his timber would make his squire crooked: in so much as the straite and vpright mind of a Iudge is the very rule of iustice till it be peruerted by affection. This no doubt is true and was by them grauely considered: but in this case because our maker or Poet is appointed not for a iudge, but rather for a pleader, and that of pleasant & louely causes and nothing perillous, such as be those for the triall of life, limme, or liuelyhood; and before iudges neither sower nor seuere, but in the eare of princely dames, yong ladies, gentlewomen and courtiers, beyng all for the most part either meeke of nature, or of pleasant humour, and that all his abuses tende but to dispose the hearers to mirth and sollace by pleasant conueyance and efficacy of speech, they are not in truth to be accompted vices but for vertues in the poetical science very commendable. On the other side, such trespasses in speach (whereof there be many) as geue dolour and disliking to the eare & minde, by any foule indecencie or disproportion of sound, situation, or sence, they be called and not without cause the vicious parts or rather heresies of language: wherefore the matter resteth much in the definition and acceptance of this word [*decorum*] for whatsoeuer is so, cannot iustly be misliked. In which respect it may come to passe that what the Grammarian setteth downe for a viciositee in speach may become a vertue and no vice, contrariwise his commended figure may fall into a reprochfull fault: the best and most assured remedy whereof is, generally to follow the saying of *Bias: ne quid nimis.*[6] So as in keeping measure, and not exceeding nor shewing any defect in the vse of his figures, he cannot lightly do amisse, if he haue besides (as that must needes be) a speciall regard to all circumstances of the person, place, time, cause and purpose he hath in hand, which being well obserued it easily auoideth all the recited inconueniences, and maketh now and then very vice goe for a formall vertue in the exercise of this Arte. . . .

SOURCE: extracts from *The Arte of English Poesie* (1589).
The first extract is from Book I, 'Of Poets and Poesie', the second from Book II, 'Of Proportion', and the third and fourth from Book III, 'Of Ornament'.

1. 'gests': tales.

2. For further discussion of the use of classical metres in English verse, see Campion and Daniel (Part One, below), Saintsbury (Part Two) and Eliot (Part Three).

3. 'nice': precise.

4. I.e., Richard Stanyhurst; see below Saintsbury (Part Two) and Hobsbaum (Part Three).

5. 'passements': trimmings.

6. 'ne quid nimis': nothing in excess.

Sir John Harington (1591)

... *Cornelius Agrippa*, a man of learning & authoritie not to be despised, maketh a bitter inuectiue against Poets and Poesie, and the summe of his reproofe of it is this (which is al that can with any probability be said against it), that it is a nurse of lies, a pleaser of fooles, a breeder of dangerous errors, and an inticer to wantonnes. I might here warne those that wil vrge this mans authoritie to the disgrace of Poetrie, to take heed (of what calling so euer they be) least with the same weapon that they thinke to giue Poetrie a blow they giue themselues a maime. For *Agrippa* taketh his pleasure of greater matters then Poetrie; I maruel how he durst do it, saue that I see he hath done it; he hath spared neither myters nor scepters. The courts of Princes where vertue is rewarded, iustice maintained, oppressions relieued, he cals them a Colledge of Giants, of Tyrants, of oppressors, warriors: the most noble sort of noble men he termeth cursed, bloodie, wicked, and sacrilegious persons. Noble men (and vs poore Gentlemen) that thinke to borrow praise of our auncestors deserts and good fame, he affirmed to be a race of the sturdier sort of knaues and lycencious liuers. Treasurers & other great officers of the common welth, with graue counsellors whose wise heads are the pillers of the state, he affirmeth generally to be robbers and peelers[1] of the realme, and priuie traitors that sell their princes fauours and rob weldeseruing seruitors of their reward. I omit, as his *peccadilia*, how he nicknameth priests, saying for the most part they are hypocrites, lawyers, saying they are all theeues, phisicians, saying they are manie of them murtherers: so as I thinke it were a good motion, and would easily passe by the consent of the three estates, that this mans authoritie should be vtterly adnihilated, that dealeth so hardly and vniustly with all sorts of professions. But for the reiecting of his writings, I refer it to others that haue powre to do it, and to condemne him for a generall libeller; but for that he writeth against Poetrie, I meane to speake a word or two in refuting thereof.

And first for lying, I might if I list excuse it by the rule of *Poetica licentia*, and claime a priuiledge giuen to Poet[s], whose art is but an imitation (as *Aristotle* calleth it), & therefore are allowed to faine what they list, according to that old verse, . . . which, because I count it without reason, I will English without rime.

> Lawyers, Hell, and the Checquer are allowed to liue on spoile;
> Souldiers, Phisicians, and Hangmen make a sport of murther;
> Astronomers, Painters, and Poets may lye by authoritie.

Thus you see that Poets may lye if they list *Cum priuelegio*.[2] But what if they lye least of all other men? what if they lye not at all? then I thinke that great slaunder is verie vniustly raised upon them. For in my opinion they are said properly to lye that affirme that to be true that is false: and how other arts can free themselues from this blame, let them look that professe them: but Poets neuer affirming any for true, but presenting them to vs as fables and imitations, cannot lye though they would.[3] . . .

SOURCE: extract from *A Preface, or rather a Briefe Apologie of Poetrie* . . ., prefixed to Harington's translation of *Orlando Furiose* (1581).

1. 'peelers': plunderers.
2. '*Cum priuelegio*': with privilege, i.e., by royal authority.
3. I.e., even if they wanted to.

Thomas Campion (1602)

THE SECOND CHAPTER, DECLARING THE VNAPTNESSE OF RIME IN POESIE.

I am not ignorant that whosoeuer shall by way of reprehension examine the imperfections of Rime must encounter with many glorious enemies, and those very expert and ready at their weapon, that can if neede be extempore (as they say) rime a man to death. Besides there is growne a kind of prescription in the vse of Rime, to forestall the right of true numbers, as also the consent of many nations, against all which it may seeme a thing almost impossible and vaine to contend. All this and more can not yet deterre me from a lawful defence of perfection, or make me any whit the sooner adheare to that which is lame and vnbeseeming. For custome I alleage that ill vses are to be abolisht, and that things naturally imperfect can not be perfected by vse. Old customes, if they be better, why should they not be recald, as the yet florishing custome of numerous poesy[1] vsed among the *Romanes* and *Grecians*? But the vnaptnes of our toongs and the difficultie of imitation dishartens vs: againe, the facilitie and popularitie of Rime creates as many Poets as a hot sommer flies.

But let me now examine the nature of that which we call Rime. By Rime is vnderstoode that which ends in the like sound, so that verses in such maner composed yeeld but a continual repetition of that Rhetoricall figure which we tearme *similiter desinentia*,[2] and that, being but *figura verbi*,[3] ought (as *Tully* and all other Rhetoritians have iudicially obseru'd) sparingly to be vs'd, least it should offend the eare with tedious affection. . . . The eare is a rationall sence and a chiefe iudge of proportion; but in our kind of riming what proportion is there kept where there remaines such a confused inequalitie of sillables? *Iambick* and *Trochaick* feete, which are opposed by nature, are by all Rimers confounded; nay, oftentimes they place instead of an *Iambick* the foot *Pyrrychius*, consisting of two short sillables, curtalling their verse, which they supply in reading with a ridiculous and vnapt drawing of their speech. As for example:

> Was it my desteny, or dismall chaunce?

In this verse the two last sillables of the word *Desteny*, being both short, and standing for a whole foote in the verse, cause the line to fall out shorter then it ought by nature. The like impure errors haue in time of rudenesse bene vsed in the Latine toong, as the *Carmina prouerbialia* can witnesse, and many other such reuerend bables.[4] But the noble *Grecians* and *Romaines*, whose skilfull monuments outliue barbarisme, tyed themselues to the strict obseruation of poeticall numbers, so abandoning the childish titillation of riming that it was imputed a great error to *Ouid* for setting forth this one riming verse,

Quot caelum stellas tot habet tua Roma puellas.

For the establishing of this argument, what better confirmation can be had then that of Sir *Thomas Moore* in his booke of Epigrams, where he makes two sundry Epitaphs vpon the death of a singing-man at *Westminster*, the one in learned numbers and dislik't, the other in rude rime and highly extold: so that he concludes, *tales lactucas talia labra petunt*, like lips like lettuce.

But there is yet another fault in Rime altogether intollerable, which is, that it inforceth a man oftentimes to abiure his matter and extend a short conceit beyond all bounds of arte; for in Quatorzens, methinks, the poet handles his subiect as tyrannically as *Procrustes* the thiefe his prisoners, whom, when he had taken, he vsed to cast vpon a bed, which if they were too short to fill, he would stretch them longer, if too long, he would cut them shorter. Bring before me now any the most self-lou'd Rimer, and let me see if without blushing he be able to reade his lame halting rimes. Is there not a curse of Nature laid vpon such rude Poesie, when the Writer is himself asham'd of it, and the hearers in contempt call it Riming and Ballating?[5] What Deuine in his Sermon, or graue Counsellor in his Oration, will alleage the testimonie of a rime? But the deuinity of the *Romaines* and *Gretians* was all written in verse; and *Aristotle, Galene*, and the bookes of all the excellent Philosophers are full of the testimonies of the old Poets. By them was laid the foundation of all humane wisdome, and from them the knowledge of all antiquitie is deriued. I will propound but one question, and so conclude this point. If the *Italians, Frenchmen*, and *Spanyards*, that with commendation have written in Rime, were demaunded whether they had rather the bookes they haue publist (if their toong would beare it) should remaine as they are in Rime or be translated into the auncient numbers of the Greekes and Romaines, would they not answere into numbers? What honour were it then for our English language to be the first that after so many yeares of barbarisme could second the perfection of the industrious *Greekes* and *Romaines*? . . .

SOURCE: extract from *Obseruations in the Art of English Poesie* (1602).

EDITOR'S NOTES

1. 'numerous poesy': poetry depending on metre, not rhyme.

2. '*similiter desinentia*': similar endings.

3. '*figura verbi*': verbal ornamentation.

4. 'bables': baubles.

5. 'Ballating': ballad-making.

Samuel Daniel   (1603)

. . . I haue wished that there were not that multiplicitie of Rymes as is vsed by many in Sonets, which yet we see in some so happily to succeed, and hath beene so farre from hindering their inuentions, as it hath begot conceit beyond expectation, and comparable to the best inuentions of the world: for sure in an eminent spirit, whome Nature hath fitted for that mysterie, Ryme is no impediment to his conceit, but rather giues him wings to mount, and carries him, not out of his course, but as it were beyond his power to a farre happier flight. Al excellencies being sold vs at the hard price of labour, it followes, where we bestow most thereof we buy the best successe: and Ryme, being farre more laborious than loose measures (whatsoeuer is obiected), must needs, meeting with wit and industry, breed greater and worthier effects in our language. So that if our labours haue wrought out a manumission from bondage, and that wee goe at libertie, notwithstanding these ties, wee are no longer the slaues of Ryme, but we make it a most excellent instrument to serue vs. Nor is this certaine limit obserued in Sonnets, any tyrannicall bounding of the conceit, but rather reducing it in *girum* and a iust forme, neither too long for the shortest proiect, nor too short for the longest, being but onely imployed for a present passion. For the body of our imagination being as an vnformed *Chaos* without fashion, without day, if by the diuine power of the spirit it be wrought into an Orbe of order and forme, is it not more pleasing to Nature, that desires a certaintie and comports not with that which is infinite, to haue these clozes, rather than not to know where to end, or how farre to goe, especially seeing our passions are often without measure? and wee finde the best of the Latines many times either not concluding or els otherwise in the end then they began. Besides, is it not most delightfull to see much excellentlie ordred in a small roome, or little gallantly disposed and made to fill vp a space of like capacitie, in such sort that the one would not appeare so beautifull in a larger circuite, nor the other do well in a lesse? which often we find to be so, according to the powers of nature in the workman. And these limited proportions and rests of stanzes, consisting of six, seuen, or eight lines, are of that happines both for the disposition of the matter, the apt planting the sentence where it may best stand to hit, the certaine close of delight with the full bodie of a iust period well carried, is such as neither the Greekes or Latines euer attained vnto. For their boundlesse running on often so confounds the Reader, that, hauing once lost himselfe, must either giue off vnsatisfied, or vncertainely cast backe to retriue the escaped sence, and to find way againe into this matter.

Me thinkes we should not so soone yeeld our consents captiue to the authoritie of Antiquitie, vnlesse we saw more reason; all our vnderstandings are not to be built by the square of *Greece* and *Italie*. We are the children of nature as well as they; we are not so placed out of the way of iudgement but that the same Sunne of Discretion shineth vppon vs; we haue our portion of the same virtues as well as of the same vices.

SOURCE: extract from *A Defence of Ryme, Against a Pamphlet entituled: Obseruations in the Art of English Poesy* . . . (1603).

PART TWO

Comment and Appraisal 1618–1887

Edmund Bolton   (1618)

. . . My judgment is nothing at all in Poems or Poesie, and therefore I dare not go far, but will simply deliver my Mind concerning those Authours among us, whose *English* hath in my Conceit most propriety, and is nearest to the Phrase of Court, and to the Speech used among the noble and among the better sort in *London*, the two sovereign Seats and, as it were, Parliament tribunals to try the question in. Brave language are *Chapman's* Iliads, those I mean which are translated into Tessara-decasyllabons, or lines of fourteen Syllables. The Works of *Sam. Daniel* contain'd somewhat aflat, but yet withal a very pure and copious *English*, and words as warrantable as any Mans, and fitter perhaps for Prose than Measure. *Michael Draiton's* Heroical Epistles are well worth the reading also, for the Purpose of our Subject, which is to furnish an *English* Historian with Choice and Copy of Tongue. Q. *Elizabeth's* verses, those which I have seen and read, some exstant in the elegant, witty, and artificial Book of the *Art of* English *Poetry*, the Work (as the Fame is) of one of her Gentlemen Pensioners, *Puttenham*, are Princely as her Prose.

Never must be forgotten St *Peter's Complaint*, and those other serious Poems said to be father *Southwell's*; the *English* whereof, as it is most proper, so the sharpness and Light of Wit is very rare in them.

Noble *Henry Constable* was a great Master in *English* Tongue, nor had any Gentleman of our Nation a more pure, quick, or higher Delivery of Conceit; witness, among all other, that Sonnet of his before his Majesty's *Lepanto*. I have not seen much of Sr *Edward Dyers* Poetry. Among the lesser late Poets, *George Gascoign's* Works may be endur'd. But the best of those Times (if *Albion's England* be not preferr'd) for our business is *The Mirrour of Magistrates* and in that Mirrour *Sackvil's* Induction, the work of *Thomas*, afterward Earl of *Dorset* and Lord Treasurer of *England*, whose also the famous Tragedy of *Gorboduc* was the best of that time, even in Sr *Phil. Sidney's* Judgment and all skilful *English* men cannot but ascribe as much thereto for his Phrase and Eloquence therein. But before in Age, if not also in Noble, Courtly, and Lustrous *English*, is that of the Songs and Sonnets of *Henry Howard*, Earl of *Surrey* (Son of that victorious Prince, the Duke of *Norfolk*, and Father of that learned *Howard*, his most lively image,

Henry Earl of *Northampton*) written chiefly by him and by Sr *Tho. Wiat*, not the dangerous Commotioner but his worthy Father. Nevertheless they who most commend those Poems and exercises of honourable Wit, if they have seen that incomparable Earl of *Surrey* his *English* Translation of *Virgil's* Æneids, which for a book or two he admirably rendreth almost Line for Line, will bear me witness that those other were Foils and Sportives.[1]

The *English* Poems of Sr *Walter Raleigh*, of *John Donn*, of *Hugh Holland*, but especially of Sr *Foulk Grevile* in his matchless *Mustapha*, are not easily to be mended. I dare not presume to speak of his Majesty's Exercises in this Heroick Kind: Because I see them all left out in that Edition which *Montague*, Lord Biship of *Winchester*, hath given us of his royal Writings. But if I should declare mine own Rudeness rudely, I should then confess that I never tasted *English* more to my liking, nor more smart, and put to the height of Use in Poetry, then in that vital judicious, and most practicable Language of *Benjamin Jonson's* Poems.

SOURCE: extract from *Hypercritica: or a Rule of Judgement, for writing or reading our History's* (written 1618, published 1722).

EDITOR'S NOTE

1. I.e., trivial by contrast.

Ben Jonson   (c. 1620)

...*Poetry*, in this latter Age, hath prov'd but a meane *Mistresse* to such as have wholly addicted themselves to her, or given their names up to her family. They who have but saluted her on the by, and now and then tendred their visits, shee hath done much for, and advanced in the way of their owne professions (both the *Law* and the *Gospel*) beyond all they could have hoped or done for themselves without her favour. Wherein she doth emulate the judicious but preposterous bounty of the times *Grandes*,[1] who accumulate all they can upon the

Parasite or *Freshman* in their friendship, but thinke an old Client or honest servant bound by his place to write and starve.

Indeed, the multitude commend Writers as they doe Fencers or Wrastlers, who, if they come in robustiously and put for it with a deale of violence, are received for the *braver-fellowes*; when many times their owne rudenesse is a cause of their disgrace, and a slight touch of their Adversary gives all that boisterous force the foyle. But in these things the unskilfull are naturally deceiv'd, and judging wholly by the bulke, thinke rude things greater then polish'd, and scatter'd more numerous then composed. Nor thinke this only to be true in the sordid multitude, but the neater sort of our *Gallants*; for all are the multitude, only they differ in cloaths, not in judgement or understanding.   . . .

SOURCE: extract from essay (written c. 1620) included in *Timber, or Discoveries made upon Men and Matters* (posthumously published in 1640).

EDITOR'S NOTE

1. I.e., time's grandees.

Edward Phillips   (1675)

. . . from Qu. *Elizabeth's* Reign the Language hath been not so unpolisht as to render the Poetry of that time ungratefull to such as at this day will take the paines to examin it well; besides, if no Poetry should Pleas but what is calculated to every refinement of a Language, of how ill consequence this would be for the future let him consider and make it his own case, who, being now in fair repute & promising to himself a lasting Fame, shall two or three Ages hence, when the Language comes to be double refin'd, understand (if Souls have any intelligence, after their departure hence, what is done on Earth) that his Works are become obsolete and thrown aside. If then their Antiquated style be no sufficient reason why the Poets of former Ages should be rejected, much less the pretence of their antiquated

mode or fashion of Poetry, which, whether it be altered for the better or not, I cannot but look upon it as a very pleasant humour, that we should be so complyant with the *French* custom as to follow set fashions, not only in Garments, but also in Music (wherein the *Lydian* Mood is now most in request) and Poetry: for Cloths, I leave them to the discretion of the Modish, whether of our own or the *French* Nation; Breeches and Doublet will not fall under a Metaphysical considera- tion: but in Arts and Sciences, as well as in Moral Notions, I shall not scruple to maintain that what was *verum & bonum*[1] once continues to be so always; now, whether the Trunck-Hose Fancy of Queen *Elizabeth*'s days or the Pantaloon Genius of ours be best, I shall not be hasty to determin, not presuming to call in question the judgment of the present Age; only thus much I must needs see, that Custom & Opinion oft times take so deep a root that Judgment hath not free power to act. To the Antient Greecs and Latins, the Modern Poets of all Nations and for several Ages have acknowledged themselves beholding for those, both Precepts and examples, which have been thought conducing to the perfection of Poetry; for the manner of its Garb and dress, which is Vers, we in particular to the *Italians*, the first of the Moderns that have been eminently Famous in this Faculty, the measure of the Greec and Latin Verse being no way suitable to the Modern Languages; & truly, so far as I have observed, the Italian *Stanza* in Heroic Poem, and the Sonnet, Canzon, and Madrigal in the Lyric, as they have been formerly more frequently made use of by the *English* than by any, so except their own proper Language they become none better then ours; and therefore having been used with so good success, I see no reason why they should be utterly rejected; there is certainly a decency in one sort of Verse more then another, which custom cannot really alter, only by familiarity make it seem better.   . . .

SOURCE: extract from the Preface to *Theatrum Poetarum, or A Compleat Collection of the Poets* (1675).

EDITOR'S NOTE

1. '*verum & bonum*': true and good.

Joseph Addison   (1694; 1711)

I

. . .
Old Spenser, next, warm'd with poetic rage,
In ancient tales amus'd a barb'rous age;
An age that yet uncultivate and rude,
Where'er the poet's fancy led, pursu'd
Through pathless fields, and unfrequented floods,
To dens of dragons, and enchanted woods.
But now the mystic tale, that pleas'd of yore,
Can charm an understanding age no more.   . . .

SOURCE: extract from 'An Account of the Greatest English Poets'
(1694).

II

. . . the sentiments in that Ballad ['of Chevy Chase'] are extremely
natural and poetical, and full of the Majestick Simplicity which we
admire in the greatest of the ancient Poets . . . I must . . . beg leave to
dissent from so great an Authority as that of Sir *Philip Sidney*, in the
Judgment which he has passed as to the rude Stile and evil Apparel of
this antiquated Song;[1] for there are several Parts in it where not only
the Thought but the Language is majestick, and the Numbers
sonorous; at least the *Apparel* is much more gorgeous than many of the
Poets made use of in Queen Elizabeth's Time.   . . .

SOURCE: extract from the *Spectator*, no 74 (25 May 1711).

EDITOR'S NOTE

1. In his *Apologie*, Sidney wrote: 'Certainly, I must confess my own
barbarousness, I never heard the old song of Percy and Douglas that I found

not my heart moved more than with a trumpet; and yet is it sung but by some
blind crowder, with no rougher voice than rude style; which, being so evil
apparelled in the dust and cobwebs of that uncivil age, what would it work
trimmed in the gorgeous eloquence of Pindar?'

Thomas Warton (1781)

. . . Sentiments and images were not absolutely determined by the
canons of composition; nor was genius awed by the consciousness of a
future and final arraignment at the tribunal of taste. A certain dignity
of inattention to niceties is now visible in our writers.[1] Without too
closely consulting a criterion of correctness, every man indulged his
own capriciousness of invention. The poet's appeal was chiefly to his
own voluntary feelings, his own immediate and peculiar mode of
conception. And this freedom of thought was often expressed in an
undisguised frankness of diction; – a circumstance, by the way, that
greatly contributed to give the flowing modulation which now
marked the measures of our poets, and which soon degenerated into
the opposite extreme of dissonance and asperity. Selection and
discrimination were often overlooked. . . .

No Satires, properly so called, were written till towards the latter
end of the queen's reign, and then but a few. Pictures drawn at large of
the vices of the times did not suit readers who loved to wander in the
regions of artificial manners. The Muse, like the people, was too
solemn and reserved, too ceremonious and pedantic, to stoop to
common life. Satire is the poetry of a nation highly polished.

The importance of the female character was not yet acknowledged,
nor were women admitted into the general commerce of society. The
effect of that intercourse had not imparted a comic air to poetry, nor
softened the severer tone of our versification with the levities of
gallantry, and the familiarities of compliment, sometimes perhaps
operating on serious subjects, and imperceptibly spreading themselves in the general habits of style and thought. I do not mean to
insinuate, that our poetry has suffered from the great change of
manners, which this assumption of the gentler sex, or rather the
improved state of female education, has produced, by giving elegance
and variety to life, by enlarging the sphere of conversation, and by

multiplying the topics and enriching the stores of wit and humour. But I am marking the peculiarities of composition: and my meaning was to suggest, that the absence of so important a circumstance from the modes and constitution of ancient life must have influenced the contemporary poetry. Of the state of manners among our ancestors respecting this point, many traces remain. Their style of courtship may be collected from the love-dialogues of Hamlet, young Percy, Henry the Fifth, and Master Fenton. Their tragic heroines, their Desdemonas and Ophelias, although of so much consequence in the piece, are degraded to the back-ground. In comedy, their ladies are nothing more than MERRY WIVES, plain and cheerful matrons, who stand upon the *chariness of their honesty*. In the smaller poems, if a lover praises his mistress, she is complimented in strains neither polite nor pathetic, without elegance and without affection: she is described, not in the address of intelligible yet artful panegyric, not in the real colours, and with the genuine accomplishments, of nature; but as an eccentric ideal being of another system, and as inspiring sentiments equally unmeaning, hyperbolical, and unnatural.

All or most of these circumstances contributed to give a descriptive, a picturesque, and a figurative cast to the poetical language. This effect appears even in the prose compositions of the reign of Elizabeth. In the subsequent age, prose became the language of poetry.

In the mean time, general knowledge was increasing with a wide diffusion and a hasty rapidity. Books began to be multiplied, and a variety of the most useful and rational topics had been discussed in our own language. But science had not made too great advances. On the whole, we were now arrived at that period, propitious to the operations of original and true poetry, when the coyness of fancy was not always proof against the approaches of reason, when genius was rather directed than governed by judgment, and when taste and learning had so far only disciplined imagination, as to suffer its excesses to pass without censure or control, for the sake of the beauties to which they were allied.   . . .

SOURCE: extracts from *The History of English Poetry* (1774–81)

EDITOR'S NOTE

1. I.e., of the Elizabethan age.

Samuel Taylor Coleridge (1807; 1817; 1831)

1 On Chapman's Translation of Homer (1807)

. . . Chapman I have sent in order that you might read the Odyssey; the Iliad is fine, but less equal in the translation, as well as less interesting in itself. What is stupidly said of Shakespeare, is really true and appropriate of Chapman; mighty faults counterpoised by mighty beauties. Excepting his quaint epithets which he affects to render literally from the Greek, a language above all others blest in the happy marriage of sweet words, and which in our language are mere printer's compound epithets – such as quaffed divine *joy-in-the-heart-of-man-infusing* wine (the under-marked is to be one word, because one sweet mellifluous word expresses it in Homer); – excepting this, it has no look, no air, of a translation. It is as truly an original poem as the Faery Queene; – it will give you small idea of Homer, though a far truer one than Pope's epigrams, or Cowper's cumbersome most anti-Homeric Miltonism. For Chapman writes and feels as a poet, – as Homer might have written had he lived in England in the reign of Queen Elizabeth. In short, it is an exquisite poem, in spite of its frequent and perverse quaintnesses and harshnesses, which are, however, amply repaid by almost unexampled sweetness and beauty of language, all over spirit and feeling. In the main it is an English heroic poem, the tale of which is borrowed from the Greek. The dedication to the Iliad is a noble copy of verses, especially those sublime lines beginning, –

> O! 'tis wondrous much
> (Though nothing prisde) that the right vertuous touch
> Of a well written soule, to vertue moves.
> Nor haue we soules to purpose, if their loves
> Of fitting objects be not so inflam'd.
> How much then, were this kingdome's maine soule maim'd,
> To want this great inflamer of all powers
> That move in humane soules! All realmes but yours,
> Are honor'd with him; and hold blest that state
> That have his workes to reade and contemplate.

In whch, humanitie to her height is raisde;
Which all the world (yet, none enough) hath praisde.
Seas, earth, and heaven, he did in verse comprize;
Out sung the Muses, and did equalise
Their king Apollo; being so farre from cause
Of princes light thoughts, that their gravest lawes
May finde stuffe to be fashioned by his lines.
Through all the pompe of kingdomes still he shines
And graceth all his gracers. Then let lie
Your lutes, and viols, and more loftily
Make the heroiques of your Homer sung,
To drums and trumpets set his Angels tongue:
And with the princely sports of haukes you use,
Behold the kingly flight of his high Muse:
And see how like the Phœnix she renues
Her age, and starrie feathers in your sunne;
Thousands of yeares attending; everie one
Blowing the holy fire, and throwing in
Their seasons, kingdomes, nations that have bin
Subverted in them; lawes, religions, all
Offerd to change, and greedie funerall;
Yet still your Homer lasting, living, raigning. –

and likewise the 1st, the 11th, and last but one, of the prefatory sonnets to the Odyssey. Could I have foreseen any other speedy opportunity, I should have begged your acceptance of the volume in a somewhat handsomer coat; but as it is, it will better represent the sender, – to quote from myself –

> A man disherited, in form and face,
> By nature and mishap, of outward grace.

. . .

SOURCE: from 'Extract of a Letter Sent With the Volume', (1807), 'communicated through Mr Wordsworth'; in *The Literary Remains of Samuel Taylor Coleridge*, ed. Henry Nelson Coleridge (London, 1836), I, p. 259.

II On Samuel Daniel (1817)

. . . Both in respect of this and of the former excellence,[1] Mr Wordsworth strikingly resembles Samuel Daniel, one of the golden

writers of our golden Elizabethan age, now most causelessly neglected: Samuel Daniel, whose diction bears no mark of time, no
distinction of age, which has been, and as long as our language shall
last, will be so far the language of the to-day and for ever, as that it is
more intelligible to us, than the transitory fashions of our own
particular age: A similar praise is due to his sentiments. No frequency
of perusal can deprive them of their freshness. For though they are
brought into the full day-light of every reader's comprehension; yet
are they drawn up from depths which few in any age are priviledged to
visit, into which few in any age have courage or inclination to
descend. If Mr Wordsworth is not equally with Daniel alike
intelligible to all readers of average understanding in all passages of
his works, the comparative difficulty does not arise from the greater
impurity of the ore, but from the nature and uses of the metal. A poem
is not necessarily obscure, because it does not aim to be popular. It is
enough, if a work be perspicuous to those for whom it is written, and,

'Fit audience find, though few.'
. . .

Source: extract from *Biographia Literaria* (1817).

editor's note

1. 'this' = 'the weight and sanity of the Thoughts and Sentiments';
'the former' = 'a perfect appropriateness of the words to the meaning'.

iii On Michael Drayton (1831)

. . . Drayton is a sweet poet, and Selden's notes to the early part of the
Polyolbion are well worth your perusal. Daniel is a superior man; his
diction is pre-eminently pure; – of that quality which I believe has
always existed somewhere in society. It is just such English, without
any alteration, as Wordsworth or Sir George Beaumont might have
spoken or written in the present day.

Yet there are instances of sublimity in Drayton. When deploring
the cutting down of some of our old forests, he says, in language which
reminds the reader of Lear, written subsequently, and also of several
of Mr Wordsworth's poems: –

... Our trees so hack'd above the ground,
That where their lofty tops the neighboring countries crown'd,
Their trunks (like aged folks) now bare and naked stand,
As for revenge to heaven each held a wither'd hand.

That is very fine.   ...

SOURCE: extract from *Table Talk* (1831).

IV On Shakespeare's *Venus and Adonis* and *Rape of Lucrece* (1817)

In the application of these principles[1] to purposes of practical
criticism as employed in the appraisal of works more or less imperfect,
I have endeavoured to discover what the qualities in a poem are
which may be deemed promises and specific symptoms of poetic
power, as distinguished from general talent determined to poetic
composition by accidental motives, by an act of the will, rather than
by the inspiration of a genial and productive nature. In this
investigation I could not, I thought, do better than keep before me the
earliest work of the greatest genius, that perhaps human nature has
yet produced, our *myriad-minded*[2] Shakespeare. I mean the *Venus and
Adonis*, and the *Lucrece*; works which give at once strong promises of
the strength, and yet obvious proofs of the immaturity of his genius.
From these I abstracted the following marks, as characteristics of
original poetic genius in general.

1. In the *Venus and Adonis* the first and most obvious excellence is the
perfect sweetness of the versification; its adaptation to the subject;
and the power displayed in varying the march of the words without
passing into a loftier and more majestic rhythm than was demanded
by the thoughts, or permitted by the propriety of preserving a sense of
melody predominant. The delight in richness and sweetness of sound,
even to a faulty excess, if it be evidently original and not the result of
an easily imitable mechanism, I regard as a highly favorable promise
in the compositions of a young man. 'The man that hath not music in
his soul'[3] can indeed never be a genuine poet. Imagery (even taken
from nature, much more when transplanted from books, as travels,
voyages and works of natural history); affecting incidents; just
thoughts; interesting personal or domestic feelings; and with these the
art of their combination or intertexture in the form of a poem, may all

by incessant effort be acquired as a trade, by a man of talents and much reading who, as I once before observed, has mistaken an intense desire of poetic reputation for a natural poetic genius; the love of the arbitrary end for a possession of the peculiar means. But the sense of musical delight, with the power of producing it, is a gift of imagination; and this, together with the power of reducing multitude into unity of effect, and modifying a series of thoughts by some one predominant thought or feeling, may be cultivated and improved, but can never be learnt. It is in these that 'Poeta nascitur non fit.'[4]

2. A second promise of genius is the choice of subjects very remote from the private interests and circumstances of the writer himself. At least I have found that where the subject is taken immediately from the author's personal sensations and experiences, the excellence of a particular poem is but an equivocal mark, and often a fallacious pledge, of genuine poetic power. We may perhaps remember the tale of the statuary, who had acquired considerable reputation for the legs of his goddesses, though the rest of the statue accorded but indifferently with ideal beauty; till his wife, elated by her husband's praises, modestly acknowledged that she herself had been his constant model. In the *Venus and Adonis* this proof of poetic power exists even to excess. It is throughout as if a superior spirit, more intuitive, more intimately conscious even than the characters themselves, not only of every outward look and act but of the flux and reflux of the mind in all its subtlest thoughts and feelings, were placing the whole before our view; himself meanwhile unparticipating in the passions, and actuated only by that pleasurable excitement which had resulted from the energetic fervor of his own spirit, in so vividly exhibiting what it had so accurately and profoundly contemplated. I think I should have conjectured from these poems that even then the great instinct which impelled the poet to the drama was secretly working in him, prompting him by a series and never-broken chain of imagery, always vivid and, because unbroken, often minute; by the highest effort of the picturesque in words of which words are capable, higher perhaps than was ever realized by any other poet, even Dante not excepted; to provide a substitute for that visual language, that constant intervention and running comment by tone, look and gesture, which in his dramatic works he was entitled to expect from the players. His Venus and Adonis seem at once the characters themselves, and the whole representation of those characters by the most consummate actors. You seem to be *told* nothing, but to see and

hear everything. Hence it is, that from the perpetual activity of
attention required on the part of the reader; from the rapid flow, the
quick change and the playful nature of the thoughts and images; and,
above all, from the alienation and, if I may hazard such an expression,
the utter *aloofness* of the poet's own feelings from those of which he is at
once the painter and the analyst; that though the very subject cannot
but detract from the pleasure of a delicate mind, yet never was poem
less dangerous on a moral account. Instead of doing as Ariosto and as,
still more offensively, Wieland has done; instead of degrading and
deforming passion into appetite, the trials of love into the struggles of
concupiscence, Shakespeare has here represented the animal impulse
itself so as to preclude all sympathy with it, by dissipating the reader's
notice among the thousand outward images and now beautiful, now
fanciful circumstances, which form its dresses and its scenery; or by
diverting our attention from the main subject by those frequent witty
or profound reflections which the poet's ever active mind has deduced
from, or connected with, the imagery and the incidents. The reader is
forced into too much action to sympathize with the merely passive of
our nature. As little can a mind thus roused and awakened be
brooded on by mean and instinct emotion as the low, lazy mist can
creep upon the surface of a lake while a strong gale is driving it
onward in waves and billows.

3. It has been before observed that images, however beautiful,
though faithfully copied from nature, and as accurately represented
in words, do not of themselves characterize the poet. They become
proofs of original genius only as far as they are modified by a
predominant passion; or by associated thoughts or images awakened
by that passion; or when they have the effect of reducing multitude to
unity, or succession to an instant; or lastly, when a human and
intellectual life is transferred to them from the poet's own spirit,

> Which shoots its being through earth, sea and air.[5]

. . .

Scarcely less sure, or if a less valuable, not less indispensable mark
. . . will the imagery supply when, with more than the power of the
painter, the poet gives us the liveliest image of succession with the
feeling of simultaneousness!

> With this he breaketh from the sweet embrace
> Of those fair arms which bound him to her breast,
> And homeward through the dark laund runs apace; . . .

Look, how a bright star shooteth from the sky,
So glides he in the night from Venus' eye.[6]

4. The last character I shall mention, which would prove indeed
but little except as taken conjointly with the former, yet without
which the former could scarce exist in a high degree and (even if this
were possible) would give promises only of transitory flashes and a
meteoric power, is depth and energy of thought. No man was ever yet
a great poet, without being at the same time a profound philosopher.
For poetry is the blossom and the fragrancy of all human knowledge,
human thoughts, human passions, emotions, language. In Shakespeare's poems, the creative power and the intellectual energy wrestle
as in a war embrace. Each in its excess of strength seems to threaten
the extinction of the other. At length in the drama they were
reconciled, and fought each with its shield before the breast of the
other. Or like two rapid streams that at their first meeting within
narrow and rocky banks mutually strive to repel each other, and
intermix reluctantly and in tumult, but soon finding a wider channel
and more yielding shores, blend and dilate, and flow on in one current
and with one voice. The *Venus and Adonis* did not perhaps allow the
display of the deeper passions. But the story of Lucretia seems to
favor, and even demand, their intensest workings. And yet we find in
Shakespeare's management of the tale neither pathos nor any other
dramatic quality. There is the same minute and faithful imagery as in
the former poem, in the same vivid colours, inspirited by the same
impetuous vigour of thought, and diverging and contracting with the
same activity of the assimilative and of the modifying faculties; and
with a yet larger display, a yet wider range of knowledge and
reflection; and lastly, with the same perfect dominion, often domina-
tion, over the whole world of language. What then shall we say? Even
this: that Shakespeare, no mere child of nature; no automaton of
genius; no passive vehicle of inspiration possessed by the spirit, not
possessing it; first studied patiently, meditated deeply, understood
minutely, till knowledge become habitual and intuitive wedded itself
to his habitual feelings, and at length gave birth to that stupendous
power by which he stands alone, with no equal or second in his own
class; to that power which seated him on one of the two glory-smitten
summits of the poetic mountain, with Milton as his compeer not
rival.[7]   . . .

SOURCE: extract from *Biographia Literaria* (1817).

NOTES

1. [Ed.] I.e., the principles of 'poetic power', which Coleridge describes in the chapter previous to this in the *Biographia*, number 14.

2. [S. T. C.] 'Aνὴρ μυριόνους, a phrase which I have borrowed from a Greek monk, who applies it to a Patriarch of Constantinople. I might have said that I have reclaimed rather than borrowed it: for it seems to belong to Shakespeare *de jure singulari, et ex privilegio naturae*.

3. [Ed.] *Merchant of Venice*, v i 83.

4. [Ed.] 'Poeta nascitur non fit': a poet is born, not made.

5. [Ed.] from 'France: an Ode': 'And shot my being thro' earth, sea and air'.

6. [Ed.] *Venus & Adonis*, 811–13 & 815–16.

John Keats   (1818)

. . . It may be said that we ought to read our Contemporaries. that Wordsworth &c should have their due from us. but for the sake of a few fine imaginative or domestic passages, are we to be bullied into a certain Philosophy engendered in the whims of an Egotist – Every man has his speculations, but every man does not brood and peacock over them till he makes a false coinage and deceives himself – Many a man can travel to the very bourne of Heaven, and yet want confidence to put down his halfseeing. Sancho will invent a Journey heavenward as well as any body. We hate poetry that has a palpable design upon us – and if we do not agree, seems to put its hand in its breeches pocket. Poetry should be great & unobtrusive, a thing which enters one's soul, and does not startle or amaze it with itself but with its subject. – How beautiful are the retired flowers! how would they lose their beauty were they to throng into the highway crying out, 'admire me I am a violet! dote upon me I am a primrose!' Modern poets differ from the Elizabethans in this. Each of the moderns like an Elector of Hanover governs his petty state, & knows how many straws are swept daily from the Causeways in all his dominions & has a continual itching that all the Housewives should have their coppers well scoured: the antients were Emperors of vast Provinces, they had only heard of the remote ones and scarcely cared to visit them.   . . .

SOURCE: extract from a letter to J. H. Reynolds (3 February 1818); reproduced in Robert Gittings (ed.), *Letters of John Keats* (London, 1970).

William Hazlitt   (1820)

. . . To return to Drummond. – I cannot but think that his Sonnets come as near as almost any others to the perfection of this kind of writing, which should embody a sentiment and every shade of a sentiment, as it varies with time and place and humour, with the extravagance or lightness of a momentary impression, and should, when lengthened out into a series, form a history of the wayward moods of the poet's mind, the turns of his fate; and imprint the smile or frown of his mistress in indelible characters on the scattered leaves. I will give the two following, and have done with this author.

> In vain I haunt the cold and silver springs,
> To quench the fever burning in my veins:
> In vain (love's pilgrim) mountains, dales, and plains
> I over-run; vain help long absence brings.
> In vain, my friends, your counsel me constrains
> To fly, and place my thoughts on other things.
> Ah, like the bird that fired hath her wings,
> The more I move the greater are my pains.
> Desire, alas! desire a Zeuxis new,
> From the orient borrowing gold, from western skies
> Heavenly cinnabar, sets before my eyes
> In every place her hair, sweet look and hue;
> That fly, run, rest I, all doth prove but vain;
> My life lies in those eyes which have me slain.

The other is a direct imitation of Petrarch's description of the bower where he first saw Laura.

> Alexis, here she stay'd, among these pines,
> Sweet hermitress, she did alone repair:

> Here did she spread the treasure of her hair,
> More rich than that brought from the Colchian mines;
> Here sat she by these musked eglantines;
> The happy flowers seem yet the print to bear:
> Her voice did sweeten here thy sugar'd lines,
> To which winds, trees, beasts, birds, did lend an ear.
> She here me first perceiv'd, and here a morn
> Of bright carnations did o'erspread her face:
> Here did she sigh, here first my hopes were born,
> Here first I got a pledge of promised grace;
> But ah! what serves to have been made happy so,
> Sith passed pleasures double but new woe!

I should, on the whole, prefer Drummond's Sonnets to Spenser's; and they leave Sidney's, picking their way through verbal intricacies and 'thorny queaches', at an immeasurable distance behind. Drummond's other poems have great, though not equal merit; and he may be fairly set down as one of our old English classics.   . . .

SOURCE: extract from *Lectures on the Dramatic Literature of the Age of Elizabeth* (1820).

A. C. Swinburne   (1875)

. . . The name of Chapman should always be held great; yet must it always at first recall the names of greater men. For one who thinks of him as the author of his best play or his loftiest lines of gnomic verse a score will at once remember him as the translator of Homer or the continuator of Marlowe. The most daring enterprise of a life which was full of daring aspiration and arduous labour was this of resuming and completing the 'mighty line' of *Hero and Leander*. For that poem stands out alone amid all the wide and wild poetic wealth of its teeming and turbulent age, as might a small shrine of Parian sculpture amid the rank splendour of a tropic jungle. But no metaphor can aptly express the rapture of relief with which you come upon it amid the poems of Chapman, and drink once more with your whole heart of that well of sweet water after the long draughts you have taken from such brackish and turbid springs as gush up among the sands and thickets of his verse. Faultless indeed this lovely fragment is not; it also bears traces of the Elizabethan barbarism, as though the great queen's ruff and farthingale had been clapped about the neck and waist of the Medicean Venus; but for all the strange costume we can see that the limbs are perfect still. The name of Marlowe's poem has been often coupled with that of the 'first heir' of Shakespeare's 'invention'; but with all reverence to the highest name in letters be it said, the comparison is hardly less absurd than a comparison of *Tamburlaine* with *Othello*. With all its overcrowding beauties of detail, Shakespeare's first poem is on the whole a model of what a young man of genius should not write on such a subject,[1] Marlowe's is a model of what he should. Scarcely the art of Titian at its highest, and surely not the art of Shakespeare at its dawn, could have made acceptable such an inversion of natural rule as is involved in the attempted violation by a passionate woman of a passionless boy; the part of a Joseph, as no less a moralist than Henri Beyle has observed in his great work on *Love*, has always a suspicion about it of something ridiculous and offensive; but only the wretchedest of artists could wholly fail to give charm to the picture of such a nuptial night as that of Hero and Leander. The style of Shakespeare's first essay is, to speak frankly, for the most part no less vicious than the matter: it is burdened and bedizened with all the heavy and fantastic jewellery of Gongora and Marino,[2] it is written throughout in the style which an Italian scholar knows as that of the *seicentisti*, and which the duncery of New Grub Street in its immeasurable ignorance would probably designate as 'Della-Cruscan'; nay, there are yet, I believe, in that quarter rhymesters and libellers to be found who imagine such men as Guido Cavalcanti and Dante Alighieri to have been representative members of the famous and farinaceous academy. Not one of the faults chargeable on Shakespeare's beautiful but faultful poem can justly be charged on the only not faultless poem of Marlowe. The absence of all cumbrous jewels and ponderous embroideries from the sweet and limpid loveliness of its style is not more noticeable than the absence of such other and possibly such graver flaws as deform and diminish the undeniable charms of *Venus and Adonis*.

With leave or without leave of a much-lauded critic who could see nothing in the glorified version or expansion by Marlowe of the little poem of Musæus but 'a paraphrase, in every sense of the epithet, of the most licentious kind', I must avow that I want and am well

content to want the sense, whatever it be, which would enable me to
discern more offence in that lovely picture of the union of two lovers in
body as in soul than I can discern in the parting of Romeo and Juliet.
And if it be always a pleasure to read a page of Marlowe, to read it
after a page of Chapman is to the capable student of high verse 'a
pleasure worthy Xerxes the great king'. Yet there is not a little to be
advanced in favour of Chapman's audacious and arduous undertak-
ing. The poet was not alive, among all the mighty men then living,
who could worthily have completed the divine fragment of Marlowe.
As well might we look now to find a sculptor who could worthily
restore for us the arms of the Venus of Melos – 'Our Lady of Beauty',
as Heine said when lying at her feet stricken to death, 'who has no
hands, and cannot help us.' For of narrative poets there were none in
that generation of any note but Drayton and Daniel; and though these
might have more of Marlowe's limpid sweetness and purity of style,
they lacked the force and weight of Chapman. Nor is the continuation
by any means altogether such as we might have expected it to be – a
sequel by Marsyas to the song of Apollo. Thanks, as we may suppose,
to the high ambition of the poet's aim, there are more beauties and
fewer deformities than I have found in any of his other poems. There
are passages indeed which at first sight may almost seem to support
the otherwise unsupported tradition that a brief further fragment of
verse from the hand of Marlowe was left for Chapman to work up into
his sequel. This for instance, though somewhat over-fantastic, has in
it a sweet and genuine note of fancy: –

> Her fresh-heat blood cast figures in her eyes,
> And she supposed she saw in Neptune's skies
> How her star wander'd, wash'd in smarting brine,
> For her love's sake, that with immortal wine
> Should be embathed, and swim in more heart's-ease
> Than there was water in the Sestian seas.

Here again is a beautiful example of the short sweet interludes which
relieve the general style of Chapman's narrative or reflective verse: –

> For as proportion, white and crimson, meet
> In beauty's mixture, all right clear and sweet,
> The eye responsible, the golden hair,
> And none is held without the other fair;
> All spring together, all together fade;
> Such intermix'd affections should invade
> Two perfect lovers.

And this couplet has an exquisite touch of fanciful colour: –

> As two clear tapers mix in one their light,
> So did the lily and the hand their white.

That at least might have been written by Marlowe himself. But the poem is largely deformed by excrescences and aberrations, by misplaced morals and mistimed conceits; and at the catastrophe, perhaps half consciously oppressed and overcome by the sense that now indeed he must put forth all his power to utter something not unworthy of what the 'dead shepherd' himself might have spoken over the two dead lovers, he puts forth all his powers for evil and for error, and gives such a narrative of their end as might have sufficed to raise from his grave the avenging ghost of the outraged poet who has been supposed – but unless it was said in some riotous humour of jesting irony, the supposition seems to me incredible – to have commended to Chapman, in case of his death, the task thus ill discharged of completing this deathless and half-accomplished work of a genius 'that perished in its pride'.   . . .

SOURCE: extract from *George Chapman: A Critical Essay* (1875); reproduced in Swinburne's posthumous collection, *Contemporaries of Shakespeare*, edited by Edmund Gosse and T. J. Wise (London, 1919).

EDITOR'S NOTES

1. Cp. Coleridge's comments in his excerpt IV, above – esp. in the first paragraph.

2. Luis de Góngora y Argote (1561–1627) and Giambaltista Marino (1569–1625), leading poets of the Spanish and the Italian Baroque, respectively.

George Saintsbury　　　(1887)

. . . William Webbe (a very sober-minded person with taste enough to admire the 'new poet', as he calls Spenser) makes elaborate attempts not merely at hexameters, which, though only a curiosity, are a possible curiosity in English, but at Sapphics which could never (except as burlesque) be tolerable. Sidney, Spenser, and others gave serious heed to the scheme of substituting classical metres without rhyme for indigenous metres with rhyme.[1] And unless the two causes which brought this about are constantly kept in mind, the reason of it will not be understood. It was undoubtedly the weakness of contemporary English verse which reinforced the general Renaissance admiration for the classics; nor must it be forgotten that Wyatt takes, in vernacular metres and with rhyme, nearly as great liberties with the intonation and prosody of the language as any of the classicists in their unlucky hexameters and elegiacs. The majesty and grace of the learned tongues, contrasting with the poverty of their own language, impressed, and to a great extent rightly impressed, the early Elizabethans, so that they naturally enough cast about for any means to improve the one, and hesitated at any peculiarity which was not found in the other. It was unpardonable in Milton to sneer at rhyme after the fifty years of magnificent production which had put English on a level with Greek and above Latin as a literary instrument. But for Harvey and Spenser, Sidney and Webbe, with those fifty years still to come, the state of the case was very different.

The translation mania and the classicising mania together led to the production of perhaps the most absurd book in all literature – a book which deserves . . . notice here, . . . because it is, though a caricature, yet a very instructive caricature of the tendencies and literary ideas of the time. This is Richard Stanyhurst's translation of the first four books of the *Æneid*, first printed at Leyden in the summer of 1582, and reprinted in London a year later. This wonderful book (in which the spelling is only less marvellous than the phraseology and verse) shows more than anything else the active throes which English literature was undergoing, and though the result was but a false birth it is none the less interesting.

Stanyhurst was not, as might be hastily imagined, a person of

insufficient culture or insufficient brains. He was an Irish Roman
Catholic gentleman, brother-in-law to Lord Dunsany, and uncle to
Archbishop Usher, and . . . author of the Irish part of Holinshed's
History, . . . [quotes two passages from Stanyhurst's prose, with its
zany language and spelling].

Given a person capable of this lingo, given the prevalent mania for
English hexameters, and even what follows may not seem too
impossible.

> This sayd, with darcksoom night shade quite clowdye she vannisht.
> Grislye faces frouncing, eke against Troy leaged in hatred
> Of Saincts soure deities dyd I see.
> Then dyd I marck playnely thee castle of Ilion vplayd,
> And Troian buyldings quit topsy turvye remooued,
> Much lyk on a mountayn thee tree dry wythered oaken
> Sliest by the clowne Coridon rusticks with twibbil or hatchet.
> Then the tre deepe minced, far chopt dooth terrifye swinckers
> With menacing becking thee branches palsye before tyme,
> Vntil with sowghing yt grunts, as wounded in hacking.
> At length with rounsefal, from stock vntruncked yt harssheth.
>   . . .
>   Hee rested wylful lyk a wayward obstinat oldgrey.
>   . . .
> Theese woords owt showting with her howling the house she replennisht.

There is perhaps no greater evidence of the reverence in which the
ancients were held than that such frantic balderdash as this did not
extinguish it. Yet this was what a man of undoubted talent, of
considerable learning, and of no small acuteness (for Stanyhurst's
Preface to this very translation shows something more than glimmer-
ings on the subject of classical and English prosody), could produce.
It must never be forgotten that the men of this time were at a
hopelessly wrong point of view. It never occurred to them that
English left to itself could equal Greek or Latin. They simply
endeavoured with the utmost pains and skill to drag English up to the
same level as these unapproachable languages by forcing it into the
same moulds which Greek and Latin had endured. Properly speaking
we ought not to laugh at them. They were carrying out in literature
what the older books of arithmetic call 'The Rule of False', – that is to
say, they were trying what the English tongue could *not* bear. No one
was so successful as Stanyhurst in applying this test of the rack: yet it
is fair to say that Harvey and Webbe, nay, Spenser and Sidney, had

practically, though, except in Spenser's case, it would appear unconsciously, arrived at the same conclusion before. How much we owe to such adventurers of the impossible few men know except those who have tried to study literature as a whole.[2]

SOURCE: extract from *A History of Elizabethan Literature* (1887).

EDITOR'S NOTES

1. Cp. Campion, on the need to imitate the 'numerous' poetry of the ancients (Part One, above). For a full study of the topic, see Derek Attridge, *Well-Weighed Syllables: Elizabethan Verse in Classical Metres* (Cambridge, 1974).

2. Cp. Eliot's discussion of Elizabethan classicism and Hobsbaum's defence of Stanyhurst, in Part Three, below.

Twentieth-Century Studies

PART THREE

Twentieth-Century Studies

T. S. Eliot   Imperfect Critics   (1920)

[In this essay Eliot discusses the approaches of two earlier critics to Elizabethan literature: Swinburne's essays collected in *Contemporaries of Shakespeare* (that on Chapman is excerpted in Part Two, above) and George Wyndham's edition of Shakespeare's poems – Ed.]

. . . In the longest and most important essay in the *Contemporaries of Shakespeare*, the essay on Chapman, there are many . . . sentences of sound judgement forcibly expressed. The essay is the best we have on that great poet. It communicates the sense of dignity and mass which we receive from Chapman. But it also illustrates Swinburne's infirmities. Swinburne was not tormented by the restless desire to penetrate to the heart and marrow of a poet, any more than he was tormented by the desire to render the finest shades of difference and resemblance between several poets. Chapman is a difficult author, as Swinburne says; he is far more difficult than Jonson, to whom he bears only a superficial likeness. He is difficult beyond his obscurity. He is difficult partly through his possession of a quality comparatively deficient in Jonson, but which was nevertheless a quality of the age. It is strange that Swinburne should have hinted at a similarity to Jonson and not mentioned a far more striking affinity of Chapman's – that is, Donne. The man who wrote

> Guise, O my lord, how shall I cast from me
> The bands and coverts hindering me from thee?
> The garment or the cover of the mind
> The humane soul is; of the soul, the spirit
> The proper robe is; of the spirit, the blood;
> And of the blood, the body is the shroud:

and

> Nothing is made of nought, of all things made,
> Their abstract being a dream but of a shade,

is unquestionably kin to Donne. The quality in question is not peculiar to Donne and Chapman. In common with the greatest – Marlowe, Webster, Tourneur and Shakespeare – they had a quality of sensuous thought, or of thinking through the senses, or of the senses thinking, of which the exact formula remains to be defined. If you look for it in Shelley or Beddoes, both of whom in very different ways recaptured something of the Elizabethan inspiration, you will not find it, though you may find other qualities instead. There is a trace of it only in Keats, and, derived from a different source, in Rossetti. . . .

. . . We should not gather from Wyndham's essay that the 'The Phoenix and the Turtle' is a great poem, far finer than *Venus and Adonis*; but what he says about *Venus and Adonis* is worth reading, for Wyndham is very sharp in perceiving the neglected beauties of the second-rate. There is nothing to show the gulf of difference between Shakespeare's sonnets and those of any other Elizabethan. Wyndham overrates Sidney, and in his references to Elizabethan writings on the theory of poetry omits mention of the essay by Campion, an abler and more daring though less common-sense study than Daniel's. He speaks a few words for Drayton, but has not noticed that the only good lines (with the exception of one sonnet which may be an accident) in Drayton's dreary sequence of 'Ideas' occur when Drayton drops his costume for a moment and talks in terms of actuality:

> Lastly, mine eyes amazedly have seen
> Essex' great fall; Tyrone his peace to gain;
> The quiet end of that long-living queen;
> The king's fair entry, and our peace with Spain.

More important than the lack of balance is the lack of critical analysis. Wyndham had, as was indicated, a gusto for the Elizabethans. His essay on the Poems of Shakespeare contains an extraordinary amount of information. There is some interesting gossip about Mary Fitton and a good anecdote of Sir William Knollys. But Wyndham misses what is the cardinal point in criticising the Elizabethans: we cannot grasp them, understand them, without some understanding of the pathology of rhetoric. Rhetoric, a particular form of rhetoric, was endemic, it pervaded the whole organism; the healthy as well as the morbid tissues were built up on it. We cannot grapple with even the simplest and most conversational lines in Tudor and early Stuart drama without having diagnosed the rhetoric in the sixteenth- and seventeenth-century mind. Even when we come across lines like:

There's a plumber laying pipes in my guts, it scalds,[1]

we must not allow ourselves to forget the rhetorical basis any more than when we read:

> Come, let us march against the powers of heaven
> And set black streamers in the firmament
> To signify the slaughter of the gods.[2]

An understanding of Elizabethan rhetoric is as essential to the appreciation of Elizabethan literature as an understanding of Victorian sentiment is essential to the appreciation of Victorian literature and of George Wyndham. . . .

SOURCE: extracts from essay in *The Sacred Wood: Essays on Poetry and Criticism* (London, 1920).

EDITOR'S NOTES

1. Webster, *The White Devil* [v vi 145].
2. Marlowe, *Tamburlaine the Great: Part Two* [v iii 47–50].

William Empson   'Sleeping Metaphors: *Nashe'*   (1930)

. . . Among metaphors effective from several points of view one may include, by no great extension, those metaphors which are partly recognised as such and partly received simply as words in their acquired sense. All languages are composed of dead metaphors as the soil of corpses, but English is perhaps uniquely full of metaphors of this sort, which are not dead but sleeping, and, while making a direct statement, colour it with an implied comparison. The school rule against mixed metaphor, which in itself is so powerful a weapon, is largely necessary because of the presence of these sleepers, who must be treated with respect; they are harder to use than either plain word or metaphor because if you mix them you must show you are conscious of their meaning, and are not merely being insensitive to the possibilities of the language.

> Beauty is but a flower
> Which wrinkles will devour.
> Brightness falls from the air.
> Queens have died young and fair.
> Dust hath closed Helen's eye.
> I am sick, I must die.
>   Lord, have mercy upon us.

[Nashe, 'In Time of Pestilence']

I call it a subdued metaphor here that *devour* should mean 'remove' or 'replace', with no more than an overtone of cruelty and the unnatural. This may seem very different from the less evident subdued metaphor in the derivation of a word like 'apprehension', say, but a reader may ignore the consequences even of so evident a metaphor as *devour*. If you go into the metaphor it may make Time the *edax rerum*, and wrinkles only time's tooth-marks; more probably it compares long curving wrinkles on the face to rodent ulcers, caterpillars on petals, and the worms that are to gnaw it in the grave. Of these, the caterpillar (from *flower*) are what the comparison insists upon, but the Elizabethan imagination would let slip no chance of airing its miraculous corpse-worm.

On the other hand

Brightness falls from the air

is an example of ambiguity by vagueness, such as was used to excess by the Pre-Raphaelites. Evidently there are a variety of things the line may be about. The sun and moon pass under the earth after their period of shining, and there are stars falling at odd times; Icarus and the prey of hawks, having soared upwards towards heaven, *fall* exhausted or dead; the glittering turning things the sixteenth century put on the top of a building may have *fallen* too often. In another sense, hawks, lightning and meteorites *fall* flashing from heaven upon their prey. Taking *brightness* as abstract, not as meaning something bright, it is as a benefit that light *falls*, diffusely reflected, from the sky. In so far as the sky is brighter than the earth (especially at twilight), brightness is natural to it; in so far as the earth may be bright when the clouds are dark, *brightness falls* from the sky to the earth when there is a threat of thunder. 'All is unsafe, even the heavens are not sure of their brightness', or 'the qualities in man that deserve respect are not natural to him but brief gifts from God; they fall like manna, and melt as soon'. One may extract, too, from the oppression in the notion of thunder the idea that now, 'in time of pestilence', the generosity of Nature is mysteriously interrupted; even at the scene of brilliant ecclesiastical festivity for which the poem was written there is a taint of darkness in the very *air*.

It is proper to mention a rather cynical theory that Nashe wrote or meant 'hair'; still, though less imaginative, this is very adequate; oddly enough (it is electricity and the mysterious vitality of youth which have *fallen* from the *hair*) carries much the same suggestion as the other version; and gives the relief of a single direct meaning. Elizabethan pronunciation was very little troubled by snobbery, and it is conceivable that Nashe meant both words to take effect in some way. Now that all this fuss has been made about aitches it is impossible to imagine what such a line would sound like.

For a final meaning of this line one must consider the line which follows it; there is another case of poetry by juxtaposition. In

> Dust hath closed Helen's eye

one must think of Helen in part as an undecaying corpse or a statue; it is *dust* from outside which settles on her eyelids, and shows that it is long since they have been opened; only in the background, as a truth which could not otherwise be faced, is it suggested that the *dust* is generated from her own corruption. As a result of this ambiguity, the line imposes on *brightness* a further and more terrible comparison; on the one hand, it is the *bright* motes dancing in sunbeams, which *fall* and become dust which is dirty and infectious; on the other, the lightness, gaiety, and activity of humanity, which shall come to *dust* in the grave. . . .

SOURCE: extract from *Seven Types of Ambiguity* (1930), pp. 25–7.

Ezra Pound (1931)　　'Italian into English'

. . . I offer you a poem that 'don't matter', it is attributed to Guido[1] in Codex Barberiniano Lat. 3953. Alacci prints it as Guido's; Simone

Occhi in 1740 says that Alacci is a fool or words to that effect and a careless man without principles, and proceeds to print the poem with those of Cino Pistoia. Whoever wrote it, it is, indubitably, not a *capo lavoro*.[2]

> Madonna la vostra belta enfolio
> Si li mei ochi che menan lo core
> A la bataglia ove l' ancise amore
> Che del vostro placer armato uscio;
>
> Si che nel primo asalto che asalio
> Passo dentro la mente e fa signore,
> E prese l' alma che fuzia di fore
> Planzendo di dolor che vi sentio.
>
> Però vedete che vostra beltate
> Mosse la folia und e il cor morto
> Et a me ne convien clamar pietate,
>
> Non per campar, ma per aver conforto
> Ne la morte crudel che far min fate
> Et o rason sel non vinzesse il torto.

Is it worth an editor's while to include it among dubious attributions? It is not very attractive: until one starts playing with the simplest English equivalent.

> Lady thy beauty doth so mad mine eyes,
> Driving my heart to strife wherein he dies.

Sing it of course, don't try to speak it. It thoroughly falsifies the movement of the Italian, it is an opening quite good enough for Herrick or Campion. It will help you to understand just why Herrick and Campion, and possibly Donne, are still with us.

The next line is rather a cliché; the line after more or less lacking in interest. We pull up on:

> Whereby thou seest how fair thy beauty is
> To compass doom.

That would be very nice, but it is hardly translation.

Take these scraps, and the almost impossible conclusion, a tag of Provençal rhythm, and make them into a plenum. It will help you to understand some of M. de Schloezer's remarks about Stravinsky's trend toward melody.[3] And you will also see what the best Elizabethan lyricists did, as well as what they didn't.

My two lines take the opening and two and a half of the Italian, English more concise; and the octave gets too light for the sestet. Lighten the sestet.

> So unto Pity must I cry
> Not for safety, but to die.
> Cruel Death is now mine ease
> If that he thine envoy is.

We are preserving one value of early Italian work, the cantabile; and we are losing another, that is the specific weight. And if we notice it we fall on a root difference between early Italian, 'The philosophic school coming out of Bologna', and the Elizabethan lyric. For in these two couplets, and in attacking this sonnet, I have let go the fervour and the intensity, which were all I, rather blindly, had to carry through my attempt of twenty years gone.

And I think that if anyone now lay, or if we assume that they mostly *then* (in the expansive days) laid, aside care for specific statement of emotion, a dogmatic statement, made with the seriousness of someone to whom it mattered whether he had three souls, one in the head, one in the heart, one possibly in his abdomen, or lungs, or wherever Plato, or Galen had located it; if the anima is still breath, if the stopped heart is a dead heart, and if it is all serious, much more serious than it would have been to Herrick, the imaginary investigator will see more or less how the Elizabethan modes came into being.

Let him try it for himself, on any Tuscan author of that time, taking the words, not thinking greatly of their significance, not balking at clichés, but being greatly intent on the melody, on the single uninterrupted flow of syllables – as open as possible, that can be sung prettily, that are not very interesting if spoken, that don't even work into a period or an even metre if spoken.

And the mastery, a minor mastery, will lie in keeping this line unbroken, as unbroken in sound as a line in one of Miro's latest drawings is on paper; and giving it perfect balance, with no breaks, no bits sticking ineptly out, and no losses to the force of individual phrases.

> Whereby thou seest how fair thy beauty is
> To compass doom.

Very possibly too regularly 'iambic' to fit in the finished poem.

There is opposition, not only between what M. de Schloezer distinguishes as musical and poetic lyricism, but in the writing itself there is a distinction between poetic lyricism, the emotional force of the verbal movement, and melopœic lyricism, the letting the words flow of melodic current, realised or not, realisable or not, if the line is supposed to be sung on a sequence of notes of different pitch.

But by taking these Italian sonnets, which are not metrically the equivalent of the English sonnet, by sacrificing, or losing, or simply not feeling and understanding their cogency, their sobriety, and by seeking simply that far from quickly or so-easily-as-it-looks attainable thing, the perfect melody, careless of exactitude of idea, or careless as to which profound and fundamental idea you, at that moment, utter, perhaps in precise enough phrases, by cutting away the apparently non-functioning phrases (whose appearance deceives) you find yourself in the English *seicento* song-books.

Death has become melodious; sorrow is as serious as the nightingale's, tombstones are shelves for the reception of rose-leaves. And there is, quite often, a Mozartian perfection of melody, a wisdom, almost perhaps an ultimate wisdom, deplorably lacking in guts.   . . .

SOURCE: extract from the essay, 'Cavalcanti' (1931); reproduced in *Make it New: Essays by Ezra Pound* (London, 1934), pp. 401–4.

EDITOR'S NOTES

1. Guido Cavalcanti (c. 1255–1300): a friend of Dante, and a leading poet of the *stil nuovo* (new style) school. Some 50 poems are attributed to him (*canzoni*, ballads and sonnets), most of them on themes of love and emotional suffering, and characterised by intensity of inspiration, introspection and the poetic expression of abstract speculation.

2. '*capo lavoro*': master-piece.

3. Boris de Schloezer, *Igor Stravinsky* (Paris, 1929).

T. S. Eliot   'Campion and Daniel'
(1932)

The literary criticism of the Elizabethan period is not very great in bulk; to the account which George Saintsbury has given there cannot in its kind be very much to add, and from his critical valuation there is not much to detract. What concerns me here is the general opinion of it which students are likely to form, in relation to the poetry of the age, on account of two 'lost causes' which that criticism championed. The censure of the popular drama, and the attempt to introduce a more severe classical form illustrated by the essay of Sir Philip Sidney, and the censure of rhymed verse, and the attempt to introduce some adaptation of classical forms illustrated by the essay of Campion, might be taken, and have been taken, as striking examples of the futility of corrective criticism, and of the superiority of irreflective inspiration over calculation. If I can show that no such clear contrast is possible, and that the relation of the critical to the creative mind was not one of simple antagonism in the Elizabethan age, it will be easier for me to demonstrate the intimacy of the creative and the critical mind at a later period.

Everyone has read Campion's *Observations in the Art of English Poesie* and Daniel's *Defence of Ryme*. Campion, who except for Shakespeare was the most accomplished master of rhymed lyric of his time, was certainly in a weak position for attacking rhyme, as Daniel in his reply was not slow to observe. His treatise is known to most people merely as the repository of two very beautiful pieces, 'Rose-cheeked Laura come' and 'Raving war begot', and of a number of other exercises most of which by their inferiority bear witness against him. . . . I do not believe that good English verse can be written quite in the way which Campion advocates, for it is the natural genius of the language, and not ancient authority, that must decide; better scholars than I, have suspected even that Latin versification was too much influenced by Greek models. . . . But the point to dwell upon is not that Campion was altogether wrong, for he was not; or that he was completely downed by Daniel's rejoinder; and we must remember that in other matters Daniel was a member of the classicising school. The result of

the controversy between Campion and Daniel is to establish, both
that the Latin metres cannot be copied in English, and that rhyme is
neither an essential nor a superfluity. Furthermore, no prosodic
system ever invented can teach anyone to write good English verse. It
is, as Mr Pound has so often remarked, the musical phrase that
matters.[1] The great achievement of Elizabethan versification is the
development of blank verse; it is the dramatic poets, and eventually
Milton, who are Spenser's true heirs. ... The second greatest
accomplishment of the age was the lyric; and the lyric of Shakespeare
and Campion owes its beauty not primarily to its use of rhyme or to its
perfection of a 'verse form', but to the fact that it is written to musical
form; it is written to be sung. Shakespeare's knowledge of music is
hardly likely to have been comparable to Campion's; but in that age a
writer could hardly escape knowing a little. I can hardly conceive
such a song as 'Come away death' being written except in collabora-
tion with the musician.[2] But, to return to Campion and Daniel, I
consider the controversy important, not because either was quite
right or wrong, but because it is a part of the struggle between native
and foreign elements as the result of which our greatest poetry was
created. Campion pushed to an extreme a theory which he did not
himself often practise; but the fact that people could then think along
such lines is significant.   ...

SOURCE: extract from 'Apology for the Countess of Pembroke'
(1932), one of the Charles Eliot Norton Lectures delivered at
Harvard (1932–33) published as *The Use of Poetry and the Use of
Criticism: Studies in the Relation of Criticism to Poetry in England*
(London, 1933), pp. 37–40.

NOTES

1. When Mr Drinkwater says (*Victorian Poetry*) 'there is now no new verse
form to be discovered in English' it is his own conception of form that
precludes novelty. He really means 'there can be no new verse form exactly
like the old ones' – or like what he thinks the old ones are. See a curious book
on the relation of poetry to music, intended for readers with no technical
knowledge of music, *Magic of Melody*, by John Murray Gibbon (Dent).

2. The real superiority of Shakespeare's songs over Campion's is not to be
found, so to speak, internally, but in their setting. I have elsewhere
commented upon the intense dramatic value of Shakespeare's songs at the
points where they occur in the plays.

Yvor Winters The Sixteenth-Century
Lyric in England (1939)

. . . If we can disengage ourselves sufficiently . . . from the preconception that sixteenth-century poetry is essentially Petrarchist, to sift the good poems, regardless of school or of method, from the bad, we shall find that the Petrarchist movement produced nothing worth remembering between Skelton and Sidney, in spite of a tremendous amount of Petrarchan experimentation during this period, if we except certain partially Petrarchan poems by Surrey and by Wyatt, and that the poetry written during this interim which is worth remembering belongs to a school in every respect antithetical to the Petrarchist school, a school to which Wyatt and Surrey contributed important efforts, perhaps their best, but which flourished mainly between Surrey and Sidney and in a few men who survived or came to maturity somewhat later, a school which laid the ground-work for the greatest achievements in the entire history of the English lyric, which itself left us some of those greatest achievements, and which is almost wholly neglected and forgotten by the anthologists and by the historians of the period, even by the editors, for the greater part, of the individual contributors to the school.[1]

The characteristics of the typical poem of the school are these: a theme usually broad, simple and obvious, even tending toward the proverbial, but usually a theme of some importance, humanly speaking; a feeling restrained to the minimum required by the subject; a rhetoric restrained to a similar minimum, the poet being interested in his rhetoric as a means of stating his matter as economically as possible, and not, as are the Petrarchans, in the pleasures of rhetoric for its own sake. There is also in the school a strong tendency towards aphoristic statement, many of the best poems being composed wholly of aphorisms, in the medieval manner exemplified by Chaucer's great ballade 'Flee from the press', or, if short, being composed as single aphorisms. If we except Chaucer's ballade, we have no high development of the aphoristic lyric in England or in Scotland before the sixteenth century, and the great aphoristic lyrics of Gascoigne and of Ralegh probably represent the highest level to which the mode has ever been brought. Further, the aphoristic lyrics of the early sixteenth century represent only one aspect of the school that I have in mind; Gascoigne, for example, cast his greatest poem, 'Gascoigne's Woodmanship', in the form of a consecutive and elaborate piece of exposition, and several other poems near his highest level are expository rather than aphoristic in outline.

The wisdom of poetry of this kind lies not in the acceptance of a truism, for anyone can accept a truism, at least formally but in the realisation of the truth of the truism: the realisation resides in the feeling, the style. Only a master of style can deal successfully in a plain manner with obvious matter: we are concerned with the type of poetry which is perhaps the hardest to compose and the last to be recognised, a poetry not striking nor original as to subject, but merely true and universal, that is, in a sense commonplace, not striking nor original in rhetorical procedure, but direct and economical, a poetry which permits itself originality, that is the breath of life, only in the most restrained and refined of subtleties in diction and in cadence, but which by virtue of those subtleties inspires its universals with their full value as experience. The best poems in the early school are among the most perfect examples of the classical virtues to be found in English poetry. I am aware that Gascoigne as a critic recommended the choice of original subject matter, but his concept of originality in this respect was naïve if regarded in the light of later practice, and his own practice must be judged in relation to later practice.

The best poems of Barnabe Googe are the following: 'Of Nicholas Grimald', 'To Dr Balle', 'To Mistress A.', 'To the Translation of Pallingenius', 'Of Mistress D.S.', 'Of Money' and 'Coming Home-ward Out of Spain'. 'Of Money' I quote entire:

> Give money me, take friendship he who list,
> For friends are gone, come once adversity,
> When money yet remaineth safe in chest,
> That quickly can thee bring from misery.
> Fair face show friends when riches do abound,
> Come time of proof, farewell they must away.
> Believe me well, they are not to be found
> If God but send thee once a lowering day.
> Gold never starts aside, but in distress
> Finds ways enough to ease thine heaviness.

The poem illustrates the qualities which I have enumerated. The sprung rhythm of this poem, which is most noticeable in the fifth line, is, while not essential to the school, very common in a few poets, especially in Googe and in Nashe, and is peculiarly expressive of their mood, in its combination of matter-of-factness with passion. By sprung rhythm, I mean the juxtaposition of accented syllables by either of two methods: by the dropping of an unaccented syllable from between two accented, as in the seven-syllable couplets of Robert Greene and in the sonnets of Wyatt; or by the raising of the accentual value of a syllable that should normally be unaccented till it is accented equally with the syllables on either side of it as in the poem just quoted. In the former type of sprung rhythm, the norm which maintains the identity of the line is accentual; in the latter it is syllabic. . . .

The greatest poet of the school is George Gascoigne, a poet unfortunate in that he has been all but irrecoverably pigeon-holed as a dull precursor in the history of certain major forms, but who deserves to be ranked, I believe, among the six or seven greatest lyric poets of the century, and perhaps higher. I base this opinion on the following poems: 'Gascoigne's De Profundis', the second and third of 'Gascoigne's Memories', 'The Constancy of a Lover', 'Dan Bartholomew's Dolorous Discourses' (from *Dan Bartholomew of Bath*), 'Gascoigne's Woodmanship', and 'In Praise of a Gentlewoman Who though She Was not very Fair Yet Was She as Hard-Favoured as Might Be'. There are a good many other poems of charm but of less power and scope.

The third of the 'Memories', a poem on the subject of the spendthrift, and bearing certain resemblances to Wyatt's poem addressed to Sir Frances Bryan, but more pointed, compact and moving, is one of the finest, and displays on a large scale the mastered hardness, the aphoristic analysis, which we have already encountered in Googe. The tone is set in the opening and never falters:

> The common speech is, spend and God will send;
> But what sends he? a bottle and a bag,
> A staff, a wallet, and a woeful end,
> For such as list in bravery to brag.
> Then if thou covet coin enough to spend,
> Learn first to spend thy budget at the brink,
> So shall the bottom be the faster bound:
> But he that list with lavish hand to link,
> In like expense, a penny with a pound,

> May chance at last to sit aside and shrink
> His hare-brained head without Dame Dainty's Door.

The most striking lines in the poem are probably those embodying the colloquial personification toward the middle:

> Yet he that yerks old angels out apace,
> And hath no new to purchase dignity,
> When orders fall may chance to lack his grace,
> For haggard hawks mislike an empty hand:
> So stiffly some stick to the mercer's stall,
> Till suits of silk have sweat out all their land,
> So oft thy neighours banquet in thy hall,
> Till Davy Debet in thy parlour stand,
> And bid thee welcome to thine own decay.

In Gascoigne's society, the destruction of the patrimony was a major catastrophe, and might well be irreparable; it was almost as serious a matter as death or moral disintegration, both of which it might easily involve. Considered in this light, the poem becomes something more than practical didacticism; it becomes a piece of moral analysis, nourished with moral perception. Davy Debet is not only debt, he is the bailiff, the new host, decay itself, and the moral judgement: he is pure terror. The poem displays a measure of the only kind of rhetorical affectation to be found in the school, the affectation of hard directness, supported in part by the traditional alliteration which later poets were to abandon.

There are perfect control and perfect directness in Gascoigne's love poetry:

> That happy hand which hardily did touch
> Thy tender body to my deep delight—

and yet again, from the poem entitled 'In Praise of a Gentlewoman':

> And could Antonius forsake the fair in Rome?
> To love his nutbrown lady best, was this an equal doom?
> I dare well say dames there did bear him deadly grudge,
> His sentence had been shortly said if Faustine had been judge,
> For this I dare avow (without vaunt be it spoke)
> So brave a knight as Anthony held all their necks in yoke:
> I leave not Lucrece out, believe in her who list,
> I think she would have liked his lure, and stooped to his fist.

What mov'd the chieftain, then, to link his liking thus?
I would some Roman dame were here the question to discuss.
But I that read her life, do find therein by fame,
How clear her courtesy did shine, in honour of her name.
Her bounty did excel, her truth had never peer,
Her lovely looks, her pleasant speech, her lusty loving cheer.
And all the worthy gifts, that ever yet were found,
Within this good Egyptian Queen, did seem for to abound.
Wherefore he worthy was, to win the golden fleece,
Which scorned the blazing stars in Rome, to conquer such a piece.
And she to quite his love, in spite of dreadful death,
Enshrined with snakes within his tomb, did yield her parting breath.

If fortune favoured him, then may that man rejoice,
And think himself a happy man by hap of happy choice,
Who loves and is believed of one as good as true,
As kind as Cleopatra was, and yet more bright of hue,
Her eyes as gray as glass, her teeth as white as milk,
A ruddy lip, a dimpled chin, a skin as smooth as silk,
A wight what could you more, that may content man's mind,
And hath supplies for every want, that any man can find,
And may himself assure, when hence his life shall pass,
She will be stung to death with snakes, as Cleopatra was.

In 'Gascoigne's De Profundis' the same qualities of style and the same
rich humanity of feeling are heightened to devotional ecstasy:

> Before the break of dawning of the day,
> Before the light be seen in lofty skies,
> Before the sun appear in pleasant wise,
> Before the watch (before the watch, I say)
> Before the ward that waits therefore alway:
> My soul, my sense, my secret thought, my sprite,
> My will, my wish, my joy, and my delight:
> Unto the Lord that sits in heaven on high,
> With hasty wing,
> From me doth fling,
> And striveth still, unto the Lord to fly.

The greatest poem of the author and of the school, a poem
unsurpassed in the century except by a few of the sonnets of
Shakespeare, is 'Gascoigne's Woodmanship'. It is addressed to Lord
Grey of Wilton, and the allegory takes the form of an apology for the
author's bad marksmanship as a huntsman: it appears that he usually

misses his deer, or else kills by accident a doe carrying or nursing young, and so unfit for food:

> My worthy Lord, I pray you wonder not,
> To see your woodsman shoot so oft awry,
> Nor that he stands amazed like a sot,
> And lets the harmless deer unhurt go by.
> Or if he strike a doe which is but carrion,
> Laugh not good Lord, but favour such a fault,
> Take will in worth, he fain would hit the barren,
> But though his heart be good, his hap is naught.

He explains this weakness, as one aspect merely of his fatal tendency to failure; he has likewise shot at law, philosophy and success as a courtier, and in every case has failed – in the case of philosophy, he admits his own weakness as the sole cause of failure:

> For proof he bears the note of folly now,
> Who shot sometimes to hit philosophy . . .

In the case of the law and in that of the court, he complains further of his incapacity in the baser arts of succeeding, and these passages have remarkable force. Then follows the sombre and powerful passage in which he introduces his next failure:

> But now behold what mark the man doth find,
> He shoots to be a soldier in his age,
> Mistrusting all the virtues of his mind,
> He trusts the power of his personage.

But he finds that he cannot free himself into the exercise of unalloyed physical strength; he has no taste for putting the innocent villager to the sword:

> He cannot spoil the simple sakeless man,
> Which is content to feed him with his bread;

and neither has he a taste for the type of corruption within the army by which officers are able to acquire wealth. There follows a general meditation upon all his failures; it concludes with a brilliant passage in which the poem is returned to the allegory:

> Now when my mind doth mumble upon this,
> No wonder then although I pine for pain:
> And whiles mine eyes behold this mirror thus,
> The herd goeth by, and farewell gentle does.

Then follows the conclusion, the greatest passage in the poem, and
one of the greatest passages in English lyrical poetry, in which the
subject is rehearsed and explained in terms of the allegory; in which
the subject is explained in terms of Christian morality; in which the
author is justified in so far as it comports with Christian humility that
he should justify himself. I wish in particular to call attention to the
rhetorical grandeur of this passage, the terseness, the subtlety of
subdued but powerful feeling:

> But since my Muse can to my Lord rehearse
> What makes me miss, and why I do not shoot,
> Let me imagine in this worthless verse,
> If right before me, at my standing's foot,
> There stood a doe, and I shall strike her dead,
> And then she prove a carrion carcase too,
> What figure might I find within my head,
> To scuse the rage which ruled me so to do?
> Some might interpret my plain paraphrase,
> That lack of skill or fortune led the chance,
> But I must otherwise expound the case.
> I say Jehovah did this doe advance,
> And made her bold to stand before me so,
> Till I had thrust mine arrow to her heart,
> That by the sudden of her overthrow,
> I might endeavour to amend my part,
> And turn my eyes that they no more behold
> Such guileful marks that seem more than they be:
> And though they glister outwardly like gold,
> Are inwardly but brass, as men may see:
> And when I see the milk hang in her teat,
> Methinks it saith, old babe learn now to suck,
> Who in thy youth couldst never learn the feat
> To hit the whites which live with all good luck.
> Thus have I told my Lord (God grant in season)
> A tedious tale in rhyme, but little reason.

Schelling states that 'George Gascoigne was held in high contemporary estimation'.[2] He cites numerous passages in support of the
assertion, which is worth remembering when we come to the
examination of later poetry.

The mature and laconic bitterness of Ralegh, and the bitter terror of
Nashe, both found their best expression in the mode established by
the poets whom I have been discussing, and continued the mode well

into the Petrarchan, and perhaps beyond the Petrarchan, era. Their best poems are 'The Lie', 'What is our Life' and 'Even such is time' by Ralegh; and 'In Time of Pestilence' and 'Autumn hath all the fruitful summer's treasure' by Nashe. 'The Lie' and 'In Time of Pestilence' employ the sequence of aphorisms in a rapid movement and at a high pitch of feeling; all five poems are too well known to require quotation. . . .

The technical range of this school, as compared with the range of the greater Petrarchans, is narrow, but this is not in itself a defect. Morally these poets display a great range and acute perceptions. A limited technique, if it is mastered, may be capable of perception as fine and as varied as a more elaborate one. In fact, the elaboration of technique may be carried considerably beyond the point at which the elaboration has any immediate usefulness, and that is more or less the service which Sidney and Spenser performed for English letters and the disservice which they performed for themselves. They are concerned largely with the pleasures of rhetoric for its own sake, though this is more true of Spenser than of Sidney, and is more true of Sidney's sonnets than of his songs, or at least than of the best of them. As a result, these poets communicate in a remarkable way the joy of purely rhetorical invention, but they spin out small themes to extreme tenuity as a result of their inventiveness, for their sensitivity to language is far in excess of their moral intelligence. Spenser developed the main outlines of a discursive and decorative rhetoric, and so taught much to the dramatists and to Milton, who commonly used the instrument with more discretion than did Spenser. Sidney perfected most of the lyrical graces, and worked out in detail the relationships between elaborate syntax (that is, the forms of logic) and a variety of beautiful stanzaic and linear structure: he thus became the schoolmaster of more than a century of lyric poets. He introduced a mode of perception too complex for his own poetic powers, which were frequently forced to seek matter in the precious and the trivial; a mode of perception too complex, indeed, for any save the greatest lyrical masters of the Renaissance, Shakespeare, Jonson, Donne and Milton, and which was not incapable of leading even those masters frequently astray. In such poems as Milton's sonnets 'On His Blindness' and 'To Cyriack Skinner', as the first of Donne's *Holy Sonnets* ('Thou hast made me'), as Shakespeare's 'Tired with all these', we have a directness, a freedom from superfluity, equal to anything in Gascoigne or in Ralegh, coupled, probably, with greater scope and greater flexibility of perception than can be found among the early Tudor poets. Or at least we can say this: that the later poets were enabled to achieve a more finished and sensitive surface through retreating from excesses which they fully understood, through suggesting by fine modulation qualities which they preferred not to pursue, than were the earlier poets who wrote relatively in ignorance of these excesses; the situation is analogous to that of human virtue, which can scarcely be said to exist in the absence of a knowledge of sin, since without such knowledge choice is impossible.

Between the extremes of Gascoigne and of Shakespeare, throughout the sixteenth and seventeenth centuries alike, we have the taint of decadence, of decoration, of means in excess of matter, usually charming, frequently beguiling in the extreme, sometimes appropriating most of the poem, sometimes scarcely discernible, but likely always to appear a little trivial if suddenly faced with one of the more classical masterpieces.

In relation to the poets who preceded them, then, Sidney and Spenser, and their fellow Petrarchans, are decadents, in the sense that their ingenuity exceeds their intelligence; they are concerned in some measure with the meaningless fabrication of procedure, and only imperfectly with moral perception. In relation to the poets who succeeded them, they are 'experimenters' and prophets, for the measure by which Shakespeare and Milton surpass Gascoigne and Ralegh is at least in part their work. This indicates that Sidney and Spenser are poets of transition, linking two periods of mastery, and are not the first flowers of Elizabethan poetry, sprung from the desert, which they are commonly reputed to be.   . . .[3]

Source: extracts from essay in *Poetry*, LIII & LIV (1939), pp. 260–5, 266–72, 323–6; reproduced, in expanded form, as 'Aspects of the Short Poem in the English Renaissance' in *Forms of Discovery: Critical and Historical Essays on the Forms of the Short Poem in English* (Chicago, 1967).

NOTES

[Reorganised and renumbered from the original – Ed.]

1. The school reached its chronological and poetical culmination in the work of George Gascoigne (1525–77) and in Sir Walter Ralegh (1552–1618),

more particularly in Gascoigne. Thomas Nashe (1567–1601) made a few of
the best contributions, and certain others were made by Barnabe Googe
(1540–94), whose only volume appeared in 1563, and by George Turbervile
(1540–1610), men who came between Gascoigne and Ralegh. . . .

   2. Felix E. Schelling: *The Life and Writings of George Gascoigne* (Publication of
the University of Pennsylvania: Series in Literature and Archeology), II-4.

   3. [Ed.] For criticism of Winters's approach, see in particular G. K.
Hunter's essay reproduced in this collection, below.

James A. S. McPeek   'Catullus's *Vivamus mea Lesbia* in Elizabethan Poetry'   (1939)

. . . The first English poet to show certain acquaintance with Carmen
v[1] appears to have been Sir Walter Ralegh.[2] His use of the poem is an
example of the tendency to employ Catullus's Epicureanism to moral
ends. In the *History of the World*, he illustrates the transiency of
mundane things by a translation of Catullus's lines on the brevity of
life (Carmen v 4–6):

> The Sunne may set and rise:
> But we contrariwise
> Sleepe after our short light
> One everlasting night.

The sentiment, borrowed from a poem quite alien to the ethical
nature of the context, is happily expressed, and it is to be regretted
that Ralegh did not give us a complete version of the poem.

   Shakespeare has the distinction of being the first English poet to
imitate, directly or indirectly, the motif of unnumbered kisses. It
cannot be said surely that Shakespeare remembered carmina v and
vii or even an imitation of them when he wrote in *Venus and Adonis*

> Here come and sit, where never serpent hisses,
> And being set, I'll smother thee with kisses,

> And yet not cloy thy lips with loath'd satiety,
> But rather famish them amid their plenty,
> Making them red and pale with fresh variety –
> Ten kisses short as one, one long as twenty.

> A summer's day will seem an hour but short,
> Being wasted in such time-beguiling sport,   [17–24]

but when a few stanzas further on we find lines which might have been inspired by the same Catullan poems,

> Be bold to play; our sport is not in sight.
> These blue-vein'd violets whereon we lean
> Never can blab, nor know not what we mean,   [124–6]

followed up later by the more significant passage,

> A thousand kisses buys my heart from me;
> And pay them at thy leisure, one by one.
> What is ten hundred touches unto thee?
> Are they not quickly told and quickly gone?
> Say, for non-payment that the debt should double,
> Is twenty hundred kisses such a trouble?   [517–22]

the temptation is great to say that the author of these excerpts knew Carmen v. Neither Lodge nor Ovid provides him this material; but Shakespeare may have known some neo-Latin or French imitation of this poem. His use of the theme anticipates Ben Jonson's by several years.

The possibilities of the influence of a secondary source, problematical in connection with these passages by Shakespeare, are richly illustrated by Samuel Daniel's use of the motif of perpetual night:

> O happy golden Age.
> Not for that Riuers ranne
> With streames of milke, and hunny dropt from trees;
> . . .
> Let's loue: this life of ours
> Can make no truce with time that all deuours.
>
> Let's loue: the sun doth set, and rise againe
> But whenas our short light
> Comes once to set, it makes eternal night.   [3]

The last three lines are essentially a translation of Carmen v 4–6; but Daniel owes their felicity to Tasso:

> O bella età dell' oro
> Non già perchè di latte
> Sen' corse il fiume, e stillò mele il bosco

. . .

> Amiam, che non ha tregua
> Con gli umana vita, e si dilegua.
> Amiam che'l Sol si muore, a poi rinasce,
> A noi sua breve luce
> S'asconde, e'l sonno eterna notte adduce.   [4]

At times when Daniel is more independent, it is much more difficult to ascertain whether he is following Catullus or some one of his imitators. Thus in the *Complaint of Rosamond*, the lines

> Now when the darke had wrapt vp all in stilnes,
> And dreadfull blacke, had dispossess'd the cleere:
> Com'd was the night, mother of sleepe and feare,
>   Who with her sable mantle friendly couers,
>   The sweet-stolne sports, of ioyfull meeting Louers

seem to be a reminiscence in part of Carmen vii 7–8:

> Aut quam sidera multa, cum tacet nox,
> Furtivos hominum vident amores.

The first line of the excerpt from Daniel's poem is a vivid equivalent for *cum tacet nox*. Other elements have entered here, however; this is a night of starless sky, a night of sable mantle, of joyful meeting lovers. Is the effect all the product of Daniel's invention or had he read passages of this nature in Italian and French poetry? The mere presence of a parallel in Catullus is not proof that Daniel knew the Catullan lines, any more than the allusion to the Minotaur (l. 478) is proof that he knew the Peleus and Thetis.

So charming a lyric could not fail to attract the attention of Ben Jonson. Not only is its influence sharply observable in several of his lyrics, but also it challenged his wit as a translator. His first essay at the theme is found in one of those few unaccountable anomalies of genius which are scattered at odd intervals throughout his work. Volpone is cast in the incongruous role of a lover; as a lover, he must sing a song. But instead of makeshift verse, designed to make him more knavish, he sings a lyric whose daintiness here is almost as shocking as Titania's sweet employment of a Catullan motif in amorous caressing of an ass's head:

> Come, my Celia, let us prove
> While we can, the sports of love,
> Time will not be ours forever,

He, at length our good will sever;
Spend not then his gifts in vain:
Suns, that set may rise again;
But if once we lose this light,
'Tis, with us, perpetual night.
Why should we defer our joys?
Fame and rumour are but toys.
Cannot we delude the eyes
Of a few poor household spies?
Or his easier ears beguile
Thus removed by our wile?
'Tis no sin love's fruits to steal;
But the sweet thefts to reveal:
To be taken, to be seen
These have crimes accounted been.

This poem represents Jonson in that midground between imitation or translation and independent composition in which he achieves nearly all his best poetic effects. The inspiration of the 'Vivamus, mea Lesbia', as it operates in this instance, is more potent than any other force, but he is, fortunately, not translating the whole poem. When he resorts to direct translation, he fails, here as elsewhere.[5] But this criticism affects only three of the eighteen lines, and these three, taken with the others, make an individual unit of highly graceful verse. Several scholars have remarked the influence of the Catullan lyric upon the whole poem, although there is nothing in Catullus to account certainly for the concluding distich.

It is not easy to analyse the Protean overtones of influence; yet it is incumbent on us to indicate as nearly as possible to what extent Jonson was influenced by Catullus in this song. It is clear that the first two lines are based on the first line of Catullus's poem. The third, fourth and fifth lines, though implicit in Carmen v 4–6, have a nearer possible source in Ausonius.[6] These lines anticipate the simpler, richer passage that Jonson has translated literally, though very flatly, from Carmen v. Up to this point Jonson has omitted the theme of censure against love (Carmen v 2–3), but he inserts it now: 'Why should we defer our joys? Fame and rumour are but toys.' The theme of the next six lines seems to trace to a passage in Ovid's *Amores* or to some imitation of Ovid.[7] Thus the whole poem appears to be a patchwork of themes from Catullus, and, more obscurely, Ausonius and Ovid.

While reading this lyric for the first time, one may mildly wonder at the omission of the 'arithmetic of kisses'[8] which Catullus so neatly manipulated to the despair of all imitators; but one's wonderment is precipitate. Jonson will not be hurried. After a short interval of romantic Marlovian promises, Volpone supplies the missing lines:

> And I will meet thee in as many shapes:
> Where we may so transfuse our wandering souls
> Out at our lips, and score up sums of pleasures,
> *Sings*) That the curious shall not know
> How to tell them as they flow;
> And the envious, when they find
> What their number is, be pin'd.

It has been demonstrated that Jonson takes his theme of the fusion of souls in kisses in this excerpt from Petronius; but the half line, 'and score up sums of pleasures' is Jonson's sensible condensation of the baffling multiplication of kisses in Carmen v, and the four lines of the Song constitute a fusion of the last three lines of the same poem with the parallel sentiment in Carmen vii. . . .

That he felt the poem worthy of recognition for itself is proved by its inclusion in *The Forest*. Even the kissing fragment was likewise preserved and incorporated in a companion poem (vi, 'To the Same' [Celia]):

> Kiss me, sweet: the wary lover
> Can your favours keep, and cover,
> When the common courting jay
> All your bounties will betray.
> Kiss again: no creature comes.
> Kiss, and score up wealthy sums
> On my lips thus hardly sundred
> While you breathe. First give a hundred,
> Then a thousand, then another
> Hundred, then unto the other
> Add a thousand, and so more:
> Till you equal with the store
> All the grass that Rumney yields,
> Or the sands in Chelsea fields,
> Or the drops in silver Thames,
> Or the stars that gild his streams,
> In the silent Summer-nights,
> When youths ply their stolen delights;
> That the curious may not know

How to tell 'em as they flow,
And the envious, when they find
What their number is, be pined.

That Jonson had not written the complete song at the time when he composed the lines in *Volpone* may be assumed, since he would have found it difficult to exclude a theme so richly consonant with the romantic 'Come live with me and be my love' thesis which Volpone is setting forth. Attracted by the kissing arithmetic of Catullus as others had been before him, and as thousands have been since, Jonson doubtless had in mind a translation of this motif when he wrote his first Celia lyric; but in *Volpone* he veered off at the very moment when he was to essay these difficult lines. One may conjecture that soon after this period he solved the problem to his own satisfaction in the lyric quoted above.

This lyric seems to be a fusion of themes from the two great kissing poems of Catullus.[9] In the first five lines, it is true, Jonson is largely independent, but even here the idea of secrecy in love may have grown out of the idea of scandal intimated in Carmen v 1–3, and the idea of stolen love and the curiosity of observers in Carmen vii 7–8, 11–12. In the next six lines [6–11], Jonson gives us his version of the multiplication of kisses. In this part of his lyric he performs a difficult task as well, perhaps, as it can be done in English; yet he falls far short of the felicity of the Latin. These lines of Jonson's are at least as good as his unimpassioned endeavor to match wits with Catullus in the rest of the lyric. The next nine lines [12–20] have obvious origin in the device of numbering kisses by sands and stars [Carmen vii 2–10]; but Jonson was almost certainly imitating Campion here:

Sooner may you count the starres,
And number hayle downe pouring,
Tell the Osiers of the *Temmes*,
Or *Goodwins* Sands deuouring,
Than the thicke-showr'd kisses here
Which now thy tyred lips must beare. [10]

To finish this patchwork, Jonson turns once more to Carmen v for the last two lines of his poem, giving the thought of Catullus a twist not sanctioned by the original [v 12–13].

This lyric of Jonson's is more important for its influence on later poets than for any merit of its own, if, indeed, it may be said to have any special quality. It is ambitious in scope; Jonson apparently felt that the twin poems of the Latin genius would make an effective unit, a mistake which Secundus and other poets had made before him. Part of the greatness of the Catullan lyrics is that they come to one with the terrific impact of a single impression of an emotion as simple and concentrated as aching new love itself. Jonson's two lyrics were destined, however, to have great influence on later writers, an influence almost comparable to that of [Skelton's] '*Phyllyp Sparowe*' on English sparrow poems.

Campion's version of Carmen v is beautiful and curious. His sense of melody kept him from essaying the difficult multiplication of kisses, and indeed, he appears never to have attempted a literal version of this theme. [Quotes 'My sweetest Lesbia let us live and love': reproduced in full in Hollander's study, excerpted in this collection, below – Ed.] . . . In this song Campion gives us the best close imitation we have of Carmen v;[11] though it is not literal, it is a noble equivalent of the Latin. In place of the mellifluous lines on kisses, he introduces a comment on the futility of war, ending with a refrain based on the Catullan sentiment concluding his first stanza. In the third stanza he very nearly achieves the effect of the 'Lugete, o Veneres' in his appeal to the lovers to grace his tomb.

No writer pays more attention to the themes of Carmen v than William Drummond; but as in his use of other Catullan motives, no author writes in a manner which more clearly indicates an indirect relationship to the work of Catullus than he does. Thus his best interpretation of the motif of perpetual night has no phrase or tag that makes it directly Catullan:

> What doth this Life bestow
> But Flowrs on Thornes which grow?
> Which though they sometime blandishing delighte,
> Yet afterwards us smite?
>
> And if the rising Sunne them faire doth see,
> That Planet setting, too beholdes them die.
> . . .
> It was for Her: and she is gone, ô Woe!
> Woods cut, againe doe grow,
> Budde doth the Rose, and Dazie, Winter done,
> But wee once dead no more doe see the Sunne.

This is an assembling of literary commonplaces, the source of which is to be sought among the many imitations of Carmen v.

His treatment of the theme of the multiplication of kisses indicates a like origin:

> Though I with strange Desire
> To kisse those rosie Lips am set on Fire,
> Yet will I cease to crave
> Sweet Touches in such store,
> As hee who long before
> From *Lesbia* them in thousands did receaue;
> Heart mine, but once mee kisse,
> And I by that sweet Blisse
> Euen sweare to cease you to importune more;
> Poore one no Number is:
> Another Word of mee yee shall not heare,
> After one Kisse, but still one Kisse, my Deare.

Here Drummond appears to allude directly to the 'Vivamus, mea Lesbia'; but it had become conventional to allude to Catullus in this fashion.   . . .

SOURCE: extract from *Catullus in Strange and Distant Britain* (Cambridge, Mass., 1939), pp. 110–20.

NOTES

[Reorganised and renumbered from the original – Ed.]

1. [Ed.] This is Catullus's poem, with an English prose translation (Loeb):

> Vivamus, mea Lesbia, atque amemus,
> rumoresque senum severiorum
> omnes unius aestimemus assis.
> soles occidere et redire possunt:
> nobis cum semel occidit brevis lux,
> nox est perpetua una dormienda.
> da mi basia mille, deinde centum,
> dein mille altera, dein secunda centum,
> deinde usque altera mille, deinde centum
> dein, cum milia multa fecerimus,
> conturbabimus illa, ne sciamus,
> aut nequis malus invidere possit,
> cum tantum sciat esse basiorum.

Let us live, my Lesbia, and love, and value at one farthing all the talk of crabbed old men.

Suns may set and rise again. For us, when the short light has once set, remains to be slept the sleep of one unbroken night.

Give me a thousand kisses, then a hundred, then another thousand, then a second hundred, then yet another thousand, then a hundred. Then, when we have made up many thousands, we will confuse our counting, that we may not know the reckoning, nor any malicious person blight them with evil eye, when he knows that our kisses are so many.

2. There are, to be sure, a few earlier English lyrics which trace in theme to Carmen v indirectly. Thus the Fourth Sonnet in *Astrophel and Stella* has lines closely related to passages in Carmina v and lxviii b, 145–6:

> Night hath closde all in her cloke,
> Twinckling starres love thoughts provoke,
> Danger hence, good care doth keepe,
> Jealozie himselfe doth sleepe;
> Take me to thee, and thee to mee:
> 'No, no, no, no, My Deare, let bee.'
> . . .
> So to raise my heart more hie;
> Feare not, els, none can us spie:
> . . .
> Niggard time threates, if we misse
> This large offer of our blisse,
> Long stay, ere she graunt the same.

Ovid – *Amores* [i iv] and *Heroides* [xvi 317–20] – might have supplied this motif in a piecemeal fashion somewhat better than Catullus; but the synthesis is neither Ovidian, nor Catullan, nor, I believe, Sidneian. The *Carpe Diem* element, which traces to Catullus through Horace, has unnumbered recensions. Sidney was probably imitating some Italian, Spanish or French poem based on Catullus and Ovid. In three consecutive sonnets on kissing in *Astrophel and Stella* [lxxix–lxxxi] Sidney does not use even one line suggestive of Carmen v. . . .

3. Samuel Daniel, 'A Pastoral' [28–30, 91–5].

4. Sir Sidney Lee demonstated that the entire pastoral is translated from Tasso (*Elizabethan Sonnets*, i. liv). See *Aminta*, chorus concluding Act i. This poem was translated by Thomas Watson in 1585, by Abraham Fraunce in 1591, and by John Reynolds in 1628. The work of Reynolds is particularly interesting because he includes with it his *Ariadne's Complaint, in imitation of Anguillara*, a flowery elaboration of Ovid's Epistle.

5. Professors Simpson and Herford – *Works of Ben Jonson* (Oxford, 1925–52), i, p. 386 – remark this peculiarity of Jonson in connection with this lyric: 'When . . . as in "To Celia" (*Forest*, v), Jonson tried the capacity of his English upon a great poet like Catullus, he rarely achieves more than mediocrity. The simple intensity of the "Soles occidere et redire possunt:

Nobis, cum semel occidit brevis lux, Nox est perpetua una dormienda"
offered no vantage ground for the salient qualities of Jonson's style, and
became "literally" rendered, merely smooth and insignificant in his "Sunnes,
that set, may rise againe: But if once we loose this light, 'Tis, with vs,
perpetuall night". Campion comes far nearer with the superb Elizabethan
romanticism of his

> Heau'ns great lampes do diue
> Into their west, and strait againe reuiue,
> But soone as once is set our little light,
> Then we must sleepe one euer-during night.'

6. Cf. the similar sentiment in the well-known lyric 'De rosis nascentibus'
[49–50] commonly ascribed to [Ausonius]: 'Collige, virgo, rosas, dum flos
novus et nova pubes, Et memor esto aevum sic properare tuum.'

7. Donne employs this same motif in a way that helps to illuminate the
general classic background (Elegie xii, 'His Parting from Her', 39–52):

> Was't not enough, that thou didst hazard us
> To paths in love so dark, so dangerous:
> And those so ambush'd round with household spies,
> And over all, thy husbands towring eyes
> That flam'd with oylie sweat of jealousie:
> Yet went we not still on with Constancie?
> Have we not kept our guards, like spie on spie?
> Had correspondence whilst the foe stood by?
> Stoln (more to sweeten them) our many blisses
> Of meetings, conference, embracements, kisses?
> . . .
> Varied our language through all dialects,
> Of becks, winks, looks, and often under-boards
> Spoak dialogues with our feet far from our words?

This is a typical example of the indirect influence of Catullus. One at once
remembers how Lesbia came with shining feet to her clandestine meeting
with Catullus at the home of Allius [lxviii 143–6]; but Ovid appreciated this
theme and expounded it in his *Amores* [i iv 15–18, 63–4] in a fashion that leaves
no room for doubt as to the source of Donne's inspiration:

> Cum premet ille torum, vultu comes ipsa modesto
> Ibis ut accumbas, clam mihi tange pedem;
> Me specta nutusque, meos vultumque loquacem,
> Excipe furtivas et refer ipsa notas.
> . . .
> Oscula iam sumet, iam non tantum oscula sumet;
> Quod mihi das furtim, iure coacta dabis.

This theme is a favorite with Ovid, recurring several times in his works, notably in the Epistle of Helen to Paris. See also Tibullus [I vi 15–20].

8. The phrase is Massinger's . . . *Fatal Dowry* [III i]:

> I have been warn'd of, touching her: – nay seen them
> Tied heart to heart, one in another's arms,
> Multiplying kisses, as if they meant
> To pose arithmetic.

9. In view of the number of imitations of these poems, it is almost hazardous to maintain that Jonson was imitating Catullus directly; but I have not found any neo-Latin imitation which accounts so well for his poem as do the *basia* of Catullus.

10. . . . Campion continues, with lines that, united with the final couplet of the passage just quoted, bespeak an acquaintance with the lyric on the harvest of kisses (Carmen xlviii):

> Such a haruest neuer was,
> So rich and full of pleasure,
> But 'tis spent as soon as reapt.
> So trustlesse is loues treasure.

Later Campion repeats this theme, with notable additions:

> What haruest halfe so sweet is
>   As still to reape the kisses
> Grown ripe in sowing?
> And straight to be receiuer
> Of that which thou art giuer,
>   Rich in bestowing?
>
> Kiss, then, my haruest Queene,
>   Full garners heaping;
> Kisses, ripest when th' are greene,
>   Want onely reaping.
>
> The Doue alone expresses
> Her feruencie in kisses,
>   Of all most louing:
>   . . .
> Let vs so loue and kisse,
>   Though all enuie us:
> That which kinde, and harmlesse is,
>   None can denie vs.

11. It is interesting to compare the first four lines of Campion's song with those of the somewhat more literal imitation of the same motif in the song 'My dearest mistress' in William Corkine's *Second Booke of Ayres*, 1612 . . .

My deerest mistrisse, let vs liue and loue,
And care not what old doting fools reproue.
Let vs not feare their censures, nor esteeme
What they of vs and of our loues shall deeme.
Old age's critticke and censorious brow
Cannot of youthful dalliance alow,
Nor euer could endure that we should tast
Of those delights which they themselves are past.

This stanza, based on the first three lines of Carmen v, reads almost like a translation of Dryden's time.

Rosemond Tuve   'Renaissance Logic and Images: *Cause*' (1947)

[In the chapter from which our extract is taken, Tuve emphasises the centrality of logical thinking in the Renaissance, especially its Ramistic reorganisation in the late sixteenth and early seventeenth centuries. (Ramistic: following the programme of Ramus, the French humanist scholar, 1515–72.) According to her argument, poetry was firmly grounded in the processes of logical thought which students learnt. They began with consideration of the ten Aristotelian categories or predicaments (e.g., 'substance', 'quality'), followed by 'Definition, Division and Method' (as in definition poems). Then followed the 'Places of Invention': 'positions and standpoints of thought from which matter for any discourse was "invented" '. This extract describes poems exemplifying 'the place *cause*' – Ed.]

... Unceasing practice in framing arguments from *cause* not only habituated poets to finding single images from this place, probably deliberately,[1] but also to inventing structural frameworks for whole poems which are essentially arguments based on this place. Such poems need not dispute or harangue. Poets with reflective or expository purposes commonly utilised such tools of dialectic, especially as Ramist ideas of the functions of logic became more pervasive.[2] It is the more fitting that I should exemplify poem structures of this type from the sonnets of Sidney, who is known to have had a lively interest in Ramistic logic – though this interest would affect only attitudes and emphases, not information or basic method.

The structure of sonnet xxvii ('Because I oft in darke abstracted guise')[3] is this: of that and that and that common effect of pride (or adjunct of the proud man), they deem the efficient cause in me to be the foul poison of bubbling pride that makes me fawn on myself and despise others (general effect embracing the specials); yet this is not the cause, for . . . (and he gives the efficient cause by the figure *aetiologia*) Rather it is ambition which makes me pass my best friends unseen, unheard (effect) *because* my thought bends all its powers to the highest place, Stella's grace. This sonnet uses *cause* to frame what is called in the list of places a *differing* or *dissentany* argument; Sidney uses it in other sonnets with equal skill. Ramist logics give it long and careful consideration; they give as the 'sign' of it *not this . . . but that*, and append poetic examples. When these are short, as in the case of single image-units, they are what rhetoricians call the 'figure of difference' (*horismos*); the example in Wotton's Ramistic logic (1626) is from *Faerie Queene* [IV ii 42].

No doubt a poet may consistently write in structures of this kind without realising that he is being a good sixteenth-century logician – though anyone who cares to try will find it oddly difficult to find, in Keats or the Pre-Raphaelites or the moderns, sonnets which might, like this one, be appended to exemplify the discussions in the logics. One has only to open Sidney to find one.

It is necessary to get rid of the modern notion that 'logic' in a poem will make it either coldly unimaginative or pedantically 'abstract', if one is to notice without prejudice the relations between the poems these men wrote and the training they were given in logical invention. It is well to keep in mind the cooperation between the learnings, the part assigned to fancy or *imaginatio* in the process of inventing, and the Renaissance respect for – simultaneously – deliberate artistry and lively freshness. One of Sidney's gayest sonnets is that beginning 'Deere, why make you more of a dogge than me?' [lix]. It is a string of suggested possible causes; all are thrown out on the ground that Sidney himself has each of the virtues of this unjustly successful animal. He alights finally upon a conclusion: not-being-these-it-must-be-*this*; very well–I'll-have-that-too (this is argued after the fashion of the disjunctive syllogism, exalted by Ramists in the teeth of peripatetic objections).[4] The pretended sternness of the dialectic carries the invention into unexpected corners, turns up particulars else passed by, so that we see Sidney, dog and all, and hear the very tone of voice with which he demands: whether the cause be the dog's lovingness? alas he himself burns in love. Whether it be that he waits so well? Sidney 'never thence would move'. Bidden, he fetches a glove? quite unbidden, here has Sidney fetched his very soul and presented it. It must be that Stella grants such delight only to things without wits – there is hope there, for he will soon be eased of his.

Sidney is fond of arguments from *cause*; they tumble over each other even in the *Arcadia*. To glance at other sonnets than his is to see, however, how naturally suited such structures were to the reflective, persuasive or 'deliberative', expository or argumentative purposes which sonnets share with certain other short kinds. Donne displays all but innumerable variations on the general pattern of an argument from *cause*, producing enormous numbers of single images using this logical base; this fact is a commentary on his conception of the uses of poetry and the functions of images. One looks at Drayton's *Idea*; the second sonnet begins with the structure which in logic produced disjunctive syllogisms ('My heart was slaine'; it must have been you or I, it was not I, it must have been you). He cites three effects, as 'evidence', and concludes, with a logical leap scarcely intended to be innocent, that 'Heav'n will still have Murther out at last'.[5]

In *Delia* (1592; the year after *Astrophel and Stella*'s appearance), Daniel's purposes are such as to be better suited by amplifying images of the simpler types; the sonnets are most of them 'demonstrative', sometimes simple praises, sometimes amplification of his pains and thus pleading but indirectly. This makes the difference in tone the more striking when occasional sonnets move toward the purposes of deliberative pieces – the general development of the sonnet as years went on. Such a one is sonnet xxix, and as the poet inquires 'O why dooth *Delia* credite so her glasse', it is the invention from the place *cause* which is responsible for the similitude, for the compression of a *mercy-wanting* storm, and for the malicious comparison with Narcissus which allows Daniel to finish, with witty insolence,

> And you are chaung'd, but not t'a Hiacint;
> I feare your eye hath turn'd your hart to flint.

Neither Daniel nor Spenser is such an acute logician as is Sidney, but the frequent examples of a tone of delicate mockery in the *Amoretti* are more than once found to accompany argument or images from the place *cause*. Both tone and image-technique are related to a shift from demonstrative to deliberative intentions, from magnifying commendation to persuasion and laughing disproof. Sonnet xviii ('The rolling wheele that runneth often round') adduces a couple of examples of common-ordinary effects of given actions, which in all conscience ought to support him in thinking that he may soften her hard heart with *enough* dropping tears and sufficiently long-*continued* entreaty. But

> . . . when I pleade, she bids me 'play my part',
> and when I weep, she sayes 'teares are but water':
> and when I sigh, she sayes I 'know the art',
> and when I waile she turnes hir selfe to laughter.   6

Or, in pursuing the knotty problem of why Nature has given such goodly gifts of beauty to so hard a heart, Spenser remarks on the otherwise reasonable conduct of that benefactress, who 'to all *other* beastes of bloody race' has at least given a dreadful countenance, thus amicably arranging a warning to possible victims [xxxi].

I could spread the net much more widely. If this quick list of sonnets whose structural framework utilises the place *cause* could rather be a careful examination of all the sonnets of all the poets mentioned, I think we should find that considerations of date and of personality are quite eclipsed by considerations of decorum. That is, we should find ourselves watching not the unconscious betrayal of differences in *psyche*, but the operation of 'laws' of decorum which govern the suitable use by any poet of certain dialectical and poetic tools, in obedience to the nature of the poem's purpose and subject. Nor is this pedantry; it is the secret inner orderliness of artistic form. The unconscious betrayals are in the poems, but we have no instrument so delicate that it can measure them, and little right to be pseudo-scientific about ultimate reasons for things while disregarding immediate ones.

Some of these examples have pursued efficient causes, some final cause (like Spenser's remarks upon Nature's arrangements for a lack of facial charm in bears and tigers, in xxxi, above). Final cause is not infrequently pursued at some length, resulting in a structural pattern like that in Sidney's 'Come let me write, and to what end?' [xxxiv]. Self-argument appears in Elizabethan literature not only in the dramatic soliloquy; in this as in numerous poems (*q.v.* Donne) a purpose to which methods of dialectic are suitable has produced a sonnet in dialogue form. It shows *stichomythia* that must be rapidly spoken, contrasted with passages in a very different tone. There is a series of neatly compressed arguments; some are similitudes based on parallel final cause ('Oh, cruell fights well pictured forth doe please'), some are simply statements of the traditional 'places' in rhetorical 'deliberations' (useful or useless to be done, hard or easy: 'What idler thing than speake and not be heard?' 'What harder thing than smart and not to speake?').[7] Sidney neatly turns the whole to a 'praise' of Stella in his last couplet, finding the efficient cause of this useless-useful writing of his in '*Stellas* great power, that so confus'd' his mind.

This 'demonstrative' intention is not infrequent in deliberations of the to-what-end variety; method obeys, the usual amplifying figures enter, and the tone is accordingly elevated rather than incisive. Single figures based on final cause, on the other hand, are likely to serve rather sternly ratiocinative functions. They are frequently sharp and short; in any case, they generally please by witty point.[8] In fact, most images utilising the place *cause* are persuasions, or support of a position. This appears to be the case regardless of date and regardless of whether the poet is 'Spenserian' or 'Metaphysical'.

Here it is wise not to allow differences in pace or verse form to draw us into false antitheses regarding the nature of *images*. It is easy to note the acuteness, the close relation of the conceit to the conceptual point, in Marvell's

> As Lines so Loves *oblique* may well
> Themselves in every Angle greet:
> But ours so truly *Paralel*,
> Though infinite can never meet.
> ['The Definition of Love',: author's italics]

If we are to perceive that Spenser, too, in the providential-storm image of *Amoretti* [xlvi] is supporting an equally precarious position on arguments from *cause*, and if we are to perceive the resultant effect on the tone of the sonnet as a whole, we shall have to read Spenser's conceit through to its finish.[9] This only begins it:

> When my abodes prefixed time is spent,
>   My cruell fayre streight bids me wend my way:
>   but then from heaven most hideous stormes are sent
>   as willing me against her will to stay.

The dilemma into which this puts a lover is one not unfamiliar to the class (and I suppose the odds are three to one that this cloudburst is *metaphor* for – anything the quick reader has the wit to imagine): whom shall he then, 'or heaven or her' obey? Horrid and dangerous choice. Quite ready to make the pious but ironical assertion that 'the heavens know best what is the best for me', he escapes on the back of an image – for who can gainsay that the governing force emanates from the nearer spheres? So

> as *she* will, . . .
> my *lower* heaven, so it perforce must bee.

Here, too, 'the conceit is itself the idea . . . when you grasp the conceit you have the idea of the poem; if you do not grasp it, you are lost'.[10] Spenser concludes his sonnet with a sestet in which he suggests with some reserve to 'ye *high* hevens' that, though their power is, to be sure, not up to the lady's, the two of them together are indeed a little more than a man can stand, and some assuagement – from the only quarter whence it can be expected – would be the part of mercy:

> Enough it is for one man to sustaine
> the stormes, which she alone on me doth raine.

This web-thin innuendo which damns with loud praise, a tiger's-paw blow which kills as it caresses, is admittedly different from Marvell's knifelike dialectic. Marvell's poem has little trace of the intention of praise-and-dispraise to which Spenser's at least pretends. The poems differ in many other ways not strictly related to an examination of imagery; line length and other formal-unit differences have subtle effect. The formal patterns which give the two images their character show dissimilarities as well as the single likeness in logical base (*cause*). Spenser uses his antithesis *sotto voce*; Marvell's comes out in the overt form of a figure of difference, a declared similitude. As an element in poetic technique, the images are comparable largely in their functional use to support a position or explain a course of action and in their contribution of witty tenuousness and delicate (or penetrating) compression; both images indicate the author's own attitude toward his subject with precision and reserve.   . . .

SOURCE: extract from ch. 11 of *Elizabethan and Metaphysical Imagery: Renaissance Poetic and Twentieth-Century Critics* (Chicago, 1947), pp. 319–27.

[Reorganised and renumbered from the original – Ed.]

1. At any rate, poets had been given practice in doing just this, deliberately, elsewhere than in logic. Rhetoric had taught them to make images thus, in, e.g., the figure *aetiologia* (Puttenham's *telcause*), in definitions, in 'confirming' by similitudes, in *metonimia* of the cause, or of the thing caused. A Ramist rhetoric like Fraunce's gives these last a careful treatment, distinguishing also *metonimia* of the subject and of the adjunct; it is interesting that Peacham added this last division when, in 1593, he enlarged by some pages his 1577 treatment of metonymy. We think of 'Death is pale' as a simple figure enough; a user of Peacham (1577) was made to realise that it was a metonymy in which the effect is understood of the efficient cause. Such divisions and awarenesses of process are natural enough to students trained as these were.

2. Ramists took exception to certain aspects of the orthodox treatment of cause and Ramist textbooks treat this place at considerable length, with separate chapters on matter, form, efficient cause, and end, and further chapters on distribution by causes, by effects.

3. [Ed.] Sidney's sonnet xxvii:

> Because I oft in darke abstracted guise,
>   Seeme most alone in greatest companie,
>   With dearth of words, or answers quite awrie,
> To them that would make speech of speech arise,
> They deeme, and of their doome the rumour flies,
>   That poison foule of bubling pride doth lie
>   So in my swelling breast that only I
> Fawne on my self, and others do despise:
>   Yet pride I thinke doth not my soule possesse,
> Which lookes too oft in his unflattring glasse:
> But one worse fault, *Ambition*, I confesse,
> That makes me oft my best friends overpasse,
>   Unseene, unheard, while thought to highest place
>   Bends all his powers, even unto *Stella's* grace.

4. Since I think that the influences of logical study upon images were chiefly exerted through habituation to certain basic processes of invention, I do not take up those portions of logic in which students learned to *dispose* arguments found by these processes into propositions or syllogisms. Although syllogistic types of reasoning frequently occur in Renaissance poems, the effects of such structures upon images would not show us anything I do not mention. Certain general notions propounded by Ramists about the very nature of proof, etc., may have affected images. . . . Ramistic emphasis upon the disjunctive syllogism may have been one such influential general point;

for a clear exposition of what this emphasis involved see Perry Miller, *The New England Mind* (New York, 1939), esp. pp. 136–9.

5. Sonnet added in 1599. For an example in which a string of possible causes is allowed to remain in generalised language, leading to an either-or conclusion, see 'Is not Love here, as 'tis in other Clymes' (No. 27; new in 1619). For one, pursuing causes, in which an argument 'from differences' entails the use of several rhetorical figures, see the charming 'Deare, why should you command me to my Rest' (No. 37; first appearance 1602).

6. I have signalised the indirect discourse by this unauthorised punctuation because I do not know of any Elizabethan sonnet series which has suffered more than the *Amoretti* by being too solemnly read, though I think that in many others as well criticism has shown itself oblivious to those indications of the *tone of voice* which contemporaries caught immediately because they were trained to perceive an author's purpose through delicate rhetorical variations. I suppose that there have even been critics who have read *Amoretti*, xxxii as though Spenser really intended 'the paynefull smith' to lead him to the serious conclusion 'What then remaines but I to ashes burne?' and as though the rhyme scheme were responsible for the metaphor and pun in the plaints he has *applyde*, and for the lacrimose reflection that this unnatural substance the 'harder growes the harder she is smit.' The lighthearted and entertaining self-criticism (in the implied comparison between the smith's *heavy sledge* and all the poems which Spenser has composed to 'beat on th' andvyle of her stubberne wit') is not noticed in this or other poems by those who are convinced that 'Spenser had no humor'.

7. The frequency with which poets use these traditional 'places' may have more to do with the fact that they are just naturally the positions of persuasion than with the fact that every poet must have written dozens of exercises based on them (on whether a thing be honest, profitable, hard or easy, necessary or not, possible, etc.). It probably pleased readers, in any case, to meet these old faithfuls. I have not tried modern poems to see whether those untrained in sixteenth-century rhetoric can avoid these 'places', for I find it more curious than important that even Donne's 'By our first strange and fatall interview' proceeds: from *profitableness*, to *honesty*, to *possibility*, to *difficulty*, and finally to the persuasive recommendation of a better course to follow [Elegy xvi].

8. A longish example is Sidney's comparison of Love's foolishness, in not seeking to get into Stella's very heart, to the naiveté of the child who does not know enough to use a book for *its own proper ends:* 'That like a Childe that some faire booke doth finde / With gilden leaves of colloured Velom, playes; / Or at the most on some faire picture staies, / But never heedes the fruite of Writers minde' [*Astrophel and Stella*, xi].

9. See Bonamy Dobrée, 'Milton and Dryden: A Comparison and Contrast in Poetic Ideas and Poetic Method', *English Literary History*, iii (1936); only the first four lines of Spenser's conceit are used for comparison with Marvell's, which is said to differ by virtue of the fact that it 'involves thought'.

10. Dobrée, op. cit., p. 86; said of Marvell. I also find difficulty in another familiar differentia for the Metaphysical conceit: 'the unexpected bringing together of ideas that seem to have nothing in common.' It is so hard to know when ideas would seem unrelated, to others, that I find this almost useless as a tool for discriminating between images. On the face of it, one of the lower spheres is no more like a woman than a line is like love. Our reactions really depend on the aptness of the *logical link which relates* the ideas, *for the given image*, and on how cunning the author may be in making us see it. Or, as Aristotle remarked, on how much genius the writer may show in seizing relationships [*Poetics*, xxii].

Donald Davie Syntax as Music in the Poetry of Thomas Sackville (1955)

[In chapter 2 of his book from which this extract is taken, Davie has explored Suzanne Langer's view, in *Philosophy in a New Key* (1942), that poetry comes closer to music than to speech or prose; 'the central act of poetry as of music, is the creation of syntax, of meaningful arrangement' – Ed.]

If we reject Mrs Langer's analysis as a full account of the nature of poetic syntax, we have still to acknowledge that to take the play of syntax on her terms can illuminate certain poetic effects which previously could not be rationalised. It is worth taking a case which shows the advantages, if also the limitations, of examining poetic syntax from her point of view. This will be all the more effective if we find a case quite remote in time and kind from symbolist and post-symbolist verse. I propose to examine from this point of view two poems by Thomas Sackville from the sixteenth-century *Mirror for Magistrates*.

Sackville in one of the best passages of the 'Complaint of Henrie Duke of Buckinghame' (which seems to me, incidentally, quite as good as the better known 'Induction') rings the changes, through several stanzas, on one simple but effective syntactical arrangement. In stanzas 142, 143, Buckingham is made to apostrophise Rome and reproach her for her ungrateful treatment of the patriot Camillus:

> Rome thou that once advaunced up so hie
> thie staie, patron, and flour of excelence
> hast now throwen him to depth of miserie
> exiled him that was thie hole defence
> ne comptes it not a horrible offence
> to reaven him of honnour and of fame
> that wan yt the whan thou had lost the same.
>
> Behold Camillus he that erst revived
> the state of Rome that dienge he did find
> of his own state is now alas deprived
> banisht by them whom he did thus detbind
> that cruell age unthankfull and unkind
> declared well their fals unconstancie
> and fortune eke her mutabilitie.

The construction 'exiled him that was thie hole defence' is natural enough and would go unnoticed were it not echoed almost at once:

> to reaven him of honnour and of fame
> that wan yt the whan thou had lost the same,

and echoed again in the next stanza:

> banisht by them whom he did thus detbind.

The little tune comes again and again, restated in each of the next three stanzas. Buckingham apostrophises Scipio, who

> art now exild as though thow not deserved
> to rest in her whom thow had so preserved.

He turns again on Rome:

> Ingratefull Rome hast shewed thie crultie
> On him by whom thow livest yet in fame.

And finally, approving Scipio's contemptuous gesture,

> his cinders yet lo doth he them denie
> that him denied amongst them for to die.

The sentence itself has a little tragic plot, with the peripeteia at the turn on the relative pronoun. As Miss Rosemond Tuve has said so well, to handle syntax with this nicety is to come as near as may be to the impossible ideal of a silent eloquence. And this is a way of handling syntax for which neither Hulme[1] nor Mrs Langer makes provision.

On the other hand, there is, in the 'Complaint', a justly famous lyrical digression on sleep and night [stanzas 159, 160, 161]. While the beauty and pathos of these stanzas is acknowledged, I do not know that anyone has tried to account for their powerful effect, coming where they do. To do so, one needs to quote not the three stanzas alone, but a block of seven; and then to have recourse to Mrs Langer:

> For by this wretch I being strait bewraied
> to one John mitton shreif of shropshere then
> all sodenlie was taken and convaied
> to Salsburie with rout of harnest men
> unto King Richard ther encamped then
> fast by the citie with a mightie host
> withouten dome wher hed and lief I lost.
>
> And with those wordes as if the ax even there
> dismembred had his hed and corps apart
> ded fell he doune and we in wofull feare
> amasd beheld him when he wold revart
> but griefes on griefes stil heapt about his hart
> that still he laie sometime revivd with pain
> and with a sigh becoming ded againe.
>
> Mid night was come and everie vitall thing
> with swete sound slepe their wearie lims did rest
> the bestes were still the litle burdes that sing
> now sweteli slept beside their mothers brest
> the old and all were shrouded in their nest
> the waters calm the cruell seas did cesse
> the woods and feldes and all things held their peace
>
> The golden stars weare whirld amid their race
> and on the erth did laugh with twinkling light
> when ech thing nestled in his resting place
> forgat daies pain withe plesure of the night
> the hare had not the gredy houndes in sight
> the ferfull dere of deth stode not in doubt
> the partridge dremd not of the sparhaukes fote
>
> The ouglie bear now minded not the stake
> nor how the cruel mastives did him tere
> the stag laie stil unroused from the brake
> the formie bore ferd not the hunters spere
> al thing was stil in desert bush and brere
> with quiet hart now from their travels cest
> soundlie they slept in midst of all their rest.

> Whan Buckingham amid his plaint opprest
> with surging sorowes and with pinching paines
> in sorte thus sowned and with a sigh he cest
> to tellen furth the trecherie and the traines
> of Banaster which him so sore distraines
> that from a sigh he fals in to a sound
> and from a sound lieth raging on the ground
>
> So twitching wear the panges that he assaied
> and he so sore with rufull rage distraught
> To think upon the wretche that him betraied
> whome erst he made a gentleman of nought
> That more and more agreved with this thought
> he stormes out sights and with redoubled sore
> Shryke with the furies rageth more and more.

It is plain that if a modern editor were to punctuate this, he would make one sentence of stanza 157 (the first quoted) and probably of 158 also. Stanza 159 however contains six sentences, 160 has four, 161 has five, 162 and 163, resuming the narrative, seem to make up one sentence between them. In fact, it seems to be Sackville's normal procedure to make the metrical unit (the stanza) the grammatical unit also. From this flowing melody, it is easy for Sackville to modulate into a plangent strain by putting into the stanza several short and simple, poignant sentences. (Of course this does not 'explain' the effect; not all the eloquence is silent, and we certainly need Dr Swart's[2] admirable account of Sackville's diction.)

It is plain that we have, in Sackville's lyrical digression on sleep, a clear example of the sort of poetic syntax that Susanne Langer led us to envisage. We admitted as much by the musical analogy we had to use – 'From this flowing melody, it is easy ... to modulate into a plangent strain.' This, of course, is something that could have occurred to any critic, whether he had read Susanne Langer or not. (In fact, I had noted it in just those terms before reading *Philosophy in a New Key*.) But this is true, I suggest, only because Sackville is working on a large scale and the machinery of his effects is correspondingly massive. The example is an obvious one; but it seems clear that effects no different in kind can be detected, once we are prepared for them, within the compass of a sonnet. And this is the value of Mrs Langer's note about musical equivalents for 'the suspensions and periodic decisions of propositional sense in poetry'.

What Sackville has to say in the stanzas about night does not exact from him the peculiar syntactical arrangements he finds for it. On the contrary the first two of the stanzas we quoted, being simple narrative, seem to demand a syntax much simpler than the complex sentences Sackville finds for them:

> For by this wretch I being strait bewraied
> to one John mitton shreif of shropshere then
> all sodenlie was taken and convaied
> to Salsburie with rout of harnest men
> unto King Richard ther encamped then
> fast by the citie with a mightie host
> withouten dome wher hed and lief I lost.

There is no articulation of meaning (e.g. of cause and effect) to compel each clause to grow out of the one before it, as each one does. Of course the syntax and the sense are not at odds, as they would have been, for instance, if we were here learning for the first time of Buckingham's death by execution. (If that had been the case, then to put the momentous information in a last subordinate clause would give it a ludicrous air, as of a careless afterthought – there is a passage in Wordsworth's 'Vaudracour and Julia' where this happens.) Still the sense does not demand a particular syntactical form, in the way that Camillus and Scipio demand the syntax Sackville gives them. The arc of their career in public life is the arc described by the sentences which describe it – 'banisht by them whom he did thus detbind'. Here the turn on the pronoun is not a matter of convenience but of necessity, if the curve of syntax is to reproduce the curve of destiny.

The distinction is not a fine one, though here it may seem to be niggling. Camillus and Scipio ride through on a syntax which is the authentic thing, which does what it appears to do. The syntax of the stanzas on night and sleep appears to be collecting *exempla*; in fact, it is the servant of a plangent rhythm, stopping and starting as the rhythm commands.

Of course I have used a musical metaphor for the Camillus-Scipio passage also. The recurrent syntactical arrangement is 'a little tune'. But this is natural. Just as Sackville takes care in the 'Induction' not to let his syntax come to blows with his sense, so here in the 'Complaint' he takes care to profit by his fidelity to the sense, to make music on a recurrent motif. No doubt in the greatest poetry sense and music go together so closely that it is impossible to say that one came before the other. Nevertheless the distinction remains, and I insist it is a crucial one.

This use of 'music' – 'the music of the poem' – is far from satisfactory. To speak of 'sense and music' in a poem is not a great deal better than saying 'sense and sound', a phrase time-honoured in other connections but quite out of place here. The trouble is that music can be heard, and so when we speak of the music of verse, we think at once of those elements in poetry, phonetic and rhythmical, that likewise appeal to the ear. But when we speak of music in relation to poetic syntax, we mean something that can be appreciated in silent reading without the reader having to imagine how the poem would sound if it were uttered aloud. This is a silent music, a matter of tensions and resolutions, of movements (but again not rhythmical movements) sustained or broken, of ease or effort, rapidity or languor. What we mean, in fact, is *empathy*. Empathy occurs in our response to the plastic arts when 'we feel ourselves occupying with our senses the *Gestalt* of the rising column or the spatial design of a picture'.[3] Sir Herbert Read warns us regarding empathy, that 'in general our use of the word in literary criticism can only be analogical'. Yet he agrees that 'there may be a true empathic relationship to the sound and shape of a poem – our response to metre, for example'. It is Susanne Langer's achievement to have shown that our response to syntax can be 'a true empathic relationship' also.

Perhaps this appears most clearly in respect of pace. We are accustomed to think, quite rightly too, that trisyllabic metre is more rapid than the iambic:

> The Assyrian came down like the wolf on the fold,
> And his cohorts were gleaming in purple and gold.

We certainly get the impression, which may even be true to fact, that in reading these lines (even silently) we have read twenty-four syllables in the time we take, in iambic verse, for sixteen. Hence we call it rapid. But now consider Pope:

> The thriving plants ignoble broomsticks made,
> Now sweep those Alleys they were born to shade

Here too, in this iambic verse, we get an impression of rapidity, but of a quite different sort. This is rapid because it expresses so much in so short a time. The rapidity of Byron is a rapid movement of lips and tongue; Pope's rapidity is a rapid movement of the mind. Pope's rapidity we perceive by empathy; Byron's we do not.

T. S. Eliot has remarked, 'I know . . . that a poem or a section of a poem tends to appear first in the shape of a rhythm before developing into words, and that this rhythm is capable of giving birth to the idea and the image'. And Schiller says, 'When I sit down to write a poem, what I most frequently see before me is its musical element and not a clear idea of the subject, about which I am often not entirely clear myself.' Both these statements are cited by Daniel-Henry Kahn-weiler, in his book on Juan Gris,[4] at a point where he is arguing that Gris, too, got the first idea for a canvas in terms of a spatial rhythm. This rhythm, worked out in preliminary drawing and then trans-ferred to the canvas, produced shapes which were only at a relatively late stage in the composition 'modified' (to use Gris's own term) into the semblance of a guitar, a bowl of fruit, a coffee-mill, or whatever else.

If Kahnweiler is right, certainly Gris's procedure is precisely analogous to what both Schiller and Eliot record as their own ways of going to work. Yet 'rhythm' and 'musical element' are not necessarily the same thing. Whatever Schiller meant by 'musical element', we cannot help but relate it to what has just been established as the soundless music of poetic syntax.

Interesting in this connection is a passage some pages earlier in Kahnweiler's book, where he considers Thierry-Maulnier's remark on rhythm in poetry, to the effect that 'it only exists where the repeated and regular shocks of an exact mechanism maintain the soul in a sort of vigilant torpor like the mysterious receptivity of a medium, so that everything is excluded which is not the pure suspense in anticipation of the unforeseeable'. The trouble with this is the emphasis on regularity, which seems to reduce rhythm to metre. Ignore this (as Kahnweiler for his quite different purposes has to do), and the 'exact mechanism', producing 'the pure suspense in anticipa-tion of the unforeseeable', could be taken to describe a piece of complex poetic syntax no less than a piece of complex and sounding rhythm. Indeed such syntax *is* rhythm, but soundless. And after all the rhythm in the head of the poet before he starts to write is soundless, in any case. We need Thierry-Maulnier's expressions to define the effect of such elaborate poetic syntax as that of F. T. Prince in his 'Epistle to a patron'. The sounded rhythm of that poem is very loose indeed. It can afford to be, but only because the unsounded rhythm of the syntax is so elaborately strict.

Thus, if all poems are born as rhythms, then some, it seems, may be born as rhythms of ideas, that is, as patterns of syntax rather than patterns of sound. And this would make of syntax the very nerve of poetry.

SOURCE: chapter extract from *Articulate Energy: An Enquiry into the Syntax of English Poetry* (London, 1955), pp. 24–32.

NOTES

[Reorganised and renumbered from the original – Ed.]

1. In his opening chapter Davie examines the claim, made by T. E. Hulme, in *Speculations* (London, 1924), that poetry needs to 'abnegate syntax'.

2. J. Swart, *Thomas Sackville: A Study in Sixteenth-Century Poetry*, Groningen Studies in English, I (Groningen, 1949).

3. Sir Herbert Read, 'The Critic as Man of Feeling', *Kenyon Review*, XII, 4 (Autumn 1950), p. 577.

4. Daniel-Henry Kahnweiler, *Juan Gris: His Life and Work*, tr. Douglas Cooper (London, 1947), p. 104.

5. Ibid, pp. 100, 101.

Wylie Sypher   'The Ornamental Surface: Spenser'   (1956)

... The renaissance has a two-dimensional as well as a three-dimensional style. The integrity of the wall surface, the profile contour, the delicate circumscription, the low-relief view of things – all these suggest that renaissance style is marked by the plane, the clear line, the 'multiplicity' of single units; they also explain why quattrocento painting uses fussy details and 'petty flourishes', giving to it an air of 'breathless complexity'. In spite of the humanist's architectural feeling for reality, enabling him to imagine a world in spacious deep perspective, it is undeniable that early renaissance art, in particular, is marked by a high degree of 'decorative isolation' and 'fractional seeing' in a flat pattern with sharp naturalistic details.

Here is a point of interference in techniques. Further, one might say that the naturalistic technique of renaissance art – which is inherited from the linear and cartographic techniques of the Middle Ages – best represents itself in shallow seeing, whereas the more intellectualist and theoretical technique of renaissance art appears in the effort to enclose the world in proportional cubic space.

In the renaissance style of decorative isolation or 'fractional seeing' Botticelli and Spenser are unequalled. So fastidiously do both perceive single flowers, leaves, hairs, wavelets and fluttering of garments that their art tends to be illustrative; their ornamental and sometimes agitated passages read like elegant excerpts from a cartographic scene. And indeed the perspective in Spenser and Botticelli seems anachronistic, as if some medieval artist had been born out of his time into the humanism of a later age. Thus the two are very self-conscious and treat allegory with a sophistication that is, at times, almost preciosity. Spenser is as 'romantic' – and as neoplatonic – as Botticelli. Berenson writes sympathetically of Botticelli's fragile, almost disembodied, vision, his 'linear decoration' and 'linear symphony' – 'and to this symphony, everything is made to yield'. Botticelli discovered a way to translate values of the flesh into values of movement, excitable, undulatory, naïve, sedulous. Thus he was able to render tactile values transparently, without having to render the volume of the body itself. Among renaissance poets Spenser has an equivalent transparency and undulation; although his art is less wiry and nervous than Botticelli's, it has the same capacity to transcribe sensuous and tactile values into values of movement, into linear symphony, working itself out through illustrative flourishes. Spenser and Botticelli have the same virginal and studied grace, the same cursive energy. The *Prothalamion* is almost a libretto for the singing contours of Botticelli's Primavera:

> There, in a Meadow, by the riuers side,
> A Flocke of *Nymphes* I chaunced to espy,
> All louely Daughters of the Flood thereby,
> With goodly greenish locks all loose vntyde,
> As each had bene a Bryde,
> And each one had a little wicker basket,
> Made of fine twigs entrayled curiously,
> In which they gathered flowers to fill their flasket:
> And with fine Fingers, cropt full featously
> The tender stalkes on hye.

> Of euery sort, which in that Meadow grew,
> They gathered some; the Violet pallid blew,
> The little Dazie, that at euening closes,
> The virgin Lillie, and the Primrose trew,
> With store of vermeil Roses,
> To decke their Bridegromes posies,
> Against the Brydale day, which was not long:
> Sweete *Themmes* runne softly, till I end my Song.

Perhaps the only comparable poet is Poliziano, whose *Giostra* also shows this sophisticate and decorative naturalism. *The Faerie Queene* retains the medieval processional movement, and in spite of Spenser's effort to impose upon this allegoric romance the discipline of some regularity and 'unity', its proportions remain capricious and its narrative ornate, anecdotal, unfocused. Spenser is so little attentive to probability that the Redcrosse Knight slays a dragon 'three furlongs' from head to tail.

The mobile and clear vision of Botticelli and Spenser belongs to the art of the earlier renaissance, before the 'grand style' of the cinquecento attained a classic dignity by simplifying the composition of painting and poetry. Many years ago Wölfflin pointed out that 'the whole conception of form possessed by the fifteenth century is two-dimensional', bound as it was by 'the spell of the flat plane, placing its figures side by side across the breadth of the picture and composing in strata'. Then, after Fra Bartolommeo and Andrea del Sarto, the painter used 'a grander kind of co-ordination' and gained 'the capacity to see parts collectively and simultaneously, the power of grasping the variety of things in the field of vision as a single unit'. Elevated by this ideal of a calm and spacious beauty, the artist 'conceived everything *sub specie architecturae*' and figures were assigned a fixed position in architectonic space, framed, enclosed and sculptured: 'Weighty masses bound together by strict rule, grandiose contrasts of direction and a mighty rhythm in the movement of the whole'. This mature composition in generous space was the triumph of renaissance humanism and the antecedent of baroque style.

Vasari's *Lives of the Painters* notes the difference between these two phases in the development of renaissance technique. After Masaccio, he says, the masters tried 'to impose rules of perspective, and to carry the foreshortenings precisely to the point which gives an exact imitation of the relief apparent in nature and the real form'. Uccello 'reduced all to strict rules, by the convergence of intersecting lines, which he diminished towards the center after having fixed the point of view higher or lower as seemed good to him'. In contrast Vasari mentions the illustrative technique of Alesso Baldovinetti, whose sensitive talent was for fluent calligraphic detail:

He drew exceedingly well, and in our book there is a mule depicted from nature by his hand, wherein every turn of each hair all over the animal is represented with much patience and considerable grace of manner. Alesso was extremely careful and exact in his works, and of all the minutiae which mother nature is capable of presenting, he took pains to be the close imitator . . .; thus we find in his pictures rivers, bridges, rocks, herbs, fruits, paths, fields, cities, castles, sands, and objects innumerable of the same kind; . . . he represented the Nativity of Christ, painted with such minuteness of care that each separate straw in the roof of a cabin figured therein, may be counted; and every knot in these straws distinguished. . . .

Because of this graceful draughtsmanship Baldovinetti's painting is almost rococo in its charming optical notations.

And indeed there is something rococo in the decorative conceited language of Elizabethan prose and verse, accepting as it does Alberti's principle that ornament is an 'auxiliary brightness' on the surface of Beauty, which consists in proportion. The renaissance literary critics were always talking about the need for 'decoration' and 'variety' in diction. Du Bellay and Ronsard wanted to 'illuminate' the French language by elegant phrases chosen from Greek and Latin poets, 'which make the verse glitter like precious stones'. Whatever were the objections to using 'inkhorn' terms, the Euphuists everywhere 'decorated' their prose with fantastic conceits, like the petty flourishes in quattrocento Italian painting, to give it an 'auxiliary brightness' and high surface tension. The Euphuistic style – for example, in Greene's *Carde of Fancie* – has the breathless complexity, restlessness and fractional accent we find in Baldovinetti; in this pre-classic phase of renaissance art the separate units, however neatly proportioned, always keep their clear identity within the composition:

. . . for as I have one childe which delights me with her vertue, so I have another that despights me with his vanitie, as the one by dutie brings me joye, so the other by disobedience breeds my annoy: yea, as the one is a comfort to my minde, so the other is a fretting corasive to my heart; for what griefe is there more griping, what paine more pinching, what crosse more cumbersome, what plague more pernitious, yea, what trouble can torment me worse, than to see my sonne, mine heire, the inheritour of my dukedom, which should be the piller of my parentage, to consume his time in roysting and ryot, in spending and spoiling, in swearing and swashing, and in following wilfullye the furie of his owne franticke fancie.

Almost any passage of conceited prose has this illustrative visibility, this dainty extravagance which is distracting in its multiplicity. We could say of Greene what is said of Pisanello's fussy paintings: all the many details are held in the same plane of interest. There is vivid naturalism, but the total effect is dilettante. In fact, like much early-renaissance painting, the conceited style elaborates its naturalistic details within a decorative surface pattern: the ornamental and learned design of the Euphuist sentence (with iso-colon, parison, paromoion) accommodates every fantastic precision and could be taken as an early phase of mannerist art if its verbal sophistication involved any psychological sophistication.

The renaissance liking for the 'gallant invention', the ornamental surface, is best expressed in the witty form of the emblem, the 'device' that appears in literature and the graphic arts. The emblem is an ornamental figure inscribed upon any surface and is defined by Geoffrey Whitney in 1586: 'The word [emblem] is as much to say in English as *To set in*, or *To put in*: properly meant by such figures or works as are wrought in plate, or in stones in the pavements, or on the walls, or such like, for the adorning of the place.' The emblem has a maximum surface vitality, and is, almost literally, the *inscription* of a decorative pattern worked out in naturalistic flourishes. Consider, for a moment, the witty Elizabethan sonnet as an overwrought inscription in low, taut relief; especially one of Spenser's *Amoretti*:

> Sweet is the Rose, but growes upon a brere;
> Sweet is the Iunipere, but sharpe his bough;
> Sweet is the Eglantine, but pricketh nere;
> Sweet is the firbloome, but his braunches rough.
> Sweet is the Cypresse, but his rynd is tough,
> Sweet is the nut, but bitter is his pill;
> Sweet is the broome-flowre, but yet sowre enough;
> And sweet is Moly, but his root is ill.
> So euery sweet with soure is tempred still,
> That maketh it be coueted the more:
> For easie things that may be got at will,
> Most sorts of men doe set but little store.
> Why then should I accoumpt of little paine,
> That endlesse pleasure shall vnto me gaine.   [XXVI]

The logic and design have a symmetry alien to mannerist art; but the images are fractional and the wit, with its busy illustration, is like the shallow ornament in the emblem. Frequently the design of the Italian painter conformed of necessity to the surface available inside some conventional framework like the triptych, the equilateral triangle, the semicircle, the rondo – frames analogous to patterns of the sonnet, the eclogue, the madrigal, and other forms.

Inherent, then, in renaissance style there is a dramatic disharmony between the foreground surface and unified deep space – the noble spaciousness that seems to be the calm signature of the classic human self. In tracing the changing styles of Shakespeare's drama, we might say that Richard II is a transparent profile, sensitively outlined, like Botticelli's figures with nervously drawn edges, and having a decorative grace. Everyone regards the melancholy figure of Richard as predecessor to Hamlet; but Hamlet exists over an abyss of malaise that has not yet opened beneath this frail king, who is seen in a sequence, almost processional, of clearly held poses: a thin helpless character wearing the haunted and decadent features of the luminous beings floating in a Botticelli scene. Richard has the charm of external appearance we see in Botticelli, whose beauty has in it 'something afflicted', so that even when he smiles, it seems, as Wölfflin says, 'only a transitory lighting up'. Amid the pageant of English history Richard is arrested in lyrical attitudes, merely a contour of royalty, who studies his worn image in the mirror he holds before him, telling, in his solemn tremolo, sad stories of the death of kings, playing the wanton with his woes, descending lithely to his little, little grave. . . .

A panoramic view of Italian renaissance painting discloses where the interferences, the transformations, occurred among the three modes of vision between 1275 and 1575:[1] the earliest mode – of the Sienese painters – was to define contour; then after Giotto there was a mode of plastic volume, of substance and flesh arranged sculpturally and architecturally in receding planes; finally there was a 'pictorial' mode, created when Giovanni Bellini and the Venetians tried to see the world as color. As soon as the world is represented by hue instead of by volume and contour, color tends to acquire the values of both contour and volume, and forms become illusions shimmering away into 'tonality'. The world does indeed shimmer away in some paintings by Titian, and in most paintings by Tintoretto and Rembrandt. It becomes musical, perhaps, instead of being architec- ture or contour or mass; then space takes on meanings that elude mathematical ratios. Space is melodic when Leonardo's renaissance science dares dissolve line ('which', says Leonardo, 'is of invisible thickness') and wherever his light is a penetrating ambience, a 'blue' perspective, a plastic dimension. Thus when Leonardo's techniques intersect, his interpretation of space is not alone mathematical; it is also a feeling for atmospheric tone – a *Stimmung*. A cubical quantity is transformed to a painterly quality. Another sort of transformation happens in Raphael's School of Athens (1509–11), where the three grand coffered vaults, the mightiest composition of renaissance painting, do not, in a sense, define architectural space in firm ratios but give it an acoustical quality, a momentum that seems to vibrate off into free energy. Here space becomes echo and motion. Even before Copernicus has imposed his mathematical symmetry upon the universe, Raphael's classic spaces are already resounding with incalculable forces. This resonance mounts to full volume in the mysterious color of Titian's painting, where all transformations occur, where all known values are changed to other values. Giorgione's pastoral landscapes are filled with transformations: the contours of hills, the intervals of space, the accents of local color, are fused into a poetic sonority. One of the most illusive structures of renaissance painting – in which techniques intersect to revise all aesthetic values – is Giovanni Bellini's Allegory of Purgatory (c. 1490). Bellini firmly grounds his composition in all the techniques of renaissance style, for the space is geometrically enclosed, the masses are sculpturally realised, the contours are tightly drawn, the color is stabilised by cool greens, browns and pale blues; yet there is a constant transforming of reality – color becomes contour, contour becomes space, space becomes mass, mass becomes color. These interferences and transformations appear at the groundwork of renaissance style in Ghiberti's bronze doors for the Florentine Baptistry, which are, at the same time, architecture, sculpture and painting.

In poetry, too, there are interferences and transformations, for Spenser's Bower of Bliss [*Faerie Queene*, VI] is contour, color, relief and music; it has both surface tension and sculptural mass, both horizontal and deep perspective, both optical texture and audible melody or 'movement'. All its values can be transvalued, as the repetition of the verb 'seemed' indicates:

> And in the midst of all, a fountaine stood,
> Of richest substaunce that on earth might bee,
> So pure and shiny, that the silver flood
> Through every channell running one might see;
> Most goodly it with curious imageree
> Was over-wrought, and shapes of naked boyes,
> Of which some seemd with lively jollitee,
> To fly about, playing their wanton toyes,
> Whilst others did themselves embay in liquid joyes.

> And over all, of purest gold was spred,
> A trayl of yvie in his native hew:
> For the rich mettall was so coloured,
> That wight, who did not well avis'd it vew,
> Would surely deeme it to be yvie trew:
> Low his lascivious armes adown did creepe,
> That themselves dipping in the silver dew,
> Their fleecy flowres they tenderly did steepe,
> Which drops of christall seemd for wantones to weepe.

Lessing's theory that poetry is not painting, that each utilises only its own technique, does not reckon with these interferences, these renaissance interchanges and correspondences between painting, relief, architecture, poetry and music. Alberti must have had some intimation of these revisions in renaissance art when he wrote that in a clever painting, which defines all its contours, the faces will 'seem to issue out from the panel like sculpture'. The languid, saturated art of Tasso – which is inherently different from the more disembodied but nevertheless elegant art of Spenser – brings to the renaissance a poetic substance generated, so to speak, from the painterly and sculptural techniques; Armida's Garden, with its luxuriant color and texture, has the ambiguous values of Correggio's painting. It was Leonardo who wrote in the *Paragone* that 'Painting is poetry which is seen and not heard, and poetry is a painting which is heard but not seen. These two arts (you may call them both either poetry or painting) have here interchanged the senses by which they penetrate to the intellect.'

The logic of renaissance techniques caused these transformations, through which there was always an escape from the algebra of the *costruzione legittima*. Sometimes the perspective opens upon a pastoral landscape, Arcadia, or on the Vale of the Arno; then space is a suffusion, not a measurement; the distance is a blue silence. These interferences bring us to the threshold of mannerism and the art of

Tintoretto, and Shakespeare at Elsinore, where the russet dawn cannot dispel Hamlet's bad dreams. . . .

SOURCE: extracts from *Four Stages of Renaissance Style* (New York, 1956), pp. 87–93, 95–8.

NOTE

1. These modes of vision are identified by Bernard Berenson in the closing pages of *The Italian Painters of the Renaissance* (1894–1907; 1932).

I. A. Richards   The Sense of Poetry: Shakespeare's 'The Phoenix and the Turtle'   (1958)

Is it not fitting that the greatest English poet should have written the most mysterious poem in English? 'The Phoenix and the Turtle' is so strange a poem – even so unlike anything else in Shakespeare, as to have caused doubts that he wrote it. And yet, no one else seems in the least likely as author.

One of the odd things about the poem is that it has engendered curiosity and praise only in relatively recent times. Emerson was among the first: 'To unassisted readers', he says, 'it would appear to be a lament on the death of a poet, and of his poetic mistress.' 'This poem', he adds, 'if published for the first time, and without a known author's name, would find no general reception. Only the poets would save it.'

Since then many notable efforts have been made to assist 'unassisted readers' without taking us perhaps very much further than Emerson himself went: 'a lament on the death of a poet'; or is it the poetic endeavour? – 'and his poetic mistress' – or could it be that whereto the poetic endeavour devotes itself: poetry?

Let us see. Let us read the poem through twice, once for detail and structure and pondering, and then again for life and motion [quotes the whole poem – Ed.] . . .

The Phoenix here is a unique bird, singular indeed – there can be but the one Phoenix. And the Turtle Dove is so devoted a lover of his Queen – so entirely hers, as she is his – that, like an Indian suttee, he is consumed, burnt up on the pyre, in the flames of her regeneration.

> Let the bird of lowdest lay,
> On the sole *Arabian* tree,
> Herauld sad and trumpet be:
> To whose sound chaste wings obay.

Who is speaking? Who is this 'bird of lowdest lay' who summons this company of birds and has this authority over 'chaste wings'? (You will note, near the end, a very strong use indeed of the word 'Chastitie'.)

I like best the suggestion that the reborn Phoenix herself is here summoning the birds to the celebration of her own (and the Turtle's) obsequies. If so, this Phoenix, this Queen, is perched on her own throne. In *The Tempest* [III iii 20–4] Sebastian cries:

> . . .   now I will believe
> . . .   that in Arabia
> There is one tree, the phoenix' throne; one phoenix
> At this hour reigning there. . . .

> [On the sole *Arabian* tree]

If so, she herself is *Herauld sad and trumpet*; and the sadness is for the Turtle – lost in the fiery rite required for the Phoenix's rebirth.

Various birds are excluded: the ill-omened, the screech-owl, say, because this is a beginning anew, another cycle of the Phoenix' life.

> But thou striking harbinger,
> Foule precurrer of the fiend,
> Augour of the feuers end,
> To this troupe come thou not neere.

Birds of prey are to be kept out too – except the symbol of authority, the Kingly Eagle, which can overawe violence as Henry VII put an end to the Wars of the Roses. Nothing arbitrary or unjust has a place here:

> From this Session interdict
> Euery foule of tyrant wing,
> Saue the Eagle feath'red King,
> Keepe the obsequie so strict.

Obsequie is a deep word here: a following after and a due compliance.

These birds are to take part in a commemorative procession, chanting the anthem, a song with the power of a spell.

> Let the Priest in Surplus white,
> That defunctive Musicke can,
> Be the death-deuining Swan,
> Lest the *Requiem* lacke his right.

Defunctive Musicke: music which has to do with death; the Swan knows how to sing its swan song before its death and knows beforehand when it is to die.

Lacke his right: lack a rightness his participation can give. Some dictionaries say *right* is just Shakespeare's misspelling of *rite* (ritual). More modern critics will call it a pun. It is better perhaps to reflect and recognise how closely interwoven the meanings of the two words can be. A rite may be the observance it is right to give, to accord.

This choral service contains an anthem, a song of praise and gladness; a requiem, a solemn dirge for the repose of the dead; and a *threne* or *thenos*, a lamentation or dirge of honour. Note, too, a curious thing about the structure of the poem: the mourning birds, when assembled and ordered, chant an anthem in which Reason (something being described, talked about, conjured up, released, in the anthem) after going through a strange change, cries out suddenly and then composes the threne, sung at the close, and this threne, so composed

> To the *Phoenix* and the *Doue*,
> Co-supremes and starres of Loue,
> As *Chorus* to their Tragique Scene

ends with directions for a pilgrimage and a prayer.

This singular involvement – each part of the poem being included in and produced by, put into a mouth created in the part before it – has a lot to do with the power and spring of this most concentred and compacted poem.

The next bird, the last of the birds, the only one to be mentioned after the Swan-Priest, may have an importance suited to this special position. The *treble dated* Crow lives, so the legend says, three times, any number of times, longer than man. A 'lived happily ever after' flavour hangs about him. Moreover, he engenders his offspring by breathing: a very ethereal mode of propagation, the mode by which poems and poetic ideas inter-inanimate and beget their successors.

He is as black as ink, dressed in proper funeral attire, and yet is directed, somewhat as though he did not belong and could not expect to be invited, to join the mourners. Perhaps, being a carrion crow, he is a kind of contaminated character. Here he is:

> And thou treble dated Crow,
> That thy sable gender mak'st,
> With the breath thou giu'st and tak'st,
> 'Mongst our mourners shalt thou go.

> Here the Antheme doth commence,
> Loue and Constancie is dead,
> *Phoenix* and the *Turtle* fled,
> In a mutuall flame from hence.

Loue and Constancie: the attraction to beauty and the attachment in truth.

Notice *is dead*: the two are so much one that even from the first mention the verb used is singular: 'is' dead, not 'are' dead. This confounds grammar, as Reason, itself, is going to be confounded in what follows.

> So they loued as loue in twaine,
> Had the essence but in one,
> Two distincts, Diuision none,
> Number there in loue was slaine.

They loved as do two people who love one another, and yet they were not two but one, and one is not a number. For this duality the same questions arise as in the Doctrine of the Trinity.

> Hearts remote, yet not asunder;
> Distance and no space was seene,
> Twixt this *Turtle* and his *Queene*:
> But in them it were a wonder.

But in them it were a wonder: in any others than 'this concordant one' all this would be 'a wonder'; not so here.

> So betweene them loue did shine,
> That the *Turtle* saw his right,
> Flaming in the *Phoenix* sight;
> Either was the others mine.

The Phoenix's eyes are traditionally of fire; they flame like the sun. But, more than that, the Turtle sees *his right* flaming in them.

His right: all he can ask or be entitled to; all that is due and just; all that he truly is, his true being.

Let me quote a few lines here from *The Birds Parliament* by Attar, the twelfth-century Persian saint and mystic, also about the Phoenix, which in Attar's poem is the leader in the soul's return to God. The poem is translated by Edward Fitzgerald, who translated Omar Khayyám.

> Once more they ventured from the Dust to raise
> Their eyes up to the Throne, into the Blaze;
> And in the Centre of the Glory there
> Beheld the Figure of THEMSELVES, as 'twere
> Transfigured – looking to Themselves, beheld
> The Figure on the Throne enmiracled,
> Until their Eyes themselves and that between
> Did hesitate which SEER was, which SEEN.

Or as in Shelley's lines from his 'Hymn of Apollo':

> I am the Eye with which the universe
> Beholds itself and knows itself divine.

Either was the others mine: diamond mine, ruby mine, yes, perhaps; but, more important, each entirely possessed and was possessed by the other.

> Propertie was thus appalled,
> That the selfe was not the same:
> Single natures double name,
> Neither two nor one was called.
>
> Reason in it selfe confounded,
> Saw Diuision grow together,
> To themselves yet either neither,
> Simple were so well compounded.
>
> That it cried, how true a twaine,
> Seemeth this concordant one,
> Loue hath Reason, Reason none,
> If what parts, can so remaine.

Any other poem, I sometimes think, would have made Reason cry

> How true a one
> Seemeth this concordant twain.

But the poem goes the further step, makes *Reason in it selfe confounded* speak in character and show itself to be confounded. Very Shakes-pearean, this dramatic actuality!

> Whereupon it made this *Threne*
> To the *Phoenix* and the *Doue*,
> Co-supremes and starres of Loue,
> As *Chorus* to their Tragique Scene.

Note that Reason is the singer

> THRENOS
>
> Beauty, Truth, and Raritie,
> Grace in all simplicitie,
> Here enclosde, in cinders lie.
>
> Death is now the *Phoenix* nest,
> And the *Turtles* loyall brest,
> To eternitie doth rest,

To the Phoenix, death is now a nest, a symbol of rebirth, but to 'the *Turtles* loyall brest' it is a place of final repose.

> Leauing no posteritie,
> Twas not their infirmitie,
> It was married Chastitie.

What these 'Co-supremes and starres of Loue' have been concerned with has not been offspring. Besides, there can be but the one Phoenix, although in this poem, we may imagine, the sacrifice, the devotion, of a Dove is needed for each new regeneration or reincarnation.

> The intellect of man is forced to choose
> Perfection of the life or of the work,

wrote W. B. Yeats. Must poets give up their lives so that poetry may be renewed?

> Truth may seeme, but cannot be,
> Beautie bragge, but tis not she,
> Truth and Beautie buried be.

As a poem may be something beyond anyone's reading or apprehension of it?

> To this vrne let those repaire,
> That are either true or faire,
> For these dead Birds, sigh a prayer.

This prayer is wordless; it is sighed only, not spoken. What it might have said is what the whole poem has been conveying, an endeavour to apprehend a mystery. And it is no good asking what this mystery is apart from this endeavour itself.

We may say if we like that this mystery is the mystery of being, which is forever dying into cinders and arising to flame and die anew; and always, perhaps, demanding a sacrifice of constancy for the sake of that to which it is loyal and true. But no remarks on this poem can be more than snapshots of something someone has thought he saw in it: helpful maybe to some but merely curiosities of opinion to others.

There are two remarks I would like, however, to make before inviting the reader to read the poem again straight through.

Beautie, Truth, and Raritie.

The truth celebrated in the poem is chiefly loyalty, faithfulness and constancy, which, as with Troilus, the true knight, the true lover, is truth spelled *Troth*. At first sight troth may not seem to have very much to do with the ways in which a statement in a science may be true (or false), or evidence offered a law court may be true (or false), or philosophical or critical or historical or literary views may be true (or false). And yet, for all of these, if we search and imagine faithfully enough, we will find that the statement or opinion, whatever it is, hangs in the midst of and is dependent upon a vast network of loyalties toward everything that may be relevant. Its truth is a matter of inter-inanimations and co-operations among loyalties, among troths.

And very significant parallels to all this hold for beauty.

This poem, one may well think, is not about any such high and remote abstractions but about two people; two people, who may be thought to have been 'the very personifications, the very embodiments', as we lightly say, of beauty and truth, though they are spoken of in the poem as two birds. That is how the poem feels, no doubt about it. But, as certainly, there is a religious quality in its movement, a feeling in it as though we were being related through it to something far beyond any individuals. This Phoenix and this Turtle have a mythic scale to them, as though through them we were to become participants in something ultimate. All this, however, is so handled that it seems as easy and as natural and as necessary as breathing.

Let us read the poem again with a wider and more relaxed attention. Was it Mr Eliot who remarked: 'There is such a thing as page fright as well as stage fright'? The very greatness of a poem can stupefy the reader.

. . .

To this vrne let those repaire,

. . .

No one who repairs to this urn will think there can be any end to wondering about it.

SOURCE: broadcast talk, WGBH–TV station, Boston, Mass. (winter season, 1957–58); printed in *Daedalus*, 87 (1958) and reproduced in Richards's *Poetries: Their Means and Ends*, ed. Trevor Eaton (The Hague, 1974), pp. 50–8.

Raymond Southall   The Decline of Court Poetry   (1964)

The influence of early-Tudor poetry upon the Elizabethans is far too pervasive and intricate to be traced in detail. But even in outline it can be seen as a process of decay in which the vigour of Wyatt and the best early-Tudor poetry is slowly but relentlessly sapped by imitators and imitators of imitators. The initial impulse of Tudor court poetry is transmitted through Surrey, Grimwald and Vaux whose falling-off is taken a stage further by the editor of Tottel and declines through a succession of anthologies – *Very Pleasant Sonnets and Stories in Meter, The Paradise of Dainty Devices, A Gorgeous Gallery of Gallant Inventions* and *A Handful of Pleasant Delights*. The decline can be seen in Surrey's translation of Petrarch, and the final collapse in that of Thomas Lodge. But evidence of the collapse is almost universal; it is there in Churchyard's handling of Wyatt's political complaint; in Hall's parodies; in Vaux's attempts to communicate an early-Tudor perturbation of mind; in the flagging effort to pretend to the vital insecurity that makes so much of Wyatt significant; in the similar attempts, from Southwell to Fletcher, to play at unquiet minds on the theme of sleepless nights. The conventions which were earlier interpreted in experience harden into Elizabethan rhetoric.

The degeneration has often been remarked in the 'sophistication' to which Wyatt's poems have been subjected by Tottel's elusive editor. Dr Tillyard, for all his metrical orthodoxy elsewhere, sharply commented upon the manner in which the rhythmical richness of 'They fle from me',

. . . slow and halting in part, but full of strange starts and surprises and on the whole astonishingly varied.[1]

has been lost as a result of editorial polishing. In the same spirit Vaux compiles his poem 'In his extreme sickness' from various lines taken from the poetry of the thirties; the 'sophistication' has been achieved at the loss of the rhythmical verve and impulse which directed the earlier poets:

> What grieves my bones and makes my body faint?
> What pricks my flesh and tears my head in twain?
> Why do I wake when rest should me attaint?
> When others laugh, why do I live in pain?
> I toss, I turn, I change from side to side,
> And stretch me oft, in sorrow's links beti'd.
>
> [in *The Paradise of Dainty Devices*]

In comparison with the manner in which the poets of the thirties made use of Chaucer, Vaux is doing nothing more than making verses out of borrowed material, none of which has been converted by any interest to which the verse-making is subordinated. Edwards, the editor of *The Paradise of Dainty Devices* is given to the same practice, and Churchyard in *A Gorgeous Gallery of Gallant Inventions* puts his recollection of the poets of the thirties to the same end:

> Is this the end of all my suit,
> For my good will to have a skorn?
> Is this of all my pains the fruit,
> To have the chaff instead of corn?
> Let them that list possess such dross,
> For I deserve a better gain;
> Yet had I rather leave with loss
> Then serve and sue – and all in vain.

In fact, the only poem in the post-Tottel anthologies that appears to be vintage 1530s is that beginning 'I smile to see how you devise' in *A Handful of Pleasant Delights*.

The sentimentality of Surrey is itself part of the attenuation of contact with present experience which turns the verse-making of Vaux, Edwards and Churchyard into an end-in-itself. The attempts of these poets to give some significance and value to their prosodising leads consequently to facile and extraneous moralising. With Wyatt the moral arises out of the action realised in the poem, as in the drama of rejection and flight, but with, for instance, Grimwald the morality is reduced to a string of precepts having no purchase upon any experience; they are not, that is to say, specific values emerging in an act of creation:

> In working well, if travail you sustain,
> Into the wind shall lightly pass the pain;
> But of the deed the glory shall remain,
> And cause your name with worthy wights to reign.
>
> [in Tottel's *Miscellany*]

Now Wyatt at times may offer good advice, but on no occasion does he only do this; there is always at least the limiting presence of some particular situation, as in the case of 'Greting to you both', which places the poem as an advice poem rather than as a piece of cant. Grimwald, on the other hand, is simply knitting together a number of moral tags which have no particular application because Grimwald does not realise them in any particular experience and they remain the outcome of a purely abstract interest.

To a lesser extent the same is true of Vaux. Vaux is indubitably a more efficient poet than Grimwald, although this impression may be due to the fact that fewer of Vaux's poems are known to us and perhaps those that are known are his best. He is as close to Wyatt as is Surrey in point of quality, and displays the same preciousness of attitude as the younger poet. His most poetical compositions are those in which his interest is most abstracted and this naturally leads him into empty moralising, as when he writes 'Of a contented mind':

> When all is done and said,
> In the end thus shall you find,
> He most of all doth bathe in bliss,
> That hath a quiet mind . . .
>
> [in *The Paradise of Dainty Devices*]

That Vaux should value the achievement of a quiet mind as 'bliss' is symptomatic; the mentality of the poem is effete:

> I can be well content,
> The sweetest time of all my life
> To deem in thinking spent.

The confession of the confected quality of the thinking is well enough born out by the saccharine quality of the sentiment. The emphasis upon sweetness, the placid smoothness of the verse, the moralistic generalities, all bespeak the ivory tower.

The last rather commonplace phrase does on this occasion appear to be justified. In one of his dream poems Hall places his narrator upon a hill from which he can look down upon a corrupt and wicked world interpreted for him by Arete (the Platonism is symptomatic). Both the elevation and the moralising mentor are typical of Wyatt's successors; life is described from a distance, it is looked down upon, and because the poetry does not participate in the life about which it generalises it has no particular existence. Not for Surrey, Harington, Vaux, Grimwald, Churchyard, and company, the doubts, perplexities and uncertainties of one trying to give value to tumultuous experience; they have their verse-making, Dame Arete, and a sufficient stock of past expressions with which to tyrannise the present moment.

The significance of the anthologies is that they establish beyond doubt that the real achievements of the courtly makers are not transmitted to the Elizabethans, and that the Elizabethans are familiar with early-Tudor court poetry only in a debased form. The complete loss of contact with a whole tradition which results can be seen by considering the way in which Thomas Lodge translates the Petrarchan poem which Wyatt gives us as 'My galy charged with forgetfulnes.' The choice of such a lightweight for comparison with Wyatt would be grossly unfair were it not for the fact that Lodge is continuing to translate in the true spirit of Surrey and that Surrey has so often, and so truly, been said to have laid the basis for Elizabethan poetry. Distance from almost any form of experience is really the only thing that gives Lodge's translation a spark of interest and that only because, upon the reader recalling Wyatt's translation, it imparts a peculiar irony to the line 'Time hath subdued art' which occurs in the final stanza. Nothing could more completely illustrate the final degeneration of courtly poetry than Lodge's opening lines:

> My boate doth passe the straights
> of seas incent with fire,

> Filde with forgetfulnesse:
>   amidst the winter's night

when compared with Wyatt's:

> My galy charged with forgetfulnes
> Thorough sharp seas in winter nights doth pass
> Twixt Rock and Rock
>   [Egerton MS. 2711 (28)]

It is true that Lodge's translation occurs in *Rosalynde*, it is Phoebe's sonnetto to Ganimede, but the context gives no reason for supposing that Lodge is not being serious and, in any case, the standard of the translation as poetry is no lower than most of the verse to be met with in the anthologies, and no lower than Lodge's 'My frail and earthly bark' in *The Phoenix Nest*.

But leaving the safety of comparison in terms of a common task – translating Petrarch – for one in terms of a common experience, the relationship between Wyatt and his successors can be more widely, if less certainly, stated. The needful experience may be found in an 'inset' complaint in Lydgate's poem 'The Complaint of the Black Knight':

> The thought oppressed with inward sighes sore
> The painful lyf, the body languisshing,
> The woful gost, the herte rent and tore,
> The pitous chere, pale in compleyning,
> The deedly face, lyk ashes in shyning,
> The salte teres that fro myn eyen falle,
> Parcel declare grounde of my peynes alle   [218–24]

Wyatt need have gone no further for a model for the poem from which the following stanza is taken (not an outstanding poem by any means):

> The restfull place Revyver of my smarte
> the labors salve incressyng my sorow
> the bodys ese And trobler off my hart
> quieter of mynd And my vnquyet foo
> fforgetter of payn Remembryng my woo
> the place of slepe wherein I do but wake
> Be sprent w^t ter*es* my bed I the forsake
>   [Devonshire MS. Add. 17492 (115)]

But he is probably also recalling Chaucer's 'A Complaint to His

Lady' in the particular reference to sleepless nights; Wyatt returns to the theme again [in 'I muste go walke the woodes so wyld']. Wyatt enhances the posture of 'disese' by substituting his own see-sawing antitheses for the older poet's inventory of woes. Where, therefore, Lydgate is simply describing a predicament, Wyatt dramatises by using his rhythmical see-saw as a means of enacting the pitch and toss of the restless mind and the tossing and turning of the sleepless lover. Lydgate, it will be noticed, uses the same divided line, but this does not become a see-saw, it does not become the expression of antithesis.

The examples which follow all, more or less, revert to the narrative simplicity of Lydgate. They fail to achieve that antithetical justification of the divided line provided by Wyatt, and consequently the perplexity of the situation which involves us in the poet's disquietude of mind remains unrealised; in its place we find a loose hold upon certain stock material. In the relevant lines from Southwell's 'Saint Peter's Complaint' the disquietude has in fact been replaced by a complacent apostrophe. Experience to Southwell, one feels forced to conclude, had in this instance none of the complication which makes life such a constant source of perplexity to most people, or at least if it had it is not being allowed to coarsen the balm of rhetoric:

> Sleepe, deaths allye: oblivion of teares:
> Silence of passions: balm of angry sore:
> Suspence of loves: securitie of feares:
> Wrathes lenitive: hartes ease: stormes calmest shore:
> Senses and soules reprivall from all cumbers:
> Benumming sence of ill, with qiet slumbers.

Despite the same phrasal use of rhythm, the predicament so essential to the effect of Wyatt's lines has disappeared, gone are the antitheses, and what for Wyatt was a turbulent but vitally apprehended situation has become, literally, a sedative. What is discerned in the remaining examples is the complacency of this kind of rhetorical handling of the situation.

Sackville's well-known 'Induction' to the *Mirror for Magistrates* is an early but standard product of Elizabethan complacency. Stanza 42 is hardly to be distinguished from the stanza from Southwell above which it closely parallels.

> The bodie's rest, the quiet of the hart,
> The trauailes ease, the still night's feere was hee
> And of our life in earth the better part,

> Reuer of sight, and yet in whom wee see
> Things oft that tyde, and oft that neuer bee:
> Without respect, esteeming equally
> King Croesus' pompe, and Irus' pouertie.

The closest that Sackville comes to a perception of experience which might ruffle the placid structure of his lines is that slight suggestion of paradox in the reference to sleep as 'Reuer of sight, and yet in whom wee see'; but this is only a rhetorical titilation of the reader's attention to be rounded off into a commonplace in the line which follows.

Even in what must be one of the better poems of the Elizabethan period we near the vital spark of experience rather through a kind of reportage which demands our sympathy than through an act of creation and direct apprehension:

> Come, Sleep, O Sleep, the certain knot of peace,
> The baiting-place of wit, the balm of woe,
> The poor man's wealth, the prisoner's release,
> The indifferent judge between the high and low!
> With shield of proof shield me from out the prease
> Of those fierce darts Despair at me doth throw.

If Sidney's lines are saved from the utter complacency of Southwell's and Sackville's, it is by the sincere but easy appeal to our sympathies contained in the last two lines. Sidney's 'Despair' is there as a compliment to Stella, it has no relationship to the ranges of experience informing the poem; coarse compliment in fact since it lacks that kind of backing in the poem and so ultimately perhaps not as sincere as has been allowed.

It may be objected that the greatest 'Elizabethan' poetry escapes the baneful confines of such inertia. This is naturally true, but a great deal of the traditionally 'greatest' poetry does not. It can be observed that once the rhetorical cue, Sleep, is given, even the greatest Elizabethan poet behaves like one of Pavlov's dogs:

> Methought I heard a voice cry 'Sleep no more!
> Macbeth does murder sleep'

Is Shakespeare able to resist the offered sedative? Here at this tense and troubled moment Macbeth's mind becomes inexplicably slack and slides into the well-worn groove:

> the innocent sleep,
> Sleep that knits up the ravell'd sleave of care,

> The death of each day's life, sore labour's bath,
> Balm of hurt minds, great nature's second course,
> Chief nourisher in life's feast, –   [II ii 36–41]

It is not a voice but a whole chorus – Southwell, Sackville, Sidney –
that is singing in Macbeth's ear. In the early part of the play Macbeth
is characterised by a sensitively relevant response to slight nuances of
meaning which frequently manifests itself in perturbed and troubled
rhythms. But in the apostrophe on Sleep he slips from this characteristic troubled immediacy into a second-hand response. The
suggestion is that once the cue, Sleep, has been given, the pull of
Elizabethan complacency diverts attention from the matter in hand,
from the specific dramatic situation, with a resultant loss of immediacy and a breach of characterisation. Shakespeare's attention has
slipped, not just Macbeth's, and his control over the play has been
temporarily subverted. It is, admittedly, a serious charge to bring
against Shakespeare and yet, unless one can subscribe to the opinion
that rhetoric on this occasion pulls Shakespeare in the dramatically
right direction, it seems an unavoidable one.

The voice which Macbeth heard does burst into song in Fletcher's
[tragedy] *Valentinian*:

> Care-charming Sleep, thou easer of all woes,
> Brother to Death, sweetly thyself dispose
> On this afflicted prince; fall like a cloud
> . . .

Here the voice is completely soporific; the phrasing still recalls to
mind Wyatt. But the vitality has gradually seeped from the experience in the course of a century; we now have poetry not as the nervous
but vivid energy it is in Wyatt but as a tranquilliser.

It would not be altogether just to leave the matter here. Sidney, for
example, at least on one occasion, proves himself capable of making
rhythmical excursions of his own, as in the following lines:

> I might! – unhappie word – Once, I might,
> And then would not, or could not, see my blisse;
> Till now wrapt in a most infernall night,
> I find how heavenly day, wretch! I did misse.

The easy Elizabethan facility is replaced by the hesitant, pausing
rhythms of Wyatt, something close to the perplexed freedom of
Shakespeare and the intricacies of Donne. But perhaps even more

immediately than Donne and Shakespeare, Sidney's lines bring to mind Hopkins. This is probably due to the recollection of

Here! creep
Wretch, under a comfort serves in a whirlwind

prompted by Sidney's fourth line. But the connection with Hopkins is deeper than that suggested by the parenthetic self-castigation of 'wretch' and lies in the disturbed, uneasy rhythms.

Where Sidney displays this kind of proximity to Wyatt he is outside the main stream of verse development of the period; his lines are no longer being manipulated primarily by 'an excessive feeling for mechanical internal regularity'.[2] The general development has already been illustrated: it is English Petrarchanism, stemming largely from Surrey and the lesser courtly makers, and illustrated in the more truly representative poems of Sidney, such as that beginning:

Queen Virtue's Court, which some call Stella's face,
Prepar'd by Nature's choicest furniture,
Hath his front built of alabaster pure:
Gold is the covering of that stately place.

which in its obvious figure-work and high polish expresses that conception of style as ornamentation which is such an essential ingredient of Elizabethan taste. Sidney himself in *An Apology for Poetry* describes such a style as 'that honey-flowing matron Eloquence apparelled, or rather disguised, in a courtesan-like painted affectation';[3] and Wythorne had expressed his moral objection to it by pointing out that only

. . . to flatter, glos, or ly . . . requyreth gloriowz and painted speech wheraz the trewth needeth but A plain and simpull vtterans withowt glozing or faining at all.[4]

The critical concern to draw up a book of rules for versifying is itself an eloquent testimonial of the Elizabethan interest in verse as ornament or decoration. Apart from Puttenham, something of this interest can be gathered from such works as Gascoigne's *Certayne notes of Instruction concerning the making of verse or ryme in English* (1575) and Spenser's and Harvey's *Three Proper and Wittie familiar Letters . . . Touching the earthquake in April last and our English refourmed Versifying* etc. (1580). The beginning of the next century saw the appearance of Campion's *Observations in the Arte of English Poesie* (1602) and, in reply,

Daniel's *Defence of Ryme* (1603). It could be argued that the concern which such works represent arose out of the recognition of the inadequacy of earlier English verse. But such an argument would be grounded in a misunderstanding of the nature of 'the problem of rhythm'. This, it has been maintained throughout, is an individual problem arising from the poet's concern to vitalise his work, that is to say to make his poetry a complete articulation of those situations and experiences in which he, the poet, is most completely involved. The reduction of this problem to a concern for rules and regulations results in a concern for facile easiness of movement which was readily elevated into decorum. It is the kind of concern displayed by Spenser when he writes to Harvey to tell him that Sidney and Dyer

. . . haue by autho[ri]tie of their whole Senate, prescribed certaine Lawes and rules of Quantities of English sillables, for English Verse: having had therof great practise, and drawen mee to their faction.[5]

It is also that of Puttenham when he enquires of his reader,

If . . . Art be but a certaine order of rules prescribed by reason, and gathered by experience, why should not Poesie be a vulgar Art with us as well as with the Greeks and Latines, our language admitting no fewer rules and nice diuersities than theirs?[6]

In such passages one can perceive the kind of connection between the Elizabethan period and the period following the Restoration which led Nott to link them together as the two best periods of English poetry.

Wyatt's sense of the delicacies of rhythm and of their evaluative function is what is lost to Elizabethan poetry as a consequence of its preoccupation with metrical polish. The concern for surface finish, smooth numbers, rich diction and ornamental figures, suggests the sense in which poetry came to be viewed as an exercise the purpose of which was to manifest a certain cultivated gentility. This, no doubt, accounts for the dressy and 'flashy' character of so much of it: Elizabethans, by and large, appear to have had the same taste in literature as they had in clothes, which is, after all, only to be expected. And this last remark is no mere figure of speech, it indicates something essentially true about Elizabethan literary taste; Puttenham thinks of a presentable poem as he thinks of a young woman of the Court dressed out in all her finery.

And as we see in these great Madames of honour, be they for personage or otherwise neuer so comely and bewtifull, yet if they want their courtly habillements or at leastwise such other apparell as custome and ciuilitie haue ordained to couer their naked bodies, would be halfe ashamed or greatly out of countenaunce to be seen in that sort, and perchance do then thinke themselues more amiable in euery mans eye, when they be in their richest attire, suppose of silkes or tyssewes & costly embroderies, then when they go in cloth or in any other plaine and simple apparell. Even so cannot our vulgar Poesie shew it selfe either gallant or gorgious, if any lymme be left naked and bare and not clad in his kindly clothes and coulours, such as may conuey them somwhat out of sight, that is from the common course of ordinary speech and capacitie of the vulgar iudgement, and yet being artificially handled must needes yeld it much more bewtie and commendation. This ornament we speake of is giuen to it by figures and figuratiue speaches, which be the flowers as it were and coulours that a Poet setteth vpon his language by arte, as the embroderer doth his stone and perle, or passements of gold vpon the stuffe of a Princely garment, or as th'excellent painter bestoweth the rich Orient coulours vpon his table of pourtraite.[7]

Needless to say, this frivolous preoccupation with a purely artificial finesse does not accord well with the spirit in which important poetry is conceived. The courtly makers appreciated show and ornament, but the pageants, the tableaux, the jousts, even the little brooch presented by Anne Boleyn to Henry, are enthused with a deeper seriousness, unfold or implicate the internal complexities of the life to which they belong, forming a sounding board for the courtly lyricist.

The change that takes place in Elizabethan poetry is more than a change in taste; it is to begin with a weakening of contact with a range of attitudes and beliefs that, associated with notions of chivalry and courtly love, gives court poetry an extended connotation that stretches backwards over at least three centuries. The individual modulations of Wyatt become, therefore, more than individual modulations; they affect the significance of a large body of previous poetry and force the reader into a reappraisal. After Wyatt the attitudes and postures of courtly love become grotesque imitations of the past, grotesque because they bring to the poetry that surface phosphoresence of a corpse; the Elizabethans, one feels, are embalming courtly love – not a far-fetched idea as can be seen by comparing Sidney's 'Queen Virtue's Court' and its description of the lady with Shakespeare's 'Full fathom five' and its description of the father.

Courtly love and chivalry are already things of the past in the Elizabethan period and, if anything, this is responsible for rather than a consequence of a change in taste. But courtly love and chivalry are not isolated phenomena; they are aspects of a much wider and more general manner of evaluating and expressing the relationships of men and women, to each other, to the world in which they lived, and to God, the whole of which was undergoing a radical, if not revolutionary, change in the sixteenth century.

SOURCE: from *The Courtly Maker: An Essay on the Poetry of Wyatt and his Contemporaries* (Oxford, 1964), pp. 148–59.

NOTES

[Reorganised and renumbered from the original – Ed.]

1. E. M. W. Tillyard, *The Poetry of Sir Thomas Wyatt* (London, 1949), p. 155.
2. George Puttenham, *The Arte of English Poesie*, ed. G. D. Willcock and Alice Walker (Cambridge, 1936), p. lxii. [The phrase is taken from the editors' introduction – Ed.]
3. Sir Philip Sidney, *An Apology for Poetry*, in E. D. Jones (ed.), *English Critical Essays*, vol. 1 (London, 1947), p. 49.
4. James M. Osborne (ed.), *The Autobiography of Thomas Wythorne* (Oxford, 1961), p. 65.
5. 'Tvvo Other, very commendable Letters', in *The Poetical Works of Edmund Spenser*, ed. J. C. Smith and E. De Selincourt (Oxford, 1924), p. 635.
6. Puttenham, op. cit., p. 5.
7. Ibid., pp. 137–8.

Arthur E. Barker   An Apology for the Study of Renaissance Poetry   (1964)

. . . It is perhaps time to consider what, historically speaking, has happened to the concept of Renaissance in the hands of cultural historians in the past century or so; and, tentatively and simple-mindedly, one might conclude thus. The concept originated, in the northern fifteenth and sixteenth centuries, in the midst of philosophical, ideological, religious, social and institutional collapse, as a description of a rebirth of the hortatory arts, and in particular the literary arts and the art of poetry. Because the humanistic literary arts and the poetry of the Renaissance were much concerned with moral philosophy and every human activity, the concept was transferred to other human activities, largely through the idealism of humanists and their educational efforts. It thus began to be applied to the philosophical, political, social conditions of its period. Cultural historians of the late eighteenth and nineteenth centuries attempted to explain this literary renaissance in terms of philosophical, political and social renaissances. The sum of what our cultural historians have succeeded in demonstrating as to literature by their cyclical reconsiderations is that, whatever the relations between literary activity and activity in these areas, there were no philosophical, political, social or economic renaissances that adequately explain the northern literary renaissance of the late sixteenth and seventeenth centuries. We may thank them heartily for this thoroughly negative evidence as to the misleading explanations of the literary renaissance provided by their nineteenth-century colleagues, and go on more intelligently with our own business, with which the merely cultural historians are obviously incapable of dealing: that is, with the appraisal and explanation of *the* English Renaissance – the literary and poetical renaissance of the late sixteenth and seventeenth centuries. As to the indubitable historicity of that renaissance as a fact, we have the conclusive evidence of our own washing-bills, of the Short-Title Catalogue, Wing, and the Stationers' Register.

As to the relation of this fact to the commercial development of the technology of printing and paper-making, it proves, as we investigate the origins of that development in the fifteenth-century North, no more sensible to say that the literary renaissance depended on the advantage of printing than that printing developed in response to the demands of the literary renaissance. Why do cultural historians nowadays so perversely insist on putting the cart before the horse and driver and on subordinating the human spirit to the instruments it demands and gets? If anything needs explaining in cultural history, it is not the failure of nerve that rendered the humanities of the later Middle Ages, as in our day, incapable of and uneasy about presenting the claims of the best values men can conceive, but what induces that failure of nerve, the unconscionable length of time it takes administrators and scientific technologists to implement the perceptions of possibilities, including the spatial and the international, formulated and given popular currency by writers from Plato to the author of *Tom Swift*.

And as to the character of this fact – the historical literary Renaissance in England – it was sixteenth-century political propaganda as revived by nineteenth-century cultural history that produced the literarily speaking unhistorical notion that the great Elizabethan explosion of literary genius was produced by euphoric post-Armada buoyancy. This notion depends on a very simple-minded reading (if any reading at all) of poems like *The Faerie Queene*, in which George may be on his way to sainthood but through a process of hard experience, amid the terrors and dangers of a by no means golden fairyland, and of falling, despairing, recovering, trying again, tripping, and trying yet again, that may be more intelligently read – like Virgil's advice to Augustus-Æneas – as a warning to Elizabeth, her courtiers and her people, that if they continue so to fumble and be found wanting, they may not be quite as providentially lucky when the next armada crisis comes. Remembering that Spenser was an efficient civil servant in that disputed Elizabethan wasteland Ireland, that Donne was a lord keeper's secretary and an ecclesiastical administrator who had devoted his studies chiefly to the points sadly in controversy between the churches, and that Milton went blind as Latin secretary to the confused Commonwealth and Protectorate Council of State, we might observe that what the philosophical and sociological historians have been telling us in their reappraisals of the period is simply what the great poets knew about it at first hand, from their experience of unwashed public linen and the rising cost of their own laundry.

The literary renaissance did not originate in the confused tensions the reappraising historians have been telling us about, though it was certainly induced by them. Great poetry does not arise from the possession of some abstract systematic philosophy, or some Miranda-like belief in a brave new world, or some expectation of plenty. The poetry of Scripture emerged from no such situation, nor the Platonic mimesis of Socratic discourse (Gilbert Murray speaks of the Greek failure of nerve), nor the Ciceronian dialogues, nor Ovid's poetry, nor the writings of Augustine; and, though there were many ineffective and idealistic humanists, and some similar poets, there were many Renaissance humanists and poets who recognised the historical situations behind such writings and the similarities in their own. What is remarkable about the great poets of the Renaissance is that they were so sensitively aware of all the tensions – religious, philosophical, ethical, political, social, economic – the historians might have saved themselves a good deal of trouble over by learning about from poetry. The literary and poetic renaissance was a response to these tensions. The tensions provide it with its materials and are the subjects of its commentary. But this renascent poetry is not to be explained or appraised simply in terms of its material or subject of comment. Many of us have made the apologetic mistake of accepting the data of the cultural historian as providing the terms in which we must evaluate, explain and sell the material of our discipline. That is a self-defeating effort, because our poets did not accept these inadequate terms but used them subordinately for their purposes while attacking their inadequacy. They did so, in the terms appropriate to the poetry of a literary renaissance, because the times, with the confused inadequacy even of moral philosophy, needed such poetry's satiric, homiletic and re-energising comment, and because men of genius were at hand capable of responding to the demand by modifying the techniques of rhetorical humanism and renewing the literary tradition through a regenerative combining of the spirits and techniques of the biblical, classical Greek, classical Roman, patristic, medieval, and even Italianate literary traditions, in a language whose continuity was dynamically renewed thereby in a new poetry. The nature and function of that literary renaissance have to be sought in appropriate literary terms which may, on the whole, be meaningless to the disdainfully unimaginative philosophical and sociological historian and may remain so for many, but were clearly not meaningless in the period of the literary renaissance and need not remain so in ours – where they are still used in everyday speech and where the techniques they represent are daily used by old and new modes of communication.

The historian may say he cannot imagine what significance such Renaissance literary terms have for us, but what they meant and how they are appliable to our times – through education, the disciplined accumulation of factual material, critical reappraisal, and the sustaining and re-energising of the tongue the English renaissance spake and the faith and morals it, however confusedly, held – is what the renaissance in Renaissance literary studies is clarifying through its various investigations and critical differences of opinion. Most historical critics, appraising in these varied ways and working in their classrooms to teach the young and the new generation of teachers of the young, would be too intelligently and modestly preoccupied (or uneasy) to offer the kind of simple-minded apology attempted here;

yet they are all in their degree and according to their abilities aware of
what we know and have seen of the disciplined and purposeful
efficiency of education on the other side of the wall – where young
teenagers can speak fluent English and skilfully misinterpret Renaissance English poems of complaint for the dialectically materialistic
purpose they have been imbued with, and aware that this demands of
North American education and especially of the humanities an
equally determined and purposeful effort to sustain and make
operative whatever is most admirable in the culture whose modern
form originated for us in the sixteenth and seventeenth centuries. It is
easy to be simple-minded about such matters; but it is useful now and
then for some simple-minded person without the perception of the
angels to dare to tread a simple path. Our present situation is
essentially comparable to the Renaissance situation – partly because,
if we extend the period as completely as we should, we shall find we
are still living in it, but more because our tensions and our risks are
comparable to those of the sixteenth and seventeenth centuries, and
chiefly because we need and are getting the kind of vigorous
reinvestigation and discussion, comparable to what went on among
rhetoricians and poets of various degrees of giftedness during the
Renaissance, of modes of communication, their defects, abuses, and
how they might be rendered more effectively human than they were in
the later Middle Ages or are now in the hiddenly persuading hands of
news-leaking politicians, journalists or advertising agencies, or in the
abstract pompositics of philosophers, moralists, reformers and many
academics.

What the study of Renaissance English poetry may contribute to
this, and what historical criticism is in process of demonstrating, may
be indicated by considering (though here all too briefly) some of the
principles developed by Sir Philip Sidney in his pre-Armada *Defence of
Poesie* written in reply to typically moralistic attacks on fantastically
seductive poetry by humanist philosophers and historians, whose title
in the apparently unauthorised of its two first printings in 1595 (in
those post-Armada years) the title of this chapter modestly echoes.
Philosophic or aesthetically oriented literary historians – like J. E.
Spingarn or René Wellek or David Daiches or M. H. Abrams, whose
perceptive attention is, however, focused on the nineteenth century
and Coleridge[1] – condescendingly describe this defence as typical of
Renaissance English self-contradiction (since, they think, it naïvely
echoes Italian Neo-Platonism and neo-Aristotelianism in regarding

the poet at once as in some sense Orphic and a seer and as an imitative artist whose operations should be controlled by consciously ordering literary principles) or as a nervously self-defensive and hence casually ironic apology by a minor poet who cannot escape from the stultifying moralism he dislikes. But, as everybody knows (and as Kenneth Muir has recently reminded us with brevity and point),[2] Sidney was a charming, sophisticated, cultivated, intelligent, humanistically well-educated, actively responsible courtier and soldier of influential family, who had seen in 1572 in Paris the Saint Bartholomew's Day massacre of Protestants (almost as bloody as the ideological massacres of our day), was deeply concerned with the secular and religious conflicts of Elizabethan England and Europe, hoped and worked at least for a union of Protestants if not for a union of Christendom that would include both his Roman Catholic recusant and French Huguenot friends, and was to die, honorably if somewhat recklessly, in the ideological and economic wars in the Netherlands. It is not wise to be condescending as to the principles of such a man, who would have appreciated the ironic Shavian definition of a gentleman as one who never unintentionally gives offence. If it is looked at in the light of current efforts to reappraise Renaissance English poetry, this seminal defence may be seen to have been sharply conscious of all the paralysing tensions of the time, and, though it never mentions England's Eliza, it may prove more than consistent with Sidney's political theory, as this is in process of being clarified,[3] and with his ecclesiastical and religious opinions, which yet demand the clarifying study that might much illuminate the premises behind his recently and perceptively re-examined poetic practice. Further, what we know of its pre-publication circulation in manuscript and may discern of its echoed influence would seem to indicate, more clearly than has been recognised, that it helped much to teach perceptive and frustrated public servants like Spenser, Donne, Milton what their poetry might do, and how, and what it should aim at, beyond what could be taught them by humanist educators, historians and moral philosophers. For, says Sidney, in caricatures in the Erasmian satiric tradition turned against unimaginative humanism itself, philosophers with their sullen gravity and contempt of ordinary outward things, sophistically speaking against subtilty, and casting largess as they go of definitions, divisions, distinctions and scornful interrogatives, can deal only with the inhumanly abstract; while the historian – loaded with old mouse-eaten records, authorising himself for the most part upon other histories built upon the notable foundation of hearsay, curious of antiquities and inquisitive of novelties, a wonder to young folk and a tyrant in table-talk as the purveyor of hard-headed, old-aged experience – is tied to the mere empirical particularity of what Henry James was to call 'clumsy life at its stupid work'. Neither, says Sidney, going beyond Aristotle, can be of any use to us unless they become poetical by, one gathers, imaginatively applying their abstractions to the human situation or imaginatively clarifying the constant significance of human experience. Poetry, for Sidney, is a realistic, imaginative, and significant 'making' or fiction (usually though not always employing the ordering and braking effect of verse) which does both. It is usual to say that this notion incoherently reflects the interminable disputes as to what poetry imitates or mirrors: existential nature and the rational Aristotelian universals or the transcendent reality of the Platonic ideas, of Italian academic theorists as these are reviewed by Spingarn and more recently by Bernard Weinberg and Baxter Hathaway (for whom Sidney appears to remain an untutored northern provincial).[4] It seems possible that Sidney was only too acutely aware of the increasingly pedantic futility of these disputes and that – thinking he had in the northern tradition a superior datum ignored by humanist Counter-Reformation Italians nervous of heresy – he was saying, with that Veronese admirer of the English Queen Mab who so much resembles him, a plague o' both your merely philosophical houses. What he says is that poetry is an imitation, *mimesis* in Aristotle's word, a representing, counterfeiting or figuring forth, which seems from the context and illustrations to mean that it represents an action, or rather the process involved in an action, though by a making of something like but not the same – 'counterfeiting' still having in Sidney's day rather more of its root than of our pejorative meaning – and that it does so in order to indicate or reveal something significant for us in the process that would not otherwise be so fully perceived. The context suggests that Sidney knew the Italian disputes and also, as I think, knew well his Aristotle and Plato through his northern Greek; but ironically, and surely not inadvertently, his definition of poetry (or proposition) does not tell us precisely what poetry imitates: we have to find that out for ourselves from reading his full defence responsively. As a northerner, he is less interested in and less certain of his power to say what poetry is than what it does. He is even willing to admit for that purpose that fiction is lies, for 'the poet never maketh any circles about your imagination, to conjure you to believe for true what he writeth', nor anything anybody, himself or any character, may morally or philosophically say in the process of the action; it is an honest admission, for it is a wise man who is certain that his telling or his acting is not partially deceptive. Some realistic Italians, like Castel-vetro, had argued that poetry was a matter not only of illusion but of counterfeiting delusion; but they had done so to prove that its sensational function was to produce wonder in vulgar minds. Sidney excludes no man and no form of poetry, even ballads, from his defence; and his defence itself illustrates the function he thinks poetry should perform. The defence is a rhetorically ordered, formally humanist forensic oration, over which (as K. O. Myrick made us see some years ago) plays the *sprezzatura*, the gracefully ironic, self-aware art of the courtier that conceals art; and through this (to go a little further than Myrick) the oration becomes itself a paradoxical fiction, a praise of lying, in which the speaker adopts (what Daiches and company have allowed themselves to be taken in by) the persona or mask of one who does not know clearly what he is talking about, in order to induce us to figure it out. Unlike most modern critics, Renaissance poets do not much care what their audiences think of them, so long as they can induce a response. I cannot here illustrate (anymore than I can imitate) Sidney's provocative irony; but what he thus figures forth is the process poetry induces, the process whereby it induces it, and the process it is imitating and counterfeiting. What is induced, Sidney thinks, is a healthily psychological process, an exercise of the whole mind whereby poetry enables men to the good actions of the whole man: a thoroughly humanistic end which, he sees from the times, merely morally philosophic humanistic rhetoric fails to achieve. For, he says in the theological terms of the time, 'our erected wit maketh us to know what perfection is, and yet our infected will keepeth us from reaching unto it'. Poetry energises the will so that a man's reach may more nearly equal his grasp; but it does so by irradiating the mind in all its rational powers which, in Sidney's still half-medieval psychology include, with the intellect and will, the memory and imagination. Sidney would accept the English Christian-Stoic suspicion of the imagination or fantasy (recently well documented)[5] as the faculty most influenced by the corrupt senses and perhaps itself the seat of original sin; but for him good poetry exercises the imagination, with the other faculties, illuminates the grounds of wisdom that, in philosophy and history, 'lie dark before the imaginative and judging power', and so enables the whole mind to respond healthily to the stimuli of experience coming through the senses and to act well through them. This is of course for Sidney a therapeutic process; but Sidney would not, no more than I, presume to contradict anyone who thinks himself not in need of the therapy of healthy exercise. By such his argument is usually reduced to an offensively elementary moralistic level by the omission (as by Daiches) of the third term of the statement in which he says poetry gives us models of virtues and vices: he says, 'notable images of virtues and vices and what else'. From the context and illustrations it appears (to imitate the philosophical jargon of our own day) that the 'whatelseness' poetry images is the human situation in which virtue and vice operate and conflict, with whatever else it is that the healthy human mind can discern as operating in that conflict, in classical, medieval or Renaissance times. Mythomystic interpreters represent Sidney – because he enjoyed ballads and bards and thought Orphic poetry drew 'wild untamed wits to an admiration of knowledge' in primitive times – as an inconsistent defender of the mythopoeic transcendentals for which they value Renaissance poetry. This may (though I doubt it) be an adequate approach to songs of innocence, Byzantium, or sonnets to Orpheus; but mythomysticism seems much inclined to hear the echo of its own Orphic voice and to seek its enthusiastic image out of time, by unhistorically reading the mythical metaphoric structure of such poems as, say, *Paradise Lost*, not only out of time but out of the context of their carefully organised poetic structures, that have a beginning, a middle and an end, designed to evoke a healthy response even to all the woe we cannot escape from. Sidney's heart responds to ballads as to a trumpet that calls to war or calls the people in the wilderness to hear a proclamation of law. His poetic world is golden and not, like nature's, brazen; but in being so it suggests the realities 'of that first accursed fall of Adam', and it induces the reader to imitate the poet's effort, through which he 'doth grow in effect into another nature'. (The preposition 'into' is significantly lacking in the unauthorised 1595 edition; but, unlike most interpreters, I quote from the authorised version.) That other nature is, as Sidney implies elsewhere, human nature as it ought to be and might be but in this world is never likely quite to be; but it is the process of effort in time that matters. Of course, for Sidney, this other nature has the support, he thinks, of his superior northern datum. The proximate source for this is in the writings in which his Huguenot friends were attempting, in line with a French tradition that goes back into the conciliar fifteenth century, to modify the rigidities of Protestant and Counter-Reformation dogmatism by philosophical Augustinian and classically humanist discourse. Sidney believed with them, though more ironically and poetically, that nature remains the art of God[6] and that history, to use Burke's phrase, is the known march of His ordinary providence. Sidney seems to be implying that good poetry or fiction is not fantastic or transcendental but, through a conscious and disciplined art making good use of the providential gifts of nature and knowing what it does and to what purpose, represents this creative process, with its corrective ironies and its sustaining energy, as it proceeds, he thinks, in time and our experience. I do not of course argue for the truth of the premise provided by Sidney's superior northern datum – or even that I myself clearly understand it and its implications. That is not the business of a merely critical literary historian. But I would argue that, historically speaking, to dismiss this premise as unintelligent and aesthetically irrelevant and to reduce it to the level of mere customary or conventional morality – with Mr Daiches and other such commentators on Sidnean Renaissance-English literary theory – is to display a failure of objective historical grasp, a lack of what the eighteenth century called 'sympathetic imagination' and what the sixteenth and seventeenth still called 'charity', and an uncritical twentieth-centric presumption as to the rightness of one's own skeptical opinions. Historically speaking, Sidney's defence has, in fact, a sharply direct, if ironic, bearing on the increasing religious tensions of the pre- and post-Armada years: that is perhaps why it remained unpublished but in circulation till 1595, because of the implications as to the extremes of both Protestant rigorism and Protestant enthusiasm in its observation (remembering the epistles) that poetry should not be 'scourged out of the church of God', its insistence on the power of what Tremellius called 'the poetical parts' of Scripture, and its constantly implied analogy between the psychology of religious and of poetic experience. It is only an analogy, not the identity some enthusiasts then as now would make it; for poetry is a human art and Sidney will have no nonsense as to any fantastic divine afflatus. But his ironic defence becomes in the end an exhortation to poets and readers not to abuse such a natural gift, but to possess themselves of the *energeia* illustrated by a poetry vitally conceived, consciously organised and controlled by art, and sensitively applied to the human situation.

Recent studies of Renaissance English poetry, especially in their concern with poetic and the function of poetry, would seem to be finding that their justification and the justification of their material lie where Sidney apologetically asserted the justification of poetry lay: in the full exercise of the mind in all its powers afforded by the historically critical study of such poetry. Since Renaissance English poetry at its best is always the product of the immediate human realities of its times, and since it aims at impinging on these realities by affecting through its art what men will and do, and since it habitually considers time and what men do in terms of the universal verities it normally ascribes to a directing and ordering Providence and finds mirrored (however distortingly) in history and experience, it is inevitable that some appraisers should regard it as a merely historical mirror of the nature of Renaissance times, others as a simple sugar-coating of morality and principles, and others as chiefly communicating a transcendent vision. Many minor poets in the period wrote verse limited to one of these functions, as many minor critics today prefer one or another of these simplifications. But the major poets of the period thought of their poetry, though fictional, as inducing a total exercise of mind, directed to sound human ends, and conducive to a healthy response to the human situation; and they did not think that uninspired, unimaginative, insensitive history and moral philosophy or any other human science could induce such an exercise. It would seem a mistake for literary humanists today to underestimate the significance of the historical fact that Renaissance English poetry represented the fullest dimensions of Renaissance *litterae humaniores*, to imitate the historians and philosophers in being content to reflect its functions only partially, while leaving the principle of preparative exercise to teachers of PE – by whom student muscles are developed through various fictional situations, including those provided by the vaulting-horse on which are practised, in the space age, what are essentially the cavalry exercises Sidney begins his apology by comparing with more necessary literary activities. The current renaissance of critically historical Renaissance literary studies, despite the disadvantages they face, illustrates the development of an intelligently and objectively appraising, humanely sensitive, high principled and informedly disciplined historical imagination. Since the spatial and international imagination involves the same exercise of mind as the historical, this is a development that should pay dividends beyond the academic.

SOURCE: extract from essay in Carroll Camden (ed.), *Literary Views: Critical and Historical Essays* (Chicago, 1964), pp. 33–43.

NOTES

[Reorganised and renumbered from the original – Ed.]

1. J. E. Spingarn, *Literary Criticism in the Renaissance* (New York, 1899 etc.), pp. 268–74; R. Wellek, *A History of Modern Criticism* (New Haven, Conn., 1955), I, p. 17; D. Daiches, *Critical Approaches to Literature* (London, and Englewood Cliffs, N. J., 1956), pp. 50–72; M. H. Abrams, *The Mirror and the Lamp: Romantic Theory and the Critical Tradition* (New York and London, 1953), pp. 14–15, 323. Daiches's concluding comment (pp. 71–2) is typical of current responses to Sidney's theory in seeing moralising as providing an escape from a Platonic dilemma which is perhaps more in the eye of the beholder than in his author's: cf. W. K. Wimsatt Jnr and C. Brooks, *Literary Criticism: A Short History* (New York, 1957), p. 170. The commentary by C. S. Lewis – in *English Literature in the Sixteenth Century* (London and New York, 1954), pp. 343–7 – remains the most perceptive, as in its insistence that the ethical is the aesthetic for Sidney, despite vagueness as to Sidney's controlling beliefs. R. L. Montgomery Jnr uses the *Defence* effectively, though without subjecting it to significant reappraisal, in his reinterpretation of Sidney's poetry in *Symmetry and Sense* (Austin, Texas, 1961); and it has of course a collateral place in the definitive edition of the poems by W. A. Ringler Jnr (Oxford, 1962).

2. K. Muir, *Sir Philip Sidney*, 'Writers and Their Work' series, No. 120 (London, 1960), though p. 11 does little more than reproduce the usual moralised view of the *Defence*.

3. The most recent examination is by E. W. Talbert, in the well-documented fourth chapter of his *The Problem of Order: Elizabethan Political Commonplaces and an Example of Shakespeare's Art* (Chapel Hill, N.C., 1962).

4. Spingarn, op. cit.; B. Weinberg, *A History of Literary Criticism in the Italian Renaissance* (Chicago, 1961); B. Hathaway, *The Age of Criticism: The Late Renaissance in Italy* (Ithaca, N.Y., 1962). Sidney of course makes no appearance in Weinberg's volumes. For evidence of Hathaway's apparent assumption that Sidney was quite incapable of recognising and attempting to resolve, from a different point of view, the theoretical cruxes of Italian criticism as Hathaway himself sees them in impressive philosophical detail, see esp. pp. 327–7.

5. W. Rossky, 'Imagination in the English Renaissance: Psychology and Poetic', *Studies in the Renaissance*, V (1958), pp. 49–73.

6. A theme whose increasing importance in criticism is reflected, among many others, in D. Bush's revisions for *English Literature in the Earlier Seventeenth-Century* (2nd edn, rev., Oxford, 1962); see *Journal of English and Germanic Philology*, LXII, no. 3 (1963).

Hallett Smith   'Poetry for Music: Thomas Campion' (1966)

. . . It is not merely in the matter of rhythmical freedom and variety that Campion's musical method in poetry is significant. He knew that the movement of poetry and its sounds are inextricably entwined. He comments in the preface to the *Two Bookes*: 'The light of this will best appear to him who hath paysed our Monasyllables and Syllables combined, both of which, are so loaded with Consonants, as that they will hardly keepe company with swift Notes, or give the Vowell conuenient liberty.'

It is this scrupulous care and sensitiveness to the movement of the line, the inflectional effects suggested by music, and the concern for the convenient liberty of the vowel that has made some of Campion's ayres among the most successful lyric poems in the language.

> I care not for these Ladies
> That must be woode and praide,
> Giue me kind Amarillis
> The wanton countrey maide;
> Nature art disdaineth,
> Her beautie is her owne;
> Her when we court and kisse,
> She cries, forsooth, let go.
> But when we come where comfort is,
> She neuer will say no.

The theme, a common one of the contrast between court and country in the matter of love, is treated with extreme simplicity. Yet Campion has managed some subtle effects within the poem, largely as a result of seeing the words in terms of a melodic line. There is a pretty contrast between the feminine endings of lines 1, 3 and 5 and the masculine endings of 2, 4 and 6; in the music they are quantitatively (in terms of time) equivalent. The last two lines, being the epigrammatic conclusion of the whole, are an example of the skilful use of rhythmical and quantitative devices which the music can support. The penultimate line is a foot longer than normal, and the music of the last line plays sportfully in the climax which has been so provocatively built up.

In great contrast to the gaiety of 'I care not for these Ladies' is the fourth ayre in the collection; its verse is as simple, but the emotions illustrated are far different and the methods used show Campion in a different light. The first stanza runs:

> Followe thy faire sunne, vnhappy shadowe,
> Though thou, though thou be blacke as night,
> And she made all of light,
> Yet follow thy fair sun, vnhappie shadowe.   [1]

The contrast between the attitude involved in the word 'shadowe' in the first line and in the fourth is strongly emphasised by the music. In the first line it is represented by two eighth notes after a succession of steady quarter notes. At the end it is set to a dotted quarter slurred to an eighth note for the first syllable and a half note for the second.[2] The melody is in the minor, but in the first instance the shadow is represented as trivial, in the second as pathetic. The line 'And she made all of light' is set to an ascending chromatic scale, a note to a syllable, suggesting the emergence from the 'blacke as night' as if one were climbing a ladder.

Campion is not always so simple as in these two examples. His remarkable utilisation of the convenient freedom of the vowel is perhaps best shown in No. 20. The delicacy of the manipulation of vowel sounds is so extraordinary that one feels that here is an ear even more sensitive than Tennyson's:

> When thou must home to shades of vnder ground,
> And there ariu'd, a newe admired guest,
> The beauteous spirits do ingirt thee round,
> White Iope, blith Hellen, and the rest,
> To heare the stories of thy finisht loue
> From that smoothe toong whose musicke hell can moue;
>
> Then wilt thou speake of banqueting delights,
> Of masks and reuels which sweete youth did make,
> Of Turnies and great challenges of knights,
> And all these triumphes for thy beauties sake:
> When thou hast told these honours done to thee,
> Then tell, O tell, how thou didst murther me.

The correspondence of 'smoothe toong' and 'O tell' indicates the careful attention of the poet to quantity; the notes are long (half notes in modern transcription) in comparison with the context. The felicity of sound arrangement in 'White Iope, blith Hellen' and elsewhere are beyond praise. But it should be observed that Campion saves the poem from monotonous ease and smoothness by appropriate but slightly 'metaphysical' epithets twice in the course of the two stanzas: '*finisht* loue' and '*banqueting* delights'.[3]

The degree and quality of this 'metaphysical' trait in Campion is perhaps best exemplified in No. 14 in the *Booke of Ayres*; it is really a development of the regular Elizabethan habits with conceits, the treatment of figures by amplification, and other devices.

> Blame not my cheeks, though pale with loue they be;
> The kindly heate vnto my heart is flowne,
> To cherish it that is dismaid by thee,
> Who art so cruell and vnsteadfast growne:
> For nature, cald for by distressed harts,
> Neglects and quite forsakes the outward partes.
>
> But they whose cheekes with careles blood are stain'd,
> Nurse not one sparke of loue within their harts,
> And, when they woe, they speake with passion fain'd,
> For their fat loue lyes in their outward parts:
> But in their brests, where loue his court should hold,
> Poore Cupid sits and blowes his nailes for cold.   [4]

Campion exploits a kind of irony possible only for the poet who is writing for music and has control over the musical setting of his words. The phrase 'For their fat love lyes in their outward parts', for example, seems to be a complex figure, startling in the context of the conventional cheeks, heart, blood and flame. But the music to the poem reveals that 'For their fat loue' corresponds to 'Who art so cruel' in the first stanza, an ascending chromatic passage followed by an octave leap downward; moreover, this is the second time the musical phrase has appeared: it was first used for 'The kindly heate' and 'Nurse not one sparke'. It might be said that the first occurrence of the musical passage produced an effect of wistfulness, but when it is repeated and insisted upon, the feeling becomes inevitably bitter.

The discussion in the opening chapter of Rosemond Tuve's . . . book, *Elizabethan and Metaphysical Imagery*, uses Campion as an example of the Elizabethan poetry which 'would come nearest to modern expectations' in utilising imagery to assist in representing a state of mind or to show just how the writer felt. Even Campion, Miss Tuve argues, does not really do this, and she contrasts with three of his best-known lyrics the opening lines from Eliot's *Preludes*. Campion's images, she maintains, are 'not sensuous in function, but they lead the poem toward generalised reflection rather than toward the more exact understanding of the writer's emotion as peculiar to him'; and 'clearly, Campion with his emphasis on conceptions and on "art" and on the ear does not think of poetic imitation as the *representation* of an emotional experience'.[5]

Apart from the question of whether modern expectation is for purely sensuous effects from imagery as Miss Tuve supposes, the general question of the emotional effects intended in an Elizabethan lyric may need clarification. It is no doubt true that the states of mind Campion was intending to reproduce by his lyrics were not states of mind or emotions 'peculiar to him'; he was drawing upon the great Renaissance storehouse of commonplaces, and his intent was probably no more autobiographical than that of any other Elizabethan poet. To say, however, that for him poetic imitation was not thought of as the *representation* of an emotional experience is to be dangerously misleading. The effect of the combination of music and words was to make the experience as vivid as possible; the marriage of diction and ayre was to result in an intensification of the feelings projected. Their particularity it is difficult to assess; but surely we are not to follow the direction of 'generalised reflection' in reading these lyrics – rather the reverse: the intensification of the emotional weight of each line, each phrase, each word in the poem as a melodic line can interpret, intensify and reveal the verse which it sets.

Most striking of all the many examples in Campion of the lines inviting music as their interpreters, standing aside for the music to carry the effect, evoking and stimulating the melodic, harmonic and rhythmic resources of music, is the poem which is usually cited only as the most interesting example of Campion's experiments in classical versification:

> Rose-cheekt Lawra, come
> Sing thou smoothly with thy beawties
> Silent musick, either other
>   Sweetely gracing. [6]

One of Campion's lyrics became so popular that it appears as a broadside ballad and is current in many different forms. Campion never published it himself, but it appeared in Richard Alison's *An Howres Recreation in Musicke* (1606) along with other lyrics of Campion, set as a madrigal. Its popularity is no doubt partly accounted for by the standard, old-fashioned nature of its sentiment – the vanity of earthly joys and the imminence of fate. It begins:

> What if a day, or a month, or a yeare
> Crown thy delights with a thousand sweet contentings?
> Cannot a chance of a night or an howre
> Crosse thy desires with as many sad tormentings?

The prosodic skill shown in this popular song combines oddly with the subject matter. But Campion was interested in popular motifs, and two of the songs from the later books of ayres exploit these very successfully. One is based on a fairy charm:

> Thrice tosse these Oaken ashes in the ayre,
> Thrice sit thou mute in this inchanted chayre;
> And thrice three times tye vp this true loues knot,
> And murmur soft, shee will, or shee will not.

As Kastendieck points out, the 'uncertainty expressed in the words finds its counterpart in the undulating melody of the piece',[7] and the modal nature of the composition fits the ancient, superstitious atmosphere which Campion has evoked in the words.

The other ayre is almost too well known to quote. It is the famous 'There is a garden in her face', perhaps the best known of all Campion's songs. Its popular derivation is in the 'cherry ripe' part of the poem, when the music imitates a London street cry and the accompaniment strikes a chord before each cry and then is silent.

Campion is the finest of the Elizabethan poets who wrote for music, and the reason is the obvious one that he was a composer at the same time. But he is in reality only an extreme example of the general situation in the late Elizabethan lyric. The lyric's shape and quality and its curious Elizabethan freshness are all determined by its close kinship to music.

SOURCE: extract from ch. v of *Elizabethan Poetry: A Study in Conventions, Meaning and Expression* (Cambridge, Mass., (1966), pp. 281–7.

NOTES

[Reorganised and renumbered from the original – Ed.]

1. . . . I have included the repetition in line 2 because it is significant in the musical development of the stanza.

2. I use E. H. Fellowes's modern transcription – *The English School of Lutenist Song Writers*, 16 vols (London, 1920–32), Pt I, vol. IV, p. 15. He has halved the note values, but this represents Campion's intention.

3. Campion's double control over music and words enabled him to provide another ditty, a religious one this time, for this melody. The two versions are compared and commented upon by Bruce Pattinson, *Music and Poetry in the English Renaissance* (London, 1948), p. 133.

4. . . . The poem was reprinted, not quite accurately, in Davison's *Poetical Rhapsody* (1602) – ed. Rollins, No. 153, and was set again by Robert Jones in his *Ultimum Vale* (1608). See E. H. Fellowes, *English Madrigal Verse, 1588–1632* (Oxford, 1920), p. 517.

5. R. Tuve, *Elizabethan and Metaphysical Imagery* (Chicago, 1947), pp. 15–17.

6. Cited as an example in Campion's *Obseruations in the Art of English Poesie* (1602).

7. M. M. Kastendieck, *England's Musical Poet, Thomas Campion* (New York, 1938), p. 145.

Barbara Herrnstein Smith   The Poetic Coda   (1968)

. . . In informal verbal situations such as chance encounters, letters to friends, or telephone conversations, the eventual obligation to conclude confronts the fact that unstructured discourse offers no handy termination point. Since abrupt cut-offs are psychologically unpleasant as well as impolite, we usually make use of some formula of conclusion to signal the approaching termination: 'Well, it's been good to talk to you – give my regards to your wife . . .', 'So, that's about it for now . . .', 'Okay, I'll be seeing you soon – Good-bye'. This last expression, 'good-bye', has become almost obligatory in telephone conversations, probably because the speaker's gestures and facial expressions cannot be seen and the only signals are vocal ones. It is a particularly interesting expression, because it has retained hardly a vestige of its original meaning and form ('God be with ye'), and the corruption suggests that its 'meaning' was always less significant than its function. It is likely that it always served the purpose of providing a genial signal of conclusion.

There is probably no language that does not have some conventional signal of this kind, and a poetic form of it is found in the Japanese *haiku*. Many of these poems conclude with a 'word' (such as *kana* or *yo*) which, we are told, has no independent meaning and functions somewhat as a punctuation mark, thus frequently translated as 'Ah', 'Oh', or simply '!'.[1] These terminal forms are called 'cutting-words' (*keriji*), and if they mean anything at all, it is simply 'this poem ends here'. The effect and even the possibility of such a poetic convention is probably related to the long tradition and rigid specifications of the *haiku*. Nothing like it is found in modern European poetry, where no linguistic element appears that does not also appear in the language of ordinary discourse.[2] Perhaps the nearest comparable convention is the envoy of the medieval ballad, which, although it is not a word but a whole stanza and contains meaningful thematic material, nevertheless serves, like the *keriji*, as a terminal signal, a poetic farewell to the reader. The envoy is best considered, however, as a particularly obvious instance of a more general kind of closural device which in form and function is the counterpart of the musical coda.

In music, the coda is a terminal section of a piece or movement, added for the specific purpose of securing closure and clearly distinguished from the preceding portion by its structure. A counterpart is found in poetry wherever the conclusion of a poem forms a more or less discrete section, involving new formal or thematic principles, or (as in the envoy) both. As a closural force, the essential characteristics of the poetic coda have already been examined [in an earlier section of the book – Ed.]: first, in the discussions of terminal modification and, later, of 'frames'.[3] As we observed, the terminal modification of formal principles arrests the reader's expectations of further development and thus prepares him for cessation. The frame could be thought of as a terminal modification of thematic principles. In any case, it achieves its closural effect by separating itself from the thematic structure of the rest of the poem and making a generalised or in some way stable comment upon it from 'outside'. (Both terminal modification and framing are characteristics of the envoy, which is commonly a truncated stanza and separates itself in various ways from the thematic structure of the poem proper.)

The following description of the function of the musical coda is suggestive:

When a number of parts or voices were made to imitate or follow one another according to rigorous rules, it would often occur that as long as the rules were observed a musical conclusion could not be arrived at. Indeed sometimes such things were constructed in a manner which enabled the piece to go on forever if the singers were so minded. . . . In order to come to a conclusion a few chords would be constructed apart from the rigorous rules, and so the coda was arrived at. . . . In a series of variations, each several variation would only offer the same kind of conclusion as that in the first theme, though in a different form; and in . . . the very nature of things it would not be aesthetically advisable for such a conclusion to be very strongly marked, because in that case each several variation would have too much the character of a complete set piece to admit of their together forming a satisfactory continuous piece of music. Therefore it is reasonable when all the variations are over to add a passage of sufficient importance to represent the conclusion of the whole set instead of one of the separate component parts.[4]

As in music, so also in poetry, the coda is most often found as a special closural device when the structure of the work does not itself adequately determine a conclusion. As we might expect, then, a poetic coda of some sort is likely to appear when the thematic structure of a poem is paratactic, associative or dialectic.

An Example from Vaux

Its effect may be illustrated . . . in the following poem, which is generally associative-paratactic in structure and concludes with an envoy-like stanza:

The Aged Lover Renounceth Love

I loathe that I did love;
In youth that I thought sweet,
As time requires for my behove,
Me thinks they are not meet.   4
   My lusts they do me leave,
My fancies all be fled,
And tract of time begins to weave
Gray hairs upon my head.
   For age, with stealing steps,
Hath clawed me with his crutch;
And lusty life away she leaps
As there had been none such.   12
   My muse doth not delight
Me as she did before,

My hand and pen are not in plight
As they have been of yore.
  For reason me denies
This youthly idle rhyme,
And day by day to me she cries,
Leave off these toys in time!   20
  The wrinkles in my brow,
The furrows in my face,
Say limping age will hedge him now
Where youth must give him place.
  The harbinger of death,
To me I see him ride;
The cough, the cold, the gasping breath,
Doth bid me to provide
  A pickaxe and a spade,
And eke a shrouding sheet;
A house of clay for to be made
For such a guest most meet.   32
  Me thinks I hear the clerk
That knolls the careful knell,
And bids me leave my woeful work
Ere nature me compel.
  My keepers knit the knot
That youth did laugh to scorn;
Of me that clean shall be forgot
As I had not been born.   40
  Thus must I youth give up,
Whose badge I long did wear;
To them I yield the wanton cup
That better may it bear.
  Lo, here the barëd skull
By whose bald sign I know
That stooping age away shall pull
Which youthful years did sow.   48
  For beauty, with her band,
These crooked cares hath wrought,
And shippëd me into the land
From when I first was brought.
  And ye that bide behind,
Have ye none other trust;
As ye of clay were cast by kind,
So shall ye waste to dust.   56

[Thomas, Lord Vaux][5]

The sequence of quatrains here is certainly not arbitrary; several of them are syntactically or in other ways thematically continuous, and the connectives 'for' and 'thus' in lines 9, 17, 41 and 49 suggest logical development. The structure is not logical, however, but associative and iterative. The poet is confronted by his own mortality, which he almost dispassionately acknowledges as it reveals itself in the signs, symptoms and visions of his own decay and death. His reflections reach a climax of sorts in lines 25–40, but the 'thus' of line 41 introduces a section that does not so much clinch as dissipate it; and since lines 41–8 are very similar to lines 21–4, they will seem either anticlimactic or repetitive. Indeed, at this point the poem threatens to become intolerably monotonous or obsessive, for the reader has been assailed by a relentless succession of 'last things', and the question 'Where do we go from here?' is beginning to press itself. The repetitive and associative structure of the poem has not yielded any principle that could determine a concluding point, and since almost every quatrain has rung with the finality of death, the closural force of any such allusion has been exhausted well before the last lines. In the conclusion of the poem, however, the poet unexpectedly turns from the incantatory evocation of his own death to a chilling envoy that sweeps the reader into the dismal fellowship of mortality. Though blunted by iteration, in this coda death's sting is sharpened once again, for here the poet has made it our own.   . . .

SOURCE extract from *Poetic Closure: A Study of How Poems End* (Chicago, 1968), pp. 186–91.

NOTES

[Reorganised and renumbered from the original – Ed.]

1. Harold G. Henderson, *An Introduction to Haiku* (New York, 1958), pp. 175–8.

2. The word '*amen*', while not strictly speaking 'European', may be regarded as an exception to this rule and is an interesting counterpart to the *keriji*. Cf. also '*selah*'.

3. [Ed.] 'terminal modification' in this discussion describes poems built on an apparently indefinitely extensible principle, which close by modifying that principle.

4. 'Coda', article by C. Hubert H. Parry, *Grove's Dictionary of Music and Musicians*, ed. Eric Blom (London, 1954), II, p. 362.

5. [Ed.] See Leonard Nathan's discussion of this poem by Vaux in his essay in this collection, below.

G. K. Hunter   Drab and Golden Lyrics of the Renaissance   (1970)

. . . It might be argued – and indeed it often is assumed – that only bad poems suffer from [the] absence of personality. The dispute between those who assume a gulf of mediocrity stretching between Wyatt and Sidney and those who defend the interim is often conducted in terms that assume the essential virtue of personality. The criticism of Yvor Winters and his followers provides a good illustration of what I mean. Winters is the founder of a modern movement asserting that the poetry not only of Ralegh and Greville but also of Gascoigne, Googe, Turberville, etc. – those that C. S. Lewis called 'Drab' – is superior to the poetry of Sidney and Spenser [For Winters' essay, see above in this collection – Ed.]. This preference is, of course, part of Winters's general admiration for poems that seem to be descriptive of objective fact. When we read 'The Sixteenth-Century Lyric in England', however, we discover that Winters's reasons for his high valuation of Ralegh and Gascoigne are closely connected with his sense of their personalities. His basic opposition is between 'rhetoric' ('the pleasures of rhetoric for its own sake') and what may be briefly described as 'honesty to experience'. He is understandably reticent about using this phrase, but when he speaks approvingly of 'the laconic bitterness of Ralegh and the bitter terror of Nashe' or of 'the moral grandeur, the grandeur of personal character to be discerned in Gascoigne and Ralegh', he is, if I understand him, asserting the value of states of mind he approves of, and assuming that these give the poems which express them their claim to value.

In his mode of valuation Winters is, of course, close to standard definitions of the lyric. We may take the definition from M. H. Abrams's handbook of literary terms: 'The term [lyric] is used for any short poem presenting a single speaker (not necessarily the poet himself) who expresses a state of mind involving thought and feeling'. The difficulty with this definition lies in the phrase 'expresses a state of mind'. Must this be confined to the meaning 'gives us the sense of a man experiencing thought and feeling'? Must the lyric (that is, the good lyric) give us the sense of a speaker inside the poem?

To pursue this question we may glance at a poem which would not, I assume, meet Winters's requirements – it does not appear in Winters's own anthology or in John Williams's *English Renaissance Poetry* – but whose claim to be a major lyric poem of the period must be generally allowed: Sidney's double sestina, 'Ye goat-herd gods that love the grassy mountains'. Even its admirers must accept that this is a highly rhetorical poem which is highly self-conscious about its rhetoric, one in which we listen in vain for signs of the individual voice speaking out to express a state of mind. But these are not defects. Awareness of the rhetoric is in fact the key to the enjoyment of the poem, whose meaning is not expressed by its statements so much as enacted by its form, acquiring existence as the formal shape of the poem unrolls. What is more, there seem to be too many good poems of this kind in the period to allow the personal voice in the poem to be thought of as the only value-conferring element. I do not wish to pursue the role of music in the lyric poetry of the period; it raises more questions than it answers. But I should like to make a single point: that music exercises a generalising effect on the words of the poem, moving the poetry away from any sense that it expresses an individual's unique feelings. In so far as the age is one in which 'music and sweet poetry agree' it is one with a bias toward generalised and impersonal lyric poetry.

Winters has attacked literary history (justifiably) for its tendency to value individual poems as representative productions of 'schools' of poetry. The attack (e.g., in his review of C. S. Lewis's Oxford History of English Literature volume, in *The Function of Criticism*) is perhaps excessively easy for him, for he assumes that all good poems are basically the same – objective descriptions from a morally approved point of view. His 'great tradition', derived from a single and repetitive criterion, is found in 'the great poems of Gascoigne and Ralegh and those most clearly resembling them by Greville, Jonson, Donne and Shakespeare'. Sidney and Spenser, on the other hand, have 'sensitivity to language ... far in excess of their moral intelligence'; they must not complicate our view of the Renaissance lyric, for they are only (as John Williams tells us) a 'temporary displacement ... an eccentric movement away from the native tradition'.

It would be easy to spend more space on Winters than on the sixteenth-century lyric; but it is not my purpose to bandy critical theories. In particular I do not wish to set against the categories of the

Winterreise – 'plain versus eloquent', 'native versus Petrarchan' – some alternative system which preserves the polarities and changes the values. This is what has happened in Winters's response to C. S. Lewis. Lewis's polarisation of 'Drab' and 'Golden' has found few defenders and Winters strenuously objects to it. But though the objection is couched as a general opposition to the categories of literary history, the structure of Winters's own categories is identical; only the values have changed.

It is of course very difficult to present separate good poems and avoid any diagram of preference between them, unless one can avoid the issue by keeping to a narrow or doctrinaire sense of what 'good' means. But let us begin by making an assumption that the sixteenth century offers different but equal kinds of lyric excellence – that (say) of the translation of Psalm CXXXIII in Byrd's *Songs of Sundry Natures* (1589):

> Behold how good a thing it is
> For brethren to agree,
> When men amongst them do no strife
> But peace and concord see.
> Full like unto the precious balm
> From Aaron's head that fell
> And did descend upon his beard
> His garment skirts until.
> And as the pleasant morning dew
> The mountains will relieve
> So God will bless where concord is
> And life eternal give.

and that (say) of the anonymous madrigal in Bateson's 1618 collection:

> Her hair the net of golden wire,
> Wherein my heart, led by my wandering eyes,
> So fast entangled is that in no wise
> It can nor will again retire;
> But rather will in that sweet bondage die
> Than break one hair to gain her liberty.

Naïvety and sophistication here face one another in such a way that they seem genuinely alternative virtues. Is it possible to speak of the Renaissance lyric so that both moods are given scope? The danger in literary history is its tendency to premature and unargued valuations.

Clearly these poems are different one from another. Clearly each belongs to a large mass of poetry which reflects the qualities it possesses individually. On the whole it may be said that the style of the first belongs to the period from the sixties to the eighties, though various features of the style are found later; while the style of the second belongs to the nineties and the following decades. Literary history offers two obvious models for dealing with this situation: either one style develops into the other (A is less good than B) or one style is a decadent form of the other (B is less good than A). A careful reading through the work of the mid-century poets, Churchyard, Golding, Howell, Googe, Turberville, Gascoigne, Edwardes, Hunnis, suggests that neither of these models will serve to describe the relationship between the style of these poets – the style of the first poem above – and the style of the second poem, which is the style of Sidney, Lodge and Daniel. I exclude Spenser from this distinction; in relation to it his position is highly ambiguous.

A careful reading suggests that neither style is a version of the other; each has as its aim a distinct image of the world, and other features are explicable in terms of this aim. What changes when poets move from one style to the other (if they move) is not only literary style but also the life-style of the persona who emerges from the body of their work.

From what was said earlier in this paper it might seem that I was now poised to advance to a distinction between the impersonal persona of a Gorges[1] and the highly personal persona of a Sidney. I must confess to some intention of this kind; but in so bald a statement the distinction would seem to be neither useful nor true. Poetry in the 'Golden' style of the second poem quoted is often as impersonal and conventional as any 'Drab' poetry; Wyatt's songs might be thought of as both 'Drab' and personal; and the poets of the mid-century are not to be described simply as men suspicious of versified egotism; their verse exhibits constantly the tension between the claims of erotic individualism and the larger claims of the society to which they belong.

It is important to note that the poets of the mid-century (I am thinking of Googe, Howell, Turberville and Gascoigne) were the first English poets to publish collections of their own lyrics. It is not surprising that they did this in volumes bearing some marks of order and design. The idea of the auto-anthology is strange; but one can see it as forced on these poets by their social situation. Their choosing to publish cuts them off from the annals of the courtly lyric; but they were already cut off in the milieux of their lives and lyrics from Wyatt, Surrey, Vaux, Ralegh, Dyer, Oxford, Essex – the real courtly makers. The verse of Googe and his fellows is poorly designed for the private entertainment of great ladies and their companions. Their love songs, when compared to Wyatt's, lack the easy support of accepted background situations and of the medieval traditions of court poem and court music. Wyatt can seem intensely personal and completely conventional at one and the same time. The mid-century poets have to be laboriously explicit in setting up a social background. The volumes seem to exist in order to create, in some sense, a cultured social world which the reader can join for the price of the book. The elaborate titles for their poems . . . are obviously part of this intention to create explicitly what the court poets evoke and assume.

These authors have many things in common: they are scholars by courtesy of a Humanist education, translators from Latin and Italian, officials by profession (Inns-of-Court men predominantly), so that the world of their verse is cut off from their professional life in a way that is not true of the courtier. Their verses are a kind of *vers de société*. They are aimed at readers of known and accepted preferences and judgements, explicitly stated by the poet himself. The persona which dominates these poems is that of the moralist, living in a world of corruption. Again and again the authors return to the commonplaces of Contempt of the World:

> What is this world, a net to snare the soul   . . .
>
> O Fortune false, how double are thy deeds   . . .
>
> Hope, whoso list, in life Hath but uncertain stay   . . .

This is the basis of their sensibilities, the common ground against which their love poems have to make their effect. It follows that the love poetry of these men describes a social view of love, where the seeming individuality of each 'I', each lover, is denied by the multiplication and monotony of Cupid's spoils:

> Where fond affection bore the chiefest sway,
> And where the blinded archer with his bow
> Did glance at sundry gallants every day.

The technique of such poets can be seen as part of this effort to express a vision of reality. The poulter's measure and the fourteener[2] are usually explained as reactions to late medieval metrical chaos; their extreme rigidity of rhythm in this view explains their vogue. But the rigidity of these metres may have a moral as well as a metrical aspect. It is not hard to imagine their attraction for the moralist who is stressing above all things the common lot that holds individual egotism in check. A highly sophisticated sensibility like Chapman's can give the fourteener a complex tread:

> Achilles' baneful wrath resound, O goddess, that imposed
> Infinite sorrows on the Greeks and many brave souls loosed
> From breasts heroic – sent them far, to that invisible cave
> That no light comforts.

But this is not what Howell and Turberville are aiming at. They aim not only at weight and solidity but also at effects of plainness. The persona they seek is that of a homespun philosopher, beloamed with proverbs and downright opinions, happy to echo the formulae that other men use and to depend on the same formulaic abstractions. Lewis, talking about the 'Drab' style, says, in a moment of unusual dyslogistic candour: 'If the poetry of the Drab Age was usually bad, that might be because new models induced minor talents to turn away from the thin, but real, trickle of poetry that still survived among the people.' It is true that the Drab poets are not ballad-writers, on the whole: but it is important to notice they do not really turn away from the rustic. These poets may aim at the court in some sense (though I suspect that the adjective 'courtly' is used much too freely and much too vaguely), but not in any sense that puts the court and the people in direct opposition. In a similar way, though we may call them men of learning, we should note that their learning is absorbed into a world where 'Maro's learned quill' or 'Senec's sappy sense' lie naturally cheek by jowl with the clodhopping integrity of country wisdom. This is not pastoral; indeed it is the opposite of pastoral, for it assumes that the tension between the images of court and country, on which pastoral depends, does not exist or should not exist.

The effort to project this same persona, to describe the same reality, probably explains vocabulary no less than metre. To modern ears their excess of Saxon monosyllables compounds the lumbering heaviness of metre, reinforced by alliteration. But pure or 'clene' English has a status in this period and among this group that relates it to shooting with the bow, hawking and hunting, and keeping open house as our forefathers did. The distaste for inkhorn terms is not only and not primarily a literary response; it is part of patriotism. As Gascoigne remarks: 'The most ancient English words are of one syllable, so that the more monosyllables that you use the truer Englishman you shall seem, and the less you shall smell of the inkhorn.' The persona I have been speaking of is, among other features, self-consciously English. . . .

SOURCE: extract from essay in Reuben A. Brower (ed.), *Forms of Lyric: Selected Papers from the English Institute* (New York, 1970), pp. 3–11.

NOTES

1. [Ed.] Sir Arthur Gorges (1557–1625), related to Sir Walter Ralegh, and the possible author of some of the poems commonly attributed to Ralegh. See H. E. Sandison, *The Poems of Sir Arthur Gorges* (Oxford, 1953).

2. [Ed.] *Poulter's measure*: rhyming couplets consisting of a line of iambic hexameter followed by a line of iambic heptameter – cf. Fulke Greville's 'Epitaph on Sir Philip Sidney'.

Fourteener: a metre of 7 iambic feet (heptameter) – cf. Chapman's *Iliad*. illustrated here in Hunter's essay.

Leonard Nathan   Gascoigne's 'Lullabie' and Structures in the Tudor Lyric   (1974)

One of the more diverting recent pastimes for those interested in Tudor lyrics is finding them a suitable taxonomy. Among the most notable – if not notorious – examples have been C. S. Lewis's Golden and Drab and Yvor Winters's Native and Petrarchan (or its less chauvinist version, Plain and Eloquent).[1] Helpful as these categories may be, they have, in their concern for stylistic discriminations, obscured other ways of making useful distinctions. One such way, structural, has been treated, if at all, in a most gingerly fashion.[2] The term *structure* itself has proved more slippery than most. I mean it here to signify the principle by which parts of a poem are related one to another, chiefly as regards larger units, for example, conclusion to body, subject or topic to the comparative material that may develop it.

It is my purpose in the following discussion to explore at least one characteristic Tudor poetic structure, and, further, to suggest that it represents an innovation that may distinguish a particular kind of sixteenth-century lyric from the dominant medieval type that preceded it far more radically than any quality of style. And I am using for my example George Gascoigne's 'The Lullabie of a Lover', a poem that has been . . . described as one 'using medieval structure'.[3] If style were the sole or even most significant determinant for understanding a poem, then such a judgement would seem right; but it is precisely in a poem whose surface might mislead on this score that the case can best be made for the conclusion that structural difference is perhaps all the difference.

An obvious characteristic of the medieval literary lyric is 'enumerative' structure.[4] But how and to what end enumeration was used in these poems needs to be explained. The following 'I Have Lived After My Lust', provides us, I believe, with a fair example of fifteenth-century poetic composition that can be called a typical handling of the topic:

Royal MS. App. 58

Now marcy, Ihe-su, I wyll amend
and neuermore displease the,
yff grace thow wylt me send.

My thoght ys full hevy
and greuith me Ryght sore;
my synnys be pesy,
whych repentyth me euer-more.
my flesh fast swetyng
my paynys to Renew,
my body besely boylyng
with hetys – lord Ihesu,
This haue I full surely
for that I was vniust
to god, the sune off mary,
and leuyd after my lust. Now mercy, Ihesu.

My fete, sume tyme more
and lesse, they do swete;

> my hert ys very pore,
>   and besyly doth bete;
> my hed ys all macy,
>   and meruelowsly dothe werke;
> my[n] yene dyme and dasy,
>   my neke ys full sterke;
> Thys haue I full surely
>   (for that I was vniust
> to god, the sune off mary,
>   and leuyd after my lust. Now mercy, Ihesu.)
>
> My hondys do me no good
>   ne-dys must I ly so
> and take no erthly fode
>   . . .
>
> now helpe me, goode lorde,
>   my stomake ys full faynt;
> I make to the acorde
>   Vppon payne off a-taynt;
> I wyll no more suerly
>   to the be so vnjust
> butt kepe thy lawes truly
>   And put a-way false lust. Now mercy Ihe[s]u.   [5]

Enumeration is clearly the dominant structural element here; the poem is a catalogue illustrating the consequence of the speaker having 'leuyd after' his 'lust'. The illustrative material, set in the figure of repetition ('my synnys', etc.), works to amplify the theme for the sake of vividness and pathos. What is interesting about the structural character of the poem is that parts are interchangeable between its beginning and end. The poet shows no concern – and this is characteristic of his type – for composing what we like to call an organic form, or, for that matter, any form that lays claim to logical or sequential coherence. Thus what might seem to later poets an almost comic breach of decorum – the juxtaposition of feet and heart – seems not to trouble him. Indeed, structure to this poet is reduced to accumulation: one thing added to another. What seems to be the overriding determinant guiding the poet's choice (aside from prosodic considerations) is what things belonged to the topic. Those things belong in the poem somewhere between the opening and closing lines.

There is a further assumption here about the character of the topic itself: that is, the poet regards it as a thing unto itself, and as such, a settled affair with its own attributes. Perhaps because of the doctrinaire quality of medieval thinking, typical subjects for literary poems – love, age, morality, divine or significant persons, for instance – were not objects for exploration or discovery so much as fixed concepts that poets could amplify, ornament or point to as exemplary. This static or categorical notion of topic leads to some predictable poetic behavior. Not only will topics be treated by the catalogue method, but the items that make up the catalogue will be arranged not because of their relations with each other, but because of their belonging to the topic; structural coherence, as we value it, is, then, beside the point. Further, topics themselves, seen as independent entities almost, will be presented with none but the most elementary relation to other topics, for example in the relation of comparison or contrast (as with youth to age). Often, whether his topic is secular or religious, the fifteenth-century poet's choice of stance is reduced to two: the encomiastic or the complaining.

It is perhaps too easy to see not just a way of perceiving literary composition, but also a way of social life, the aristocratic. Poetry, in this milieu, becomes a social pastime reflecting a rigid hierarchy in which status relationships ideally have precedence over and give value to personal relationships. It is no accident that the French *ballade* was so obsessively preoccupied with classes of things, of beautiful women, flowers, virtues, heroes, lovers; and that these individuals illustrate something typical about the class – its qualities or limits. Writing in this tradition, Lydgate provides us with an example of its English counterpart in the second stanza of an encomium to a lady:

> Wyfly trouthe with Penelope,
>   And with Gresylde parfyt pacyence,
> Lyche Polixcene fayrely on to se,
>   of bounte beaute having th'excellence
> Of qweene Alceste, and al the diligence
>   Of fayre Dydo pryncesse of Cartage –
>   Al this hathe nature sett in your ymage! [6]

Penelope, like all other elements of such lists, has no function beyond personifying a virtue and whether or not she precedes or follows Dido is not at issue. Her presence in the poem is simply to help exemplify and exhaust a certain category of women for the purpose of elementary comparison with the object of the poet's praise.

The limits of this method of composition are many and obvious, as any collection of fifteenth-century poetry will testify. The few truly gifted literary poets of the period manage, at best, charm and wit. The most important limit for our purposes, however, is that the enumerative structure, used in the way medieval poets tended to use it, implies a static and isolated treatment of topics. What makes 'Lullabie' a Renaissance poem and not a medieval one is, as I hope to show, that Gascoigne's use of enumeration does not imply such a view of topics.

Before considering 'Lullabie', however, I should like to discuss another poem, the well-known 'The Aged Lover Renounceth Love' by Lord Vaux. Its topic, like that of the medieval poem already quoted, is age and its attributes [Nathan quotes the whole poem, reproduced in Barbara Herrnstein Smith's study in this collection, above – Ed.] . . .

The first stanza establishes a typical antithesis, youth against age. The antithesis is absolute: the attributes of the topic of youth are in no way seen as connected to or resulting in the topic of age. The former is perceived merely as contrastive material to heighten the interest of the latter. The antithesis, further, along with enumeration or accumulation, provides the structural principle of the poem which unfolds as a series of then/now contrasts, interspersed with descriptions of age.

There is in all this very little sense of logical or dramatic development. While it might be argued that there is something like a progress in the poem, the movement from stanza to stanza is considerably less than inevitable. Stanzas 1–4 serve as background representing the negative effects of the loss of youth; 5 is a transition between the first section and the next; 6–9 present the character of age; 10, the proper stance toward age, though it overlaps 5 in this function; 12 intensifies the reason for the self-exhortation in 11 by offering a *memento mori* figure, though seeming to repeat the effects of 6–10; 13 reverts to the opening stanza as a reminder that the vices of youth bring the troubles of age, perhaps as a preparation for the last stanza that generalises the speaker's experience.

Though point by point, it is more lucid and its prosody is under better control than that of the usual among its fifteenth-century counterparts, 'The Aged Lover Renouncethe Love', it is fair to say, hardly represents much of an advance on the late medieval literary lyric. Indeed, certain stanzas can be excised with no damage to the poem – 1 or 2, 3 or 4 and 5; 12 or 13. And if certain stanzas were shifted it would make no important difference: for instance, 12 back to 11. The apparent looseness of the construction is to some degree concealed by the heavily patterned metre and clarity of each stanza, as well as by the familiarity of the topic. But measured against the structural integrity of, say, Marvell's 'To His Coy Mistress', 'The Aged Lover Renounceth Love' is slack.

Its slackness, however, is less the result of incompetence than the poet's commitment to a principle of composition that gave him as structural means only the simplest kind of antithesis and enumerative accumulation, and, moreover, his commitment to a way of viewing experience that was static and categorical, so that topics like that of love and age could seem connected only by crude opposition.[7]

The principle of composition arising from this view probably has little effect on epigrammatic verse; in longer poems enumeration and contrast are seldom enough to provide full structural control. Vaux, working from this principle, produces a series of sententious propositions about the dreadfulness of old age, vivified by a sort of low-profile personification, ending in the climactic apostrophe to the reader. That is, he has addressed a settled topic, located in it its characteristic attributes in a 'poetic' fashion, and nothing more. This is the way of much poetry, of course, and particularly the literary lyric of fifteenth-century England.[8]

It is not the way of Gascoigne's 'Lullabie'. Yet a failure to see this is at least understandable, for Gascoigne composes in the same tradition as Vaux – at least with respect to topic, prosody, diction and figure – a tradition fixed primarily by Tottel's *Miscellany*, which includes 'The Aged Lover Renounceth Love'. A cursory reading of 'The Lullabie of a Lover' might suggest more likeness than difference between Gascoigne and Vaux:

The Lullabie of a Lover

Sing lullaby, as women doe,
Wherewith they bring their babes to rest,
And lullaby can I sing to,
As womanly as can the best.
With lullaby they still the childe,
And if I be not much beguild,
Full many wanton babes have I,
Which must be stild with lullabie.

First lullaby my youthfull yeares,
It is nowe time to go to bed,
For croocked age and hoary heares,
Have wone the haven [within] my head:
With Lullaby then youth be still,
With Lullaby content thy will,
Since courage quayles, and commes behind,
Go sleepe, and so beguile thy minde.

Next Lullaby my gazing eyes,
Which wonted were to glaunce apace.
For every Glasse maye nowe suffise,
To shewe the furrowes in my face:
With Lullaby then winke awhile,
With Lullabye your lookes beguile:
Lette no fayre face, nor beautie brighte,
Entice you efte with vayne delighte.

And Lullaby my wanton will,
Lette reasons rule, nowe reigne thy thought,
Since all to late I finde by skyll,
Howe deare I have thy fansies bought:
With Lullaby nowe tak thyne ease,
With Lullaby thy doubtes appease:
For trust to this, if thou be styll,
My body shall obey thy will.

Eke Lullaby my loving boye,
My little Robyn take thy rest,
Since age is colde, and nothing coye,
Keepe close thy coyne, for so is best:
With Lulla[b]y be thou content,
With Lullaby thy lustes relente,
Lette others pay which hath mo pence,
Thou art to pore for such expence.

Thus Lullabye my youth, myne eyes,
My will, my ware, and all that was,
I can no mo delayes devise,
But welcome payne, let pleasure passe:
With Lullaby now take your leave,
With Lullaby your dreames deceive,
And when you rise with waking eye,
Remember then this Lullabye.

Ever or Never. [9]

The typical metrical regularity, the addiction to alliteration, the reliance on repetition (enumeration) and personification – all these, as well as the deliberately idiomatic character of the language, show, if nothing else, that Gascoigne learned his lessons well and that one of his basic texts was *Songes and Sonettes* [Tottel's *Miscellany*].

Yet the differences between 'Lullabie' and its models are far more striking than the resemblances. First, there is the controlling metaphor of the poem, the invention of the lullaby, though this itself has been viewed as a proof of the poem's medievalness.[10] One might as well assert that the topic of *King Lear* marks it as somehow medieval because the fall of princes was a topic much used in medieval poetry. In fact, when the fifteenth-century literary poet used the lullaby it was not a metaphor in the strict sense but a literal attempt to represent what was regarded as an historical event in Christian lore; thus, in Harley MS. 2380, the poet exploits the topic to create a dramatic context for the doctrine he aims to communicate and the pathos he wishes to evince:

> Sco sayd, 'sweit sone, wen sal this be [don],
> that ye sal suffir al this vo?'
> 'Moder fre, al sal ye se
> With xxx yer & thrio –
> It is no nay.'
> > He sayd ba-bay;
> > sco sayd lullay,
> > the virgin fresch as ros In may.   [11]

The lullaby here does no more than reaffirm a well-established and categorical relation between the virgin and her divine offspring. That relation was fixed and static with its appropriate attributes long before the poem was written. Nor did the poet tamper with it; his aim was to work within the limits imposed by such a tradition.

Gascoigne's use of the lullaby is far more complex and figures forth a relation between categories heretofore linked, if at all, only in the simple connection proposed by 'The aged louer renounceth loue'. If Vaux's speaker sees the acceptance of the miseries of age as the total and denunciatory rejection of the works of youth, Gascoigne, when he looks at the topic of age, sees something far less simple and, if one can use the phrase, less self-deceivingly facile. The metaphorical use of the lullaby is not quite paraphrasable, but it clearly establishes a relation between youth and age that is not simple contrast, but rather like that of the deepest kinship – mother to child – and the complex of feelings implied: fondness, indulgence, tenderness, irony, and a sense of duty. The topics are joined far more realistically or at least less abstractly than they are in Vaux. For men surely do not often give up their youth willingly; indeed, one suspects in Vaux's stance too much protest, an over-violent rejection of what, as Gascoigne plainly realises, is part of one's self. Gascoigne's use of the lullaby, in fact, makes available to him a far more complex and accurate moral perception of the topic, an advantage reflected in his control and a complexity of tone as compared, say, to the flatness and simplicity of Vaux's voice.[12]

Gascoigne has, by his use of the lullaby metaphor, found a profound link between what before were perceived as mere opposites; this link presupposes a specific way of seeing experience and how it might be represented in poetry. And this way is far different from that underlying the enumerative method. Topics here are not simply abstract conceptions by which to judge experience as if it could be isolated into atomic units of significant substance. Thus, the possibility is opened for a different kind of poem, a true alternative to the still prevalent literary modes of the fifteenth-century lyric: the cataloguing encomium or complaint. Such poems might provide the wherewithal to examine relationships not as if they were fixed and static, but rather as the result of a process that paralleled the relational character of actual experience. Many of Wyatt's poems are precisely the kind that make relationship itself the center of interest, often the relation between the old way of composing and perceiving the experience of love set against something new and painfully difficult to apprehend, which he calls by many names, among them newfangledness or change.[13] Newfangledness, as a topic, was long familiar to the medieval poets, but never treated by them as fit for analysis in complex relation to other topics. Like Wyatt, Gascoigne sees complex relationship itself as a vital subject for poetry. More particularly, he sees that through available poetic structure, he can connect apparently antithetical aspects of experience. The poet's task for him, then, is to invent a controlling figure of sufficient richness and appropriateness to give the poet tonal scope to do justice to the complexity of the experienced relation.[14] And that 'Lullabie' is not a mere accident is attested to by another of Gascoigne's poems, 'Woodsmanship', which links youth and age (or at least middle age) in a yet richer and more serious way.

A closer look at 'Lullabie' indicates that, while the controlling metaphor does not provide Gascoigne with a particular means of organisation, it does give him tonal control, stanza by stanza, throughout which he is able to maintain the stance of a mother singing her babes to sleep: a loving fondness made ironic by the underlying acceptance of the necessity to put youth to sleep. Moreover, it is wholly appropriate for the poet to make use of the principle of enumeration since a lullaby by nature is repetitive; so that if no other principle were at work in the poem the lullaby metaphor would have given Gascoigne considerable structural coherence.

There is another principle at work, however; the psychological, as understood by the Renaissance poet and his audience.[15] After the opening stanza that proposes the controlling metaphor, a second stanza extends the meaning of the metaphor to a literal situation; the next three stanzas are ordered so as to parallel the process involved in the experience of sexual passion. This artful organisation is not in itself the inevitable sign of a Renaissance lyric, but the structural frame of the lullaby metaphor gives it a fine irony missing from the medieval lyrics. Thus what could have been – the middle stanza – medieval enumeration is indeed a witty little liturgy of renunciation, whose climax is the indulgently good-humored dismissal of 'little Robyn', the most difficult and perhaps spoiled child of all. This, structured by the lullaby metaphor, achieves a complexity of perception simply unavailable through the conventions underlying fifteenth-century lyrics.

It remains to be said that the last stanza rounds off the poem in a summary statement qualified by the psychologically accurate admission that the speaker, because of his reluctance to give up his youth, has been inventing ways to forestall having to do so: 'I can no mo delayes devise.' This humane honesty is followed by an apostrophe accepting pain and a final farewell to his 'babes', with the injunction that they remember the lullaby when they awaken and, by implication, submit to the new dispensation.

Compared with this affectionately delicate and yet toughly candid poem, 'The Aged Lover Renounceth Love', seems flat and frigid. And this is not because Vaux is incompetent or Gascoigne the immeasurably superior writer. If 'The Aged Lover Renounceth Love' could do with some cutting and maybe even rearrangement, 'Lullabie' is not flawless; for example, the last stanza, particularly in its sixth line, contains some unhelpful ambiguity. It is rather that the principles of composition – particularly with respect to structure – that inform 'The Aged Lover Renounceth Love' set very severe limits to what the practitioner can do with any topic. The principle of composition Gascoigne employs, however he came upon it, gave him an instrument of considerable range in dealing with common human experience. Moreover, each of these principles assumes a way of perceiving reality. The mannered and schematic tonality in Vaux's poem is the direct result of a categorical way of seeing reality, while Gascoigne's more open, subtle (though no less formal) voice is the direct consequence of a more fluid and relational way of seeing things. Indeed, it might be said that the topic of poems that come from this mode of seeing is always relationship itself. And it is this latter kind of poem that seems to me to appear in the Renaissance for the first time in numbers that suggest it is as characteristic of the time as it is uncharacteristic of fifteenth-century poetry. I have already mentioned its presence in Wyatt and have noted that Gascoigne's most impressive poem, 'Woodsmanship', partakes of the mode, as does also Ralegh's 'Even Such as Time', Sidney's 'With How Sad Steps', and Jonson's 'On My First Son'. It might be argued that the structure of Shakespeare's great tragedies is akin to that of these poems, leading the auditor to a perception not of categories but of relationships. That may perhaps be too extensive a claim for one kind of structure; in any case, it is plainly visible at the end of the sixteenth century and carries over into some of the most important work of the seventeenth century in elaborate and subtle variations like Herbert's 'The Collar' and Marvell's 'The Garden'.

At the beginning of this essay I asserted that enumeration was a characteristic structural principle of medieval poetry. At this point, I think it is possible to go further: enumeration itself is based upon a more fundamental principle, what one might call the principle of simple juxtaposition in which the elements of a poem are related both in temporal order and conceptually on the basis of a nearly one-to-one comparison or contrast or both, and rarely anything between. This principle, which obviously leads to an accumulative structure of which enumeration is one kind, strongly persists into the sixteenth century; but along with it another principle comes into play which replaces the simple antithesis and catalogue of comparisons with a more complex relating of elements where the attention is not so much on any element as on the relation between them, as in the relation between youth and age in Gascoigne. This latter kind of mode differs also in that it is less concerned with stance (encomium, complaint, precation, exhortation) than with communicating a perception about experience, about how the parts of the world fit together.

It is understanding this mode that I think may give us at least as much help in understanding the sixteenth-century lyric as categories like Drab and Golden. Drab and Golden or Plain and Eloquent poets can also be looked at structurally with some benefit. For example, Sidney and Jonson turn out to share more than late Tudor sophistication by this criterion: a turn of mind that habitually seeks the meaning of relationship, that explores the discontinuities in experience for some connection that will hold, at least in poetry. It is perhaps for this reason that they, like Wyatt and Gascoigne, rely so heavily on irony, that figure which implies doubleness and ambivalence and which is so foreign to Lydgate, Orleans, Suffolk and the myriad minor writers of fifteenth-century lyrics. In any case, the poetry whose topic is relationship itself is one of the important kinds that appears in the sixteenth century. And, as I have tried to show, it can best be understood if we look to the principles that bind elements into coherency.

SOURCE: essay in Thomas O. Sloan and Raymond S. Waddington (eds), *The Rhetoric of Renaissance Poetry* (Berkeley, Cal., 1974), pp. 58–72.

NOTES

[Reorganised and renumbered from the original – Ed.]

1. See G. K. Hunter's 'Drab and Golden Lyrics of the Renaissance', [for the first half of this essay, see the preceding item in this collection – Ed.] Professor Hunter, refining on both Winters and Lewis, makes his division along historical lines; he finds two modes: one is the plain-spoken social poem dominant at mid-century and dependent for its full meaning on its narrative context; the other, coming to prominence at century's end, is the aesthetically autonomous lyric, the emblem of some particular brilliant personality.

2. The exception is Douglas L. Peterson's *The English Lyric from Wyatt to Donne* (Princeton, 1967), in which structure is given a great deal of attention, but, alas, to the end of confusing the reader. For Professor Peterson seems sometimes to mean by structure a principle of arrangement, sometimes the arrangement itself; this shift of definition brings him to curious conclusions,

not the least curious of which is the conflation of rhetorical with poetic intention when he reads certain poems from Tottel's *Miscellany* as though they were translations of the school rhetorics of the time (see, for instance, pp. 55–61). It is one thing to note that Tudor poets found rhetorical handbooks useful sources for arrangement, quite another to see some sort of equivalence between the rhetorical and the poetic usage of common material.

3. Professor Peterson again, who goes on to explain his judgement by asserting that 'both the theme and the lullaby as a convention are common in collections of secular and religious medieval lyric' and that the 'enumerative repetitive structure is also medieval' (p. 161). This reading engages in a gross reduction. The intention of the medieval poet in enumerating is, as I hope to show, far different from Gascoigne's intention in doing so; just as the view of poetry and of experience underlying medieval enumeration is different from that underlying Gascoigne's enumeration.

4. Professor Peterson's term (see note 3). It should be understood that I exclude from my consideration non-literary verse such as the popular song, occasional and practical verse since the Tudor lyrics under consideration were literary.

5. Carleton Brown (ed.), *Religious Lyrics of the XVth Century* (Oxford, 1939), no. 139, pp. 213–14.

6. Russell H. Robbins, *Secular Lyrics of the XIVth and XVth Centuries* (Oxford, 1952). From the poem titled 'The All-Virtuous She', no. 131, pp. 129–30.

7. The opposition – a simplistic reading of Petrarch and a commonplace in the anthologies – is handsomely represented in microcosm by two complementary epigrams of George Turberville:

> Maister George His Sonet of the Paines of Loue
>
> Two lines shall tell the griefe,
>   that I by loue sustaine:
> I burne, I flame, I faint, I freeze,
> of Hell I feele the paine.

and

> Turberuile's Aunswere and Distich to the Same
>
> Two lines shall teach you how
>   to purchase loue anewe:
> Let reason rule where Loue did raigne
>   and ydle thoughts eschewe.

8. I do not mean to imply that poems informed by the principle of enumeration are necessarily slack or loose mixtures of these elements. Ralegh's 'The Lie', written with a polemic intention, is but one example of enumeration working with powerful unitary effect. Any structural principle

can be put to telling use. What separates 'The Lie' from typical lyrics of the fifteenth century is that the latter, besides exhibiting less sophistication and skill, direct their language away from the experience they purport to encompass; to put it another way, they are all too often formularies. Because the poet sees poetic composition as gathering all that is appropriate to a topic, which is itself an abstraction, he can hardly help regarding his craft as something of a polite game. If religious poets were invested with more imaginative seriousness, they seldom show it except in the solemnity of their effort.

9. George Gascoigne, *The Posies* in *The Complete Works of George Gascoigne*, ed. John W. Cunliffe (Cambridge, c. 1907), i, pp. 44–5.

10. Professor Peterson regards this invention, as we have seen, as one mark of the poem's medieval character (see note 3), but it is fair to say that he also finds it, as Gascoigne uses it here, part of what sets the poem off 'as an example of the refined plain style', along with its 'extraordinary control of the refrain technique' (Peterson, p. 162). Professor Peterson's preoccupation with the thesis of plain versus eloquent proposed by Winters makes him overlook important and, for his case, relevant points. By emphasising questions of style in a way that seems to imply that Renaissance plain style is somehow more sophisticated than medieval, he further implies some sort of notion of progress as the underlying category for assessing poetry, when, in fact, as I am arguing, it is in some instances the far more radical matter of different modes of perception.

11. Brown, op. cit., p. 6. It is interesting to compare John Phillip's 'Lullaby', written before 1562, with both the fifteenth-century literary lullabies and Gascoigne's lyric – cf. Norman Ault (ed.), *Elizabethan Lyrics* (New York, 1949), p. 41. While Phillip uses the device for a secular poem and has achieved something like Tudor eloquence, his aim is perhaps even simpler than his fifteenth-century predecessors, though Gascoigne may have remembered Phillip's phrase, 'I will not delay me', when writing 'I can no mo delayes devise'.

12. I think Professor Peterson insists on the wrong emphasis when he asserts (concerning the lines: 'And lullaby can I sing to, / As womanly as can the best') that Gascoigne's 'admission here that with the loss of those powers which have made him a vigorous lover he approaches effeminacy is nicely ironic' (Peterson, p. 162). Ironic yes, but not because of effeminacy. This is to overread the figure. The focus is on the relation between youth and age, not on Gascoigne's womanliness. Nor is he in any way making fun of the inability of age. Womanliness is a counter to the youthful qualities personified as children. To make it anything more is to misplace emphasis.

Another misreading of the lullaby metaphor is William Tydeman's 'He sings his declining faculties to rest, with the amused air of a content and mellowed philanderer' – *English Poetry, 1400–1580* (London, 1970), p. 62. This judgement entirely ignores the moral understanding of the poem, enforced by

the last stanza; it also ignores the generous sympathy of the stance toward
youth, rare in a time when the commonplace position of the poet writing
about age was a flat condemnation of youth as a total waste, or worse.

13. See my 'Tradition and Newfangledness in Wyatt's "They Fle From
Me" ', *English Literary History*, 32 (1965), pp. 1–16.

14. This controlling figure may very well be what Gascoigne meant – but
did not have the terms for – when he speaks in 'Certayne notes of Instruction'
of invention that is posed against *'oratione perpetua'*, which sounds suspiciously
like the sort of medieval poem I have described in which the poet's chief
structural principle is enumeration (see Gascoigne, I, pp. 65–66).

15. This fact has been noted before. See, for example, Tydeman who says:
'Gascoigne . . . follows standard Renaissance sex psychology. The
Elizabethans believed that love, contracted through the eyes, stimulated the
passions, in alliance with the fancy, to gain control of the will, overthrow it,
and achieve physical satisfaction' (p. 256). With some qualification and less
summary simplicity, this was the general view of the literate Englishman of
the sixteenth century. That 'little Robyn', the sexual organ, should be treated
in the favored climactic position is wittily proper, both to the allegory and to
the then current view of the matter.

Alastair Fowler   'Elizabethan Conceits:
Spenser, Sidney and Drayton'   (1975)

Future historians of criticism may well be struck by how much more
interest our age has shown in Metaphysical imagery than in
Elizabethan. The different rates of scholarly publication in the two
fields will certainly provide them with some remarkable contrasts.[1]
Statistics hardly seem necessary, if one thinks how hard it would be to
find books on Elizabethan poetry comparable with those of William-
son, Warnke, Summers, Miner, Stein, Alvarez, Miller, Richmond
and Fish, to name only a few. There are, of course, many works on
individual Elizabethan writers; but almost none that treat their style
in general, unless as a preliminary to Metaphysical style. No doubt
our successors may see the preference as manifesting some movement
of taste, even of thought, which it would be ridiculous to think of
escaping, if we ever became aware of it. But they will possibly also
wonder why we took so long to remove obstacles well within our

lesser reach, which hamper appreciation of Elizabethan imagery needlessly.

Metaphysical and Spenserian Conceits

In 1946 Rosemond Tuve detected 'a growing tendency to forsake Elizabethan for Jacobean poets'.[2] Since then· neglect of the Elizabethans has become almost total, interrupted only by a partial recovery of Spenser and by some diachronic forays tracing motifs or intellectual traditions. Shakespeare is the great exception: his *Sonnets* have not lost favour.[3] They have been lumped awkwardly with Metaphysical poetry, however; and interpreters have found great difficulties in them, not all due to the privacy of their social context.

Rosamond Tuve was surely right in arguing that we misconstrue the rhetorical functions of Renaissance imagery. But that hardly explains why a barrier obstinately separates Tudor and Stuart poetry, with only Shakespeare by his genius obscurely breaking it. The powerful demonstrations of her *Elizabethan and Metaphysical Imagery* mostly go to bring the two periods of literature together, rather than to distinguish between them in any way that could explain or counteract an unreasonable preference for one. It is much the same with J. A. Mazzeo's connection of seventeenth-century imagery with a poetic of universal analogy.[4] We may agree with his critique of attempts to explain the Metaphysical style in terms of Petrarchism, the emblem tradition, Ramistic logic, or the Baroque.[5] And we may accept, with reservations, his theory that the Metaphysical poets 'possessed a view of the world founded on universal analogy and derived habits of thought which prepared them for finding and easily accepting the most heterogeneous analogies'.[6] (T. E. May's point – that *correspondencia* in Gracián is not a metaphysical concept – may be thought a local objection, hardly impairing the general theory.) Few will doubt that cosmic analogies, both familiar and occult, played a great part in Metaphysical poetry, even if no-one can reasonably believe that every conceit enshrined a serious philosophical correspondence. However, Professor Mazzeo's theory applies to the sixteenth century no less than to the seventeenth. Giordano Bruno, with whom the practice and theory of the heuristic use of analogy coincide, comes in the earlier period.[7] And on the other hand the English Reformers increasingly challenged the doctrine of *analogia entis*, from the late sixteenth century onwards. Mazzeo might have used his Hegel *symbolon* ('When philosophy paints its gray in gray, a shape of life has grown old') more narrowly, to imply that much seicento theory was retrospective, based on cinquecento practice. At any rate, we are left with the question why Elizabethan conceits should be less accessible than Metaphysical ones. The habit of cosmic analogy, however applicable, was common to both periods. True, later analogies were often pressed farther; but that need not have made them more attractive.

We begin to wonder how far the distaste for Elizabethan imagery rests on informed value preferences, and whether some of the inaccessibility may not be self-created. Have critics possibly made their approach with an inappropriate mental set? At least they seem to have had an expectation that they would find Elizabethan conceits to be comparatively simple. Occasionally this is given a rationale in terms of contemporary theory: 'The relation between the object and its representation was relatively clear in the criticism of the cinquecento. For our [seicento] theorists the relationship was more complex'.[8] When in fact a critic finds late Elizabethan conceits intricate and oblique, he is liable to call them 'diffuse, vague, atmospheric' and 'shadowy' – the terms F. T. Prince applies to [Spenser's] *Amoretti*.[9] Alternatively, he may deny that there is much in them besides their vehicles; as when Allen Tate writes of Spenser's 'ornamental decoration of image'; or when Jean Hagstrum thinks that 'the iconic poetry of Drayton . . . contents the eye' only.[10] In the same way, Austin Warren contrasts Spenser and Donne: the former's epic simile 'is fully pictorial; the intent . . . is decorative. On the other hand, the "sunken" and the "radical" types of imagery – the conceits of Donne . . . expect scant visualisation'.[11] But visualisation is far too limited a notion to be helpful with late Elizabethan imagery.[12] And a reader of dark conceits is unlikely to find the lights hidden beneath their surfaces, if he believes that plain superficiality bounds them.

Concentrate on the sensuous particulars of the vehicle in *Amoretti* 6, for example, and you might condemn such a phrase as 'gentle breast' for its stock epithet, or the whole sonnet for imprecision:

> The dureful oak, whose sap is not yet dried,
>   Is long ere it conceive the kindling fire:
>   But when it once doth burn, it doth divide
>   Great heat, and makes his flames to heaven aspire.
> So hard it is to kindle new desire,
>   In gentle breast that shall endure for ever: [13]

But trace the correspondences of tenor and vehicle, and you find their members performing fairly complex functions. Thus, the vehicular oak, which holds out against attempts to ignite it but then burns greatly with lasting flames, resembles the virtuous lady, in that she resists easy lusts but may at last love devotedly and faithfully. The comparison selects meanings of *gentle* and modulates them to convey a particular excellence of courteous generosity which will not change troth once plighted.[14] Any contrariety between 'dureful' and 'gentle' is muted by the emblematic associations of the oak as *fortitudo* or moral virtue,[15] and by the common application of *gentle* to domestic varieties of trees.[16] When, however, we try to trace out the rest of the tenor and vehicle chains – a project that would be easy enough with a Metaphysical conceit – the difficulties of embedded, doubled and inverted metaphors are encountered. 'Divide / Great heat' unquestionably implies some such tenor as 'share great love': a comparison depending on the conventional fire of love.[17] But one can hardly keep 'divide' (or, in another way, 'dureful') out of the abruptly changed metaphor that follows:

> Deep is the wound, that dints the parts entire
> With chaste affects, that naught but death can sever.

The wound of deep love paradoxically joins together and makes one flesh ('entire'; 'knits the knot'), so that oak-splitting turns out not to be a preliminary to burning. The resistent firmness of the tree's knotted grain, revalued in retrospect, is now seen to be insisted on by the extraordinarily-sustained *traductio* 'nought . . . not . . . not . . . naught . . . not . . . knot'. In this way the almost-unsplittable slow-burning fierce-burning divided-undivided oak corresponds to multiple tenors, distinct though not incompatible. Through these rhetorical labyrinths we are guided by traditional figurative applications, such as the proverbs 'heart of oak' and 'one stroke fells not an oak',[18] conveying the moral soundness of the lady and the magnitude of the work of courtship. Or consider 'makes his flames to heaven aspire'. The flames rise just as the love aspires to a heaven beyond its mortal reach, perhaps beyond it altogether. But take *aspire* to carry the implication 'die',[19] and the breast if not the love may reach heaven to endure indeed for ever. The entirely wounded tree and the funerary but amorous fire interrelate in a way that eludes logic.[20] Yet the effect is far from imprecise: these flames positively crackle with intelligence of passion.

G. K. Hunter's interesting account of *Amoretti* partly rests on prescriptive assumptions about what 'the English sonnet form, with its epigrammatic structure' ought to be, as it moves to 'final denouement', preferably in a couplet.[21] Like J. W. Lever, he blames Spenser for the generic error of attempting in sonnets what can only be accomplished in long poems; unjustly, since Elizabethan 'sonnet sequences' sometimes were long poems in quatorzain stanzas, with ample room for unresolved suspensions and prolonged meditation.[22] Nevertheless, Professor Hunter's perceptive descriptions of Spenser's 'characteristically self-involuted' syntax (p. 135) deserve close attention. The observation that 'the effortless flow of analogies . . . often involves a genuine ambiguity between tenor and vehicle, between the point of comparison and the thing compared' (p. 138) applies with equal force to *The Faerie Queene* and to many *Amoretti* stanzas. Instead of at once deploring this feature, however, we may wish to defer judgement a little.

Spenser's Complex Conceit

Amoretti 1, which Hunter thinks deficient in argument, calls for rather extended treatment, as a fine but not uncharacteristic example of the neo-Petrarchan manner Spenser shared with Sidney and Shakespeare. As we should expect with a poem in such a well-developed tradition, the means to its passionate sensuousness are not simple, even if its effect seems so:

> Happy ye leaves when as those lily hands,
>   Which hold my life in their dead doing might
> Shall handle you and hold in love's soft bands,
>   Like captives trembling at the victor's sight.
> And happy lines, on which with starry light,
>   Those lamping eyes will deign sometimes to look
> And read the sorrows of my dying spright,
>   Written with tears in heart's close bleeding book.
> And happy rhymes bathed in the sacred brook,
>   Of Helicon whence she derived is,
> When ye behold that angel's blessed look,
>   My soul's long lacked food, my heaven's bliss.
> Leaves, lines, and rhymes, seek her to please alone,
> Whom if ye please, I care for other none.

The opening quatrain compares the white vibrating leaves of *Amoretti* held in the lady's hands to captives white and trembling before a triumphator who may take their lives. Ordinary captives' hard bonds, in the vehicle, correspond in the tenor to the soft fingers holding the book (and perhaps secondarily, if the book is bound, to the cords binding its quires).[23] But since the lady's hands are those 'which hold my life in their dead doing might', the simile functions as a complex metaphor,[24] in whose embedded comparison it is the lover, conquered in an *amorosa guerrera*, who pretends to dread his mistress' mood. Thus, vibrating leaves held in fingers resemble captives held in physical bonds and trembling with fear, who in turn resemble the poet trembling with emotions of love, whether at the thought of Elizabeth's touch or of his life being figuratively in her hands:

vibrating leaves		trembling captives		trembling poet
tenor 1	*resembling*	*vehicle 1*		
		tenor 2	*resembling*	*vehicle 2*

Moreover, since poet and book belong to the same field of discourse, the complex metaphor is of a very special form, in which the more distant vehicle returns to the proximate literal chain. So far we can be reasonably sure of having constructed the conceit correctly – except possibly for some uncertainty as to whether tenor and vehicle may not be inverted, the sonnet being more about the lover than the book. But even at this stage of reading we have depended on the positiveness or congruence of the comparisons, which rest on the love-triumph tradition familiar from such works as Ovid's *Amores*, Petrarch's *Trionfi* and Colonna's *Hypnerotomachia*, and returned to in sonnets 29 and 52 of the present sequence.[25] If the metaphor submerged in 'love's soft bands' had been more novel or difficult in itself, it would have lessened the possibility of farther, superstructural effects.

Taking the metaphor of 'lily hands' into account brings us to stranger ground. Lilies hold leaves too, so that there is almost some thought of a double vehicle. At least, trembling of the lilies' leaves is suggested, and with it an idea that Elizabeth's hands may shake a little (like her proud heart in *Amoretti* 10) with the emotion the printed leaves are designed to arouse. The leaves will be happy, obviously, according to the poetic convention whereby a lover regards the 'experience' of objects enjoying physical contact with his mistress as enviable.[26] Less obviously, they will be fortunate when the trembling they engender indicates the successful effect of the poet's courtship. Ambiguity here expresses a reciprocity of relation that distinguishes *Amoretti* from most sonnet sequences: when Elizabeth is 'pleased' by the leaves (a stage very different from that of Sonnet 48, where she burns a confession of the poet's love), he as much as she will be 'victor'.[27]

To call the metaphoric structure circular or involuted would not do justice to its robust though gentle movement. Succeeding conceits of *Amoretti* 1 become more abstract as they rise towards the world of Ideas. One sequence of discourse runs through aspects of the book: the material 'leaves'; the communication of 'lines' looked on and 'sorrows' read; the poetic form, 'rhymes', drawn from higher vision. And corresponding aspects of the beloved ascend from 'hands', through 'eyes', to the 'angel's look' in them – that is, from physical through animate to spiritual levels. Each quatrain has an inset figure whose vehicle anticipates the next level. 'Victor's sight' looks on to 'lamping eyes' and optical activity in the second quatrain; copious tears and blood flow towards the 'sacred brook' of the third. Finally, 'bliss' makes the end of the *askesis* of souls (vegetable, animal, rational), just as it is the final cause of literary composition. The concluding summation can hardly be said to lack foundation in poetic logic.[28] The couplet asserts Spenser's seriousness, even his preference for instrumental values, at the same time as it refers, like *Astrophel and Stella* 1, after the manner of mannerism, to its own form. One could divide many narrow questions about ambiguities in this complicated sonnet. For the present purpose, we need only note the frequent switches from tenor to vehicle chains. A few words (*bold*, *trembled*) belong to both; but lexical as distinct from syntactical ambiguities are not specially noticeable.

Amoretti 15 seems at first to have a much simpler figurative structure. Consisting of a catalogue or blazon of features, visually compared each to some precious material, it might have been written to confirm Raymond Southall's thesis about commercial materialism in Elizabethan love poetry. Indeed, he discusses it as such: Spenser is like an enthusiastic salesman, and the sonnet 'flatters the lady by treating her as a precious but as yet unexploited commodity'.[29] But this appearance is deceptive. Spenser in fact criticises the vain efforts of the 'tradeful merchants':

> Ye tradeful merchants, that with weary toil,
>   Do seek most precious things to make your gain;
>   And both the Indias of their treasures spoil,
>   What needeth you to seek so far in vain?
> For lo my love doth in her self contain

> All this world's riches that may far be found,
>   If sapphires, lo her eyes be sapphires plain,
>   If rubies, lo her lips be rubies sound:
> If pearls, her teeth be pearls both pure and round;
>   If ivory, her forehead ivory ween;
>   If gold, her locks are finest gold on ground;
>   If silver, her fair hands are silver sheen:
> But that which fairest is, but few behold,
> Her mind adorned with virtues manifold.

The opening apostrophe, moreover, alludes to *Revelation* 18. 10–16 and *Ezekiel* 27–8, which list the same materials among the wealth of a once-beautiful city (Babylon, Tyre). Tyre has claimed 'perfect beauty', but her merchants or suppliers will be terrified by her downfall.[30] In the Biblical exegetic tradition, some of the riches were allegorised as individual virtues; others grouped as the clothing of prelapsarian integrity.[31] No doubt some of Spenser's readers would not get farther than the jewels-features matrix of the blazon, and 'but few behold' the additional jewels-virtues matrix. But the uncertain would be helped by his concluding hint: 'her mind adorned with virtues manifold'. Again the conceit depends on complex metaphors. Spenser does not mean that Elizabeth's mind is adorned with virtues as her body with jewels (the proportional metaphor of Aristotle's *Poetics*),[32] since her features do not merely wear, but are, figuratively, the jewels. The implication is rather that *feature* (vehicle) resembles *jewel* (tenor, secondary vehicle) which resembles *virtue* (secondary tenor). In this light, *adorned* may not seem exactly lacking in compression.

The flowers of the *baiser-blason* Sonnet 64, in appearance artlessly sensuous, mere Archimbaldi-like collage, open on inspection into figures of another sort. Behind their swooning synaesthesia, an elusive wit matches each to its feature in unexpected ways. Elizabeth's neck smells like 'a bunch of columbines' because these are white – but also because *collum* means neck. And 'her snowy brows like budded belamours' preserves the continuity of the list by inventing a plausible flower name: the *belamour* is not a bell flower but a love glance, which will bloom as the young lady's 'budded' brow opens.[33] The most complex of the comparisons is also the most erotic: her goodly bosom's resemblance to 'a strawberry bed'. No doubt its main point lies with the concealed nipple-berries; but surely we are also meant to explore the farther association of 'bed' (in a literal sense) with the white pillows to which breasts were commonly likened?[34] Logical analysis in terms of multiple grounds of comparison can hardly be thought adequate. The conceit is a highly impacted metaphor, involving three discourse sets (breasts, nipples), (pillows, bed) and (strawberry bed, berries), with several members submerged. The link between the first vehicle, pillows, and the second tenor, strawberries, depends on no more than the shared word 'bed'. Metaphoric intricacy here allows an unsuggestive lightness of sensuous suggestion.

In a work so various as *Amoretti* we naturally find sonnets of other sorts, from which figurative complexity is absent. But there are also many comparable passages. We need look no farther than a sonnet already discussed for several instances of the obliquity noted in *Amoretti* 64. Subsidiary to the main conceit of *Amoretti* 15 there may be submerged pun in 'her forehead ivory *ween*' ('think', 'fair'); a half-punning aptness to lips in 'rubies *sound*'; and a medical propriety in the choice of sapphires for eyes so good to look at.[35] It would be tasteless to analyse these fugitive graces in logical terms; yet one can scarcely think their semantic structure less complex than that of many a metaphysical conceit. Such incidentally witty decorums are everywhere in *Amoretti*, even though we may think its larger effects, its deeply-meditated complex metaphors, more characteristic of Spenser at his best.

Doubled and Circular Metaphors: Sidney and Drayton

Sidney's conceits, if sometimes more dramatic and forceful than Spenser's, are seldom much simpler. *Astrophel and Stella* Sonnet 9 is a characteristic example, possessed of far more complexity than it has been credited with:

> Queen Virtue's court, which some call Stella's face,
>   Prepared by Nature's chiefest furniture,
>   Hath his front built of alabaster pure;
>   Gold is the covering of that stately place,
> The door by which sometimes comes forth her Grace,
>   Red porphir is, which lock of pearl makes sure:
>   Whose porches rich (which name of cheeks endure)
>   Marble mixed red and white do interlace.

A double *allegoria* allows architectural features to stand simultaneously for physical features and for moral qualities. In one, the court is

Stella's face, an equation less arbitrary when *face* meant 'façade';[36] in the other, it is virtue's earthly home. That it is the best design of an architect called Nature means both that Stella's face needs no cosmetic embellishing and that she owes her mental qualities to nature in a high philosophical sense.[37] Similarly the court 'hath his front [entrance side] built of alabaster pure' not only because Stella's forehead ('front') is white and smooth, but also because her demeanour is morally pure (the symbolic meaning of alabaster).[38] And the queen ('her Grace') leaving a door of porphiry resembles a spoken grace enunciated by Stella's lips, as well as a favour shown to Astrophel.[39] Such an allegory with double tenors would have been incomprehensible unless some of its component metaphors were already known. Here, Sidney takes for granted not only the familiar blazon motif, which correlated a fairly restricted range of precious materials with physical features,[40] but also the allegorical house motif, based on dream symbolism, which correlated architectural and bodily or moral properties.

In addition, schemes linking riches and virtues underlie the thought, as in *Amoretti* 15. But in *Astrophel and Stella* word-plays that clench the various chains of discourse together are more frequent. Sidney's fondness for *antanaclasis*, *adnominatio* and pun may even be judged excessive: his rhetoric, though brilliant and powerful, lacks something of Spenser's delicacy. In the present sonnet, indeed, the play on *touch* is notorious for its manneristic extremity; without ever, perhaps, having received adequate interpretation:

> The windows now through which this heavenly guest
> Looks over the world, and can find nothing such,
> Which dare claim from those lights the name of best,
> Of touch they are that without touch doth touch,
> Which Cupid's self from Beauty's mine did draw:
> Of touch they are, and poor I am their straw.

The 'lights' or 'windows' that the guest looks out from have been applied to Stella: their black touchstone resembles the darkness of her eyes, which emotionally 'touch' and attract Astrophel as rubbed jet attracts straw by the action of its electrostatic field – only 'without touch', without rubbing, without sexual contact.[41] Perhaps also there is the more bitter implication that Stella affects Astrophel injuriously, that is, touches him, without having any imagination – any 'sense of inward touch' – about his feelings.[42] But all of this lies within the court-face allegory: we should also follow out the allegory of Queen Virtue. In it, the 'lights' are moral lights or examples, and the 'touch' is true touchstone, which 'doth touch' (i.e., tests) and finds the world around to be of inferior metal.[43] The final couplet may well introduce a farther application, with Cupid igniting Astrophel's straw, by 'lights' from touch-powder, to kindle the familiar fire of passion.[44] But in any event the sestet clearly offers alternative rather than complementary grounds for comparison. Doubling of metaphors by *antanaclasis* and pun, a favourite local device with Sidney, here determines the overall effect. We have to choose between a virtuously testing and a magnetically attractive Stella, with some sense of unresolved contradiction.[45] Is this really a Court of Virtue or (as Cupid's participation suggests) a Court of Love? The building materials confirm the latter identification: they would once have been recognisable as quarried from the pseudo-Chaucerian *Court of Love*.[46] Yet the tone will not easily allow reconciliation of the two aspects in terms of the Venus-Virgo or any such composite figure. On the contrary, once 'Queen Virtue' is understood dramatically, like Astrophel's sarcasm, other phrases too may acquire ironic force. Do 'some' call Stella's virtue *only* her 'face' or outward show?[47] Does Astrophel consciously imagine theological grace leaving Stella as she grants him a favour? Does he regard her as not just 'stately' but vain, incapable as she is of seeing anything her superior? At least in Astrophel's view the choice of an opaque material for the windows (Cupid's doing, not Nature's) may be a little ridiculous. No wonder Queen Virtue can see so little.[48]

Appreciation of *Astrophel and Stella* 1 depends no less heavily on multiple relations of tenor and vehicle. No reader will get far without grasping that poetical composition is simultaneously allegorised as childbirth ('came forth . . . great with child') and as stumbling ('came halting . . . wanting Invention's stay'). The first *allegoria* develops a traditional personification of Nature as the mother of Art by making Invention (also a traditional mother of Art) a would-be assistant at the birth, prevented from helping by Study (only a stepmother, since she unlike Nature cannot produce anything new).[49] The second *allegoria* presents the words associated with Study. They stumble, whether from *vieux-jeux* decrepitude or unsteady inexperience, against the obstacle of other poets' irrelevant models (metrical 'feet').[50] Invention, again, cannot help, inhibited as she is by the daunting regime of laborious Study. We have to notice at least the entangle-

ment of these metaphors, before we can appreciate Astrophel's
passion, let alone Sidney's art:

> But words came halting forth, wanting Invention's stay,
> Invention, Nature's child, fled step-dame Study's blows,
> And others' feet still seemed but strangers in my way..
> Thus great with child to speak, and helpless in my throes,
> Biting my truant pen, beating my self for spite,
> 'Fool', said my Muse to me, 'Look in thy heart and write'.

Two or more discourse sets (childbirth and first or second childhood)
separately resemble Astrophel's difficulties of expression when he
allows Invention to be neglected. The vehicular chains are linked by
pun ('came forth'), by shared personifications ('Study', 'Invention'),
and perhaps by a scheme of Ages of Man corresponding to stages of
composition in the tenor. But they remain distinct metaphors, as their
non-sequential arrangement – with postnatal tripping followed by
throes of childbirth – makes plain. Here, figurative structure is more
than a display of Sidney's penchant for ambiguity: it deliberately
mimes the impatient disorder of Astrophel's mind.[51]

We have discussed only two forms of compound metaphor: Spenser's
complex embedded conceits, and Sidney's doubled vehicles or tenors.
But other forms were also cultivated. Michael Drayton, in particular,
produced a great variety, including multiple conceits, and a circular
complex type in which the distant vehicle returns to literal tenor
discourse:

> All fence the tree which serveth for a shade,
>   Whose great grown body doth repulse the wind,
> Until his wasteful branches do invade,
>   The straighter plants, and them in prison bind,
>   Then like a foul devower of his kind:
> Unto his root all put their hands to hew,
> Whose roomth but hinder other which would grow.   [52]

This *allegoria* [in his *Mortimeriados*] for human orgulousness obviously
becomes complex metaphor when the figurative tree is itself likened,
because of its habit, to a human traitor. Similarly, *invade* and *prison*
introduce complex metaphors, since they are figurative words so far
as arboreal discourse is concerned. However, they also return to
literal discourse, in which powerful barons might well invade and
imprison. Several circular conceits come within the few stanzas

190   A. FOWLER (1975):   ON CONCEITS (SPENSER, SIDNEY, DRAYTON)

narrating Edward II's subterranean mission. Perhaps the finest is an evocation of

> These gloomy lamps, by which they on were led,
>   Making their shadows follow at their back,
> Which like to mourners, wait upon the dead,
>   And as the dead, so are they ugly black,
>   Like to the dreadful images of wrack;
> These poor dim-burning lights, as all amazed,
> As those deformed shades whereon they gazed.   53

Here *wrack*, revenge, is quite literally the journey's purpose, so that the second vehicle reverts to the first tenor. The recursive comparisons of *Mortimeriados* sometimes achieve remarkable compression, as in the hyperbole praising the queen: 'That lily hand, rich Nature's wedding glove'.[54] To say that such poetry contents the eye is true, but it is also a staggering oversimplification.

It would not be difficult to carry this review of metaphoric types a great deal farther. But we must beware: classifying Elizabethan conceits easily works against their grain of unexpectedness, their proclivity to surprise precisely by the copiousness of their formal obliquity.

SOURCE: extract from *Conceitful Thought: The Interpretation of English Renaissance Poems* (Edinburgh, 1975), pp. 87–103.

NOTES

[Resystematised, retaining numbering, from the original – Ed.]

1. E.g., the bibliography in K. K. Ruthven *The Conceit* (1969), pp. 61–4, which lists twice as many studies in the later period.

2. R. Tuve, *Elizabethan and Metaphysical Imagery* (Chicago 1947), p. 6.

3. Generic descriptions include L. C. John, *The Elizabethan Sonnet Sequences: Studies in Conventional Conceits* (New York 1938) and K. K. Ruthven, 'The Poet as Etymologist', *Critical Quarterly*, II (1969), pp. 9–37. Shakespeare is only partly an exception: J. M. Nosworthy, e.g., finds 'altogether too much of the working out of conceits' – S. Wells (ed.), *Shakespeare: Select Bibliographical Guides* (London, 1973), p. 48.

4. J. A. Mazzeo, *Renaissance and Seventeenth-Century Studies* (New York, 1964), chs 1, 2; also his 'A Critique of Some Modern Theories of Metaphysical Poetry', in W. R. Keast (ed.), *Seventeenth-Century English Poetry* (New York, 1962), pp. 63–74.

5. Mazzeo, in Keast, pp. 65–9.

6. Ibid., p. 73.

7. See: ibid., pp. 63–4; F. A. Yates, 'The Emblematic Conceit in Giordano Bruno's *De gli eroici furori* and in the Elizabethan Sonnet Sequences', *J. of the Warburg Institute*, 6 (1943), pp. 101–21, and *Giordano Bruno and the Hermetic Tradition* (London, 1964); and L. S. Lerner & E. A. Gosselin, 'Giordano Bruno', *Scientific American*, 228 (April 1973), pp. 86–94.

8. Mazzeo, *Studies*, p. 43.

9. F. T. Prince, 'The Sonnet from Wyatt to Shakespeare', in J. R. Brown & B. Harris (eds), *Elizabethan Poetry* (London, 1960), pp. 18–19.

10. A. Tate, *Reactionary Essays* (New York, 1936), p. 74, cited in Tuve, *E. & M. Imagery*, p. 216 n.; J. H. Hagstrum, *The Sister Arts* (Chicago and London, 1958), p. 100. On the indispensable terms *vehicle* and *tenor*, taken from I. A. Richards, see D. M. Miller, *The Net of Hephaestus* (The Hague and Paris, 1971), p. 42.

11. E. A. Warren, *Richard Crashaw: A Study in Baroque Sensibility* (Baton Rouge, La., 1939), p. 177, discussed by Mazzeo, 'A Critique' in Keast, p. 70.

12. Mazzeo, ibid., rightly deprecates stress on visualisation; as does Tuve, *E. & M. Imagery*: ch. 5, 'The Criterion of Sensuous Vividness'.

13. Spenser, *Amoretti*: Variorum text; orthography modernised but not punctuation – *Complete Works* (Variorum), ed. E. Greenlaw et al. (Baltimore, Md, completed 1949, rev. edn 1958).

14. See *OED*: s.v. *Gentle* – A 1 'noble', A 1d 'excellent', A 3 'generous, courteous'.

15. See Guy de Tervarent, *Attributs et symboles dans l'art profane, 1450–1600*: s.v. *Chêne*, col. 91.

16. *OED*: s.v. *Gentle*, A 4 cites Holland (1601): 'the gentle garden cornel tree'; and Shakespeare, *Winter's Tale* [IV iv 93]: 'We marry / A gentler scion to the wildest stock'.

17. Possibly punning *divide* = 'share' (*OED*: 8b) and = 'give out in all directions' (*OED*: 8c, but with no earlier example). Several other puns in the sonnet are discussed in W. C. Johnson, 'Spenser's *Amoretti* 6', *Explicator*, 38 (1971).

18. M. P. Tilley (ed.), *Dictionary of Proverbs* . . . (Ann Arbor, 1950): H 309, e.g., 'my heart is as sound as a bell, heart of oak' (1609); and T 496, e.g., 'It is but a simple oak, that [is] cut down at the first stroke' (1477), and 'It is not one stroke that can fell an oak' (1631). Submerged idioms like these often make local intention uncertain: cf. Miller (note 10 above), pp. 58, 80, 86.

19. *OED*: s.v. *Aspire*, 5 'mount up'; also *ad fin.*, =*Expire*, e.g. Hellowes (1574): 'Christ aspiring upon the cross'; cf. Johnson, *Poetaster* [I i 83–4]: 'Then, when this body falls in funeral fire, / My name shall live, and my best part aspire.'

20. See Tervarent, col. 184: s.v. *Flamme*, 5, a funerary motif expressing death's finality. On the fire of love, see Mario Praz, *Studies in Seventeenth-Century Imagery* (Rome, 1964), Index: s.v. *Fire*; *Flame*; *Cupid (Love) as stoker*; *Cupid blows the coals*.

192   A. FOWLER (1975):   ON CONCEITS (SPENSER, SIDNEY, DRAYTON)

21. G. K. Hunter, 'Spenser's *Amoretti* and the English Sonnet Tradition', in J. M. Kennedy & J. A. Reither (eds), *A Theatre for Spenserians* (Toronto and Buffalo, 1973), pp. 134, 139; cf. pp. 142–3. L. L. Martz has fortunately felt the need to defend Spenser's sonnets against the objection that they lack 'wit and compression'; the brilliant result is his 'The *Amoretti*: "Most Goodly Temperature"', in W. Nelson (ed.), *Forms and Convention in the Poetry of Edmund Spenser* (New York, 1961), pp. 146–68.

22. Hunter, in Kennedy & Reither, pp. 142–3; cf. J. W. Lever, *The Elizabethan Love Sonnet* (London, 1956), pp. 102–3: 'Why then did Spenser confound two distinct ways of writing?' For reasons why sonnets should be regarded as stanzas, see: (a) A. Dunlop, 'Calendar Symbolism in the *Amoretti*', *Notes and Queries*, 214 (1969), pp. 24–6, and 'The Unity of Spenser's *Amoretti*', in A. Fowler (ed.), *Silent Poetry: Essays in Numerological Analysis* (London, 1970), pp. 153–69: (b) T. P. Roche, in C. Ricks (ed.), *English Poetry and Prose, 1540–1674* (London, 1970), pp. 101–18; (c) W. C. Johnson, 'Rhyme and Repetition in Spenser's *Amoretti*', *Xavier University Studies*, 9 (1970), pp. 15–25; (d) A. Fowler, *Triumphal Forms: Structural Patterns in Elizabethan Poetry* (Cambridge, 1970), ch. 9.

23. *OED*: s.v. *Band*, sb I 1 'fetter'; I 2 'loose tie', e.g., Shakespeare, *Venus and Adonis*, st. 38, 'Her arms infold him like a band'; I 2b 'the cords crossing the back of a book' (no example before 1759, but cf. *Bind*: v. III 11, common from c. 1400).

24. I use *compound metaphor* in the sense defined in G. N. Leech, *A Linguistic Guide to English Poetry* (London, 1969), pp. 159–61 (the 'overlapping of two or more individual metaphors'), but distinguish *complex* (embedded) metaphors and *double* or multiple metaphors with more than one vehicle or tenor. Contrast *compound* in Miller (note 10, above), p. 131. Leech's account is useful; though adequate description would have to deal with grammatic and semantic aspects of chains of discourse, considered literally and metaphorically.

25. See Fowler, *Triumphal Forms* (note 22, above), pp. 38–61. Superstructural effects allowed by congruent comparison offset the arguments against congruence of C. Brooks & W. K. Wimsatt – *Literary Criticism: A Short History* (New York, and London, 1957) – e.g., that reliance on positive metaphor leads to *cliché*. See Miller, pp. 96–7, 196; also p. 123, arguing that Neocritical criteria inevitably favoured Metaphysical poetry. Advantages of positive metaphor include a larger creative role for the reader (ibid., p. 133) and (I would add) greater communicative possibilities.

26. See Ruthven (note 1, above), pp. 20–2.

27. Martz (note 21, above), pp. 152ff., finds the relationship characterised by a rare mutuality of affection. *Amoretti* 17 uses the ambiguous application of *trembling* again.

28. On the summation schema, see Ernst Robert Curtius, *European*

Literature and the Latin Middle Ages, trans. W. R. Trask (London, 1953), pp. 289–90.

29. R. Southall, 'Love Poetry in the Sixteenth Century', *Essays in Criticism*, 22 (1972), p. 377.

30. See esp. *Ezekiel* 27.3 ('O Tyrus, thou hast said, I am of perfect beauty') and 27.6, 12, 16, 22, listing ivory, silver, emeralds and gold. In *Revelation* 18.11–12 'the merchants of the earth' are to regret former merchandise of gold, silver, pearls and ivory. For analogues, see Variorum edn (note 13, above), *Minor Poems*, II pp. 424–5. Closest is Desportes, *Diane* 1.32, where the riches are perhaps allegorised as 'graces'; cf. also G. Marino's elegiac variation, *Rime* (Venice, 1608), 1.153: 'le perle, e i rubini e l'ostro, e l'oro/Dove dove son hor? .../Quante ricchezze un picciol marmo involve,/Quant'honor ...'. W. Drummond of Hawthornden – *The Poetical Works*, ed. L. E. Kastner, 2 vols (Edinburgh and London, 1913), I p. 52 – imitates both Marino and *Amoretti*: 'Those pearls, those rubies, which did breed desire,/Those locks of gold, that purple fair of Tyre,/Are wrapt (aye me!) up in eternal night'. His mention of Tyre shows appreciation of Spenser's biblical allusion.

31. Allegorising *Ezekiel* 28.13: 'Thou has been in Eden the Garden of God: every precious stone was in thy garments, the ruby . . . the sapphire, emerald, and the carbuncle and gold [side-note: "my people Israel which shined as precious stones"]' – Geneva version. Following *Genesis* 2.10–12, which connects gold and bdellium (Geneva note: 'or pearl') with the River Pison, the 4 rivers of Paradise were correlated with the cardinal virtues (Pison with Prudence): e.g., Philo, *De leg. alleg.*, 1.19–20, trans. F. H. Colson & G. H. Whitaker, vol. I (New York, and London, 1929), pp. 187–9; Jerome, *Comm. in Ezech*, in J. P. Migne, *Patrologia Latina*, xxv, pp. 270–1 (identifying the jewels of *Ezekiel* 28.11ff., *Isaiah* 54.11–13, *Revelation* 21 as the sacerdotal stones and Gifts of the Spirit); and (still) Valeriano 21.13: pp. 254–5. Also cf. 2 *Chronicles* 9 on mutual gifts of Solomon and Sheba: esp. verse 21, 'gold, and silver, ivory'.

32. Aristotle, *Poetics* 1457 b 11: see Ruthven, p. 5.

33. *OED*: s.v. *Belamour*, 2 e.g., G. Fletcher, *Christ's triumph after death*, st. 48: 'eyes,from whence are shed / Infinite belamours, where to express / His love'. Gerard's *Herbal* lists several flowers with *bell* in their name, including one also called Venus's looking-glass. See Drayton, *Polyolbion* 15.170ff. – *Works*, ed. J. W. Hebel et al. (2nd edn, Oxford, 1962), IV, pp. 307–8 – for a description of Isis's bridal crown: groups of red roses, gillyflowers and pinks as specifically garden flowers, suitable for the bride. On the columbine's theological symbolism, see G. Schiller, *Iconography of Christian Art*, trans J. Seligman (London, 1971), I, p. 51.

34. *Les blasons anatomiques du corps féminin . . . composez par plusieurs poètes contemporains* (1550), ed. A. [van] B[ever] (Paris, 1907), itself a blazon of erotic

blazons: cf. Marot's *Blason du beau tétin*: 'Une fraise, ou une cerise, / Que nul ne voit, ne touche aussi'; and *Faerie Queene*, vi 8 42: 'Her paps, which like white silken pillows were'.

35. Cf. Du Bartas, trans J. Sylvester (1592–99), p. 563: 'Sapphires, cure eyes'. But the correlation of sapphires with eyes was common.

36. *OED*: s.v. *Face, sb* iii 12b.

37. *OED*: s.v. *Furniture*, 1a 'the action of accomplishing a design'; 1b 'embellishing'; 5b 'intellectual faculties, mental furniture', e.g. Dekker (1609): 'That quality is . . . the only furniture to a courtier'.

38. *OED*: s.v. *Front*, ii 6; cf. i 1 'forehead'; i 3a 'demeanour'. *Cheeks* could mean the side pieces (cf. 'porches') of a doorway (*OED* 9). Alabaster was the pure receptacle of the ointment of faith: see Rabanus Maurus on *John* 12.3, in Migne (note 31, above), cvii, pp. 1101–2; and cf. Sidney, *Old Arcadia*, Poem 62, line 80 (Robertson edn, p. 240; Ringler edn, p. 88): 'a spotless mine of alabaster'; cf. also Diana's oratory in Chaucer's *Knight's Tale*, i (a), 1910.

39. *OED*: s.v. *Grace*, ii 8 & 16b. Grace was a blazon item: see *Les blasons anatomiques* (note 34, above), p. 85.

40. On the amorous blazon, see Ruthven, 'The Composing Mistress' (relating it to schemes of planetary gifts) in op. cit. (note 1, above); Sidney, *Poems* (Ringler edn), p. 410; R. L. Montgomery, *Symmetry and Sense: The Poetry of Sir Philip Sidney* (New York, 1969), p. 125; M. B. Ogle, 'The Classical Origin and Tradition of Literary Conceits', *American J. of Philology*, 34 (1913),. pp. 125–52.

41. See Sidney, *Poems* (Ringler edn), pp. 463–4, which rightly identifies these touch eyes with Sonnet 91's 'seeing jets', and so detects electrostatically-charged lignite. *OED*: s.v. *Touch*, sb ii 6 'touchstone'; vb i 24 'stir the feelings'; sb ii 'magnetising'; vb i 6c 'magnetise by rubbing with a magnet'; sb i 1a, b 'physical touch', 'sexual contact'. See Alan Sinfield, 'Sexual Puns in *Astrophel and Stella*', *Essays in Criticism*, 24 (1974), p. 346.

42. *OED*: s.v. *Touch*, vb i 7 'affect injuriously'; sb iii 14 'moral perception'.

43. *OED*: s.v. *Light*, sb 8a, b 'moral luminary'; *Touch*, vb i 8a 'test the fineness of (esp. gold or silver)'. Jet was also used in the ancient guilt-divining ritual of axinomancy.

44. *OED*: s.v. *Light*, sb i 4a 'spark igniting any combustible substance' (earliest example, 1684); s.v. *Touch*, sb iv 21 'touch-powder'; and s.v. *Touch-powder*.

45. B. Twyne's contemporary misreading (Bodleian ccc, ms 263, fols 114b–120; quoted in Ringler edn of Sidney's *Poems*, pp. 463–4) shows him ready to fault the reasoning – perhaps Astrophel's, however, not Sidney's.

46. *Court of Love*: Sidney would have read this in Stowe's Chaucer (1561), fol. 348ff. See *Chaucerian and Other Pieces*, ed. W. W. Skeat (Oxford, 1897), p. 411.

47. *OED*: s.v. *Face*, sb ii 10 'outward show; factitious appearance; pretence'.

48. In confirmation, 'Gold is the covering of that stately place' indicates a House of Pride; cf. too 'windows of kindness', *Quio amore langueo*, st. 13. But contrast *Isaiah* 51.11–12, a key text for the blazon subgenre: 'I will make thy windows of emeralds [Authorised Version, "agates"], and thy gates shining stones' – Geneva version.

49. On Natura and Invenzione as mothers of art in Vasari, see E. Panofsky, *Renaissance and Renascences in Western Art* (New York and London, rev. edn, 1972), p. 31, n.2. Sidney may follow Ficino's genealogy, in which Natura's first-remove images claim seniority both to *natura naturata* and to art's imitations: Plato, *Opera omnia additis Marsilii Ficini ... commentariis* (Basel, 1561), p. 683, the fine passage beginning 'ascende age Platonice contemplator ... ad naturam formarum eiusmodi genetricem'. By this metaphysic, the poet's image of Stella had independent status.

50. The reference to the sonnet's un-English alexandrines makes a further pun.

51. Taine's notorious account of *Astrophel and Stella* as the expression of Sidney's obsession ('in every extreme passion ordinary laws are reversed. . . . Our logic cannot pass judgement on it. . . . Common sense and good language cannot penetrate') would not be ridiculous if we read 'Astrophel' for 'Sidney': Taine, *History of English Literature*, trans. H. van Laun (Edinburgh, 1873), I, p. 169. For a recent discussion, see R. A. Lanham, '*Astrophel and Stella*: Pure and Impure Persuasion', *English Language Review*, 2 (1972), pp. 100–2.

52. *Mortimeriados*, 2282–5: in Drayton, *Works*, ed. J. W. Hebel et al. (Oxford, 2nd rev. edn, 1962), I, p. 374. Either *devower = devourer*, or it means 'one who devows, i.e., gives up by oath, sacrifices'. A typical instance of multiple comparisons comes at *Mortimeriados*, 2423ff.; Hebel et al. edn, I, p. 378.

53. Ibid., 2465–71; Hebel et al. edn, I p. 379.

John Hollander   The Case of Campion
(1975)

... By the 1580s, a variety of poetic conventions had become assimilated to the notion of 'lyric poem', including 'sonnets' in both the strict and loose senses (that is, the familiar fourteen-line iambic pentameter poems as well as any short, Petrarchan love poem), epigrams, pastoral lyrics, and so forth. A musician (as Donne puts it in 'The Triple Fool'), 'his art and voice to show,/Doth set and sing my pain' – and composers frequently raided miscellanies and anthologies as well as published books and poems in manuscript. Almost any poem might, after publication, show up in a musical setting, sometimes altered for the convenience of the composer.

Although the composers of these songbooks used to be credited, in older and unscholarly anthologies, with the words to their songs, this was rarely the case. Except for an occasional amusing anomaly, like Captain Tobias Hume in his *Poetical Music*, there is only Thomas Campion to maintain, in the English Renaissance, the ancient traditions of the poet-composer. The reputation of another such figure, Chaucer's great contemporary Guillaume de Machaut, has undergone a strange revision in the last fifty years. Before then, philological scholars thought of him as a lyric poet, and it is only modern musicology that has shown how much more interesting his ballades, virelais and rondeaux were as musical structures than as verse patterns. In short, Machaut is ranked as one of the great composers, and his musical glory has eclipsed his fame as a poet.

Not so with Campion. As a composer he is idiomatic and graceful, seldom tactless but seldom inspired. He worked within the framework of the strophic air always, and never responded to the influence of the new Italian *stilo recitativo* like Alfonso Ferrabosco, or developed an insistent and personal chromaticism, like John Daniel (brother of the poet Samuel, who refuted Campion's prosodic theories). Neither did he, like John Dowland – who was a virtuoso lutenist of great fame – do anything remarkable with his lute accompaniments: for the most part, they lie easily under the hand, with a minimum of fugal writing and a rather four-square texture.

His minor talents as a composer are most exposed, perhaps, when we can compare his setting of one of his own texts with that of another composer. In the case of a little song from Campion's fourth book,[1] we have just such an opportunity. The text itself works through a rather hackneyed Elizabethan theme, but presents one feature of interest for the setting:

> I must complain, yet doe enjoy my Love.
>   She is too faire, too rich in bewty's parts.
> Thence is my grief; for Nature, while she strove
>   With all her graces and divinest arts
> To form her too too beautifull of hue,
> She had no leasure left to make her true.

The degree of enjambment of the third line would hardly be noticeable were it not for the exigencies of setting, where in the style Campion usually employs, a musical period coincides with a line. Not only is Dowland's setting superior in every way – the lute accompaniment, for example, is polyphonic and inventive – but the better composer approaches the transition from line 3 to line 4 with great musical and metrical sophistication. His lute accompaniment covers the enjambed break 'strove/With' by a rapidly moving figure, but picks out the *contre-rejet* 'With' with a single bass note. It is a bit of musical setting that would correspond almost exactly to a sophisticated oral performance of the poem. And yet this all occurs within the convention of the Jacobean strophic lute song: this is not yet a matter of the breaking up of lines of verse into syntactic and rhetorical units by the kind of declamatory setting that comes to be a Caroline vogue (settings of Carew by Lawes would be a case in point).

But as a master of the structure of the stanzaic lyric song text, Campion is unsurpassed in English. He is Sidneyan to the degree that he is absorbed with elements of what the earlier poet called *architectonike* – the patterning and symmetry of parts of language: lines, grammatical structures, stanzas, and so forth. He is Jonsonian in his response to Latin lyric and elegiac poets, rather than to Sidney's shaping Italian. But he is in a different lyric world from John Donne's, dominated as it is by a rhetorical necessity which overrides repetitive stanzaic principles in the generation of its rhythms and its images. 'Strong lines' was the seventeenth-century critical term for metaphysical verse of the Donne tradition. Campion's remain always smooth.

But by no means weak. If his model was not the skewed, the emphatic and the paradoxical, it remained all the more the delicate, the precise and the epigrammatic. We tend to think of epigram or aphorism primarily in terms of written inscriptions, rather than chant or song – and indeed, Classical tradition assigned epigram to the metre of the elegiac couplet. Yet there were lyrical poems – like the Anacreontea – which Renaissance writers assimilated to such poems as those of the Greek Anthology, and it is not strange to find Campion remarking as follows about the poetic form he made his own:

Short Ayres, if they be skilfully framed, and naturally exprest, are like quicke and good Epigrammes in Poesie, many of them shewing as much artifice, and breeding as great difficultie as a large Poeme.

Let us look at an instance of this. Catullus's famous lyric 'Vivamus, mea Lesbia, atque amemus' was a background text for many seventeenth-century poems of erotic invitation. Shakespeare reworked some of it in *Venus and Adonis*. Ben Jonson's adaptation of it occurs first as a song in *Volpone* and later in his selection of his own favorite poems called *The Forest*. It was set by Ferrabosco . . . but it remains most powerful as a spoken text [quotes 'To Celia': reproduced in full in McPeek's study, excerpted in this collection, above – Ed.] . . .

Campion's reworking of the same Latin original is another matter. Here, he abandons Catullus after the first strophe, and turns the *nox est perpetua una dormienda* from the middle of the poem into a slightly varying refrain, seeing in it unfulfilled lyrical and expository possibilities:

> My sweetest Lesbia let us live and love,
> And though the sager sort our deedes reprove,
> Let us not way them: heavn's great lamps doe dive
> Into their west, and strait againe revive,
> But soone as once set is our little light,
> Then must we sleepe one ever-during night.
>
> If all would lead their lives in love like mee,
> Then bloudie swords and armour should not be,
> No drum nor trumpet peaceful sleepes should move,
> Unles alarme came from the campe of love:
> But fooles do live, and wast their little light,
> And seeke with paine their ever-during night.
>
> When timely death my life and fortune ends,
> Let not my hearse be vext with mourning friends,
> But let all lovers rich in triumph come,
> And with sweet pastimes grace my happie tombe:
> And Lesbia close up thou my little light,
> And crowne with love my ever-during night.

This is the *carpe diem* theme further humanised and matured by an awareness of the *memento mori* aspect of it: the vision of dying in love, and for it, and having love made on one's tomb, is a sweeter one than we find in Jonson's 'let us do it while we can', or, later on in the century, the sardonic energy of Marvell's 'To his Coy Mistress'.

In this poem, too, it is as if the stanzaic limitation were a source of creative energy for Campion, rather than a restraint. Throughout the corpus of songs we can see this energy at work – whether in a hymn, like the lovely 'Never Weather-Beaten Saile', a magic spell like 'Thrice Toss These Oaken Ashes in the Aire', or a half-parodic comment on the burning brands of Eros in 'Fire, Fire, Fire Fire'. The development of a theme and its disposition throughout the successive strophes is always his forte. Take, for example, the justly famous 'Cherry-Ripe', which takes off from the most common of street cries, the '*Cherry ripe ripe ripe!*' of the cherry vendor, sung, as we know from other early seventeenth-century evidence, through an ascending third . . . [from B to D in the treble clef, above middle C – Ed.] Whether the sung phrase as Campion recalled it suggested the garden conceit (Herrick wrote a little poem starting with the same repeated words of the street cry), or whether it crept in as the basic image was unfolding, the result was a wonderful transformation of a whole series of commonplaces:

> There is a Garden in her face,
> Where Roses and white Lillies grow;
>   A heav'nly paradice is that place,
> Wherein all pleasant fruits doe flow.
>   There Cherries grow, which none may buy
>   Till Cherry ripe themselves doe cry.
>   Those Cherries fairly does enclose
>
> Of Orient Pearle a double row;
>   Which when her lovely laughter showes,
> They look like Rose-buds fill'd with snow.
>   Yet them nor Peere nor Prince can buy,
>   Till Cherry ripe themselves doe cry.
>
>   Her Eyes like Angels watch them still;
> Her Browes like bended bowes doe stand,
>   Threatning with piercing frownes to kill
> All that attempt with eye or hand
>   Those sacred Cherries to come nigh,
>   Till Cherry ripe themselves doe cry.

In the first strophe, we may let the significance of 'heav'nly paradice' go by, thinking it a mere hyperbole as conventional as the roses and lilies of the blazon, or Petrarchan catalogue of delights – the red of feeling and the white of purity which combine in the 'carnation' or flesh tone in emblematic color language (the Elizabethans seem not to have had our term 'pink'). We may even miss an echo in the use of

'flow' for 'abound', of the Biblical 'flowing with milk and honey', seeing only the image extending through the refrain: the lady's lips, which alone are able to say 'yes' for her, are like wares that advertise themselves. But then, in the second stanza, both rosebuds filled with snow and pearl jewels growing in a vegetative garden underline the neglected 'paradice'. Here are all seasons at once, and the natural and artificial are confounded: we are in the neighborhood of the earthly paradises of Spenser and his followers. The final stanza, in which the cherries become 'sacred' and assimilated mythologically to the golden apples of the Hesperides, shows us the garden as being angelically protected (the old Petrarchan cliché about frowning eyebrows being like drawn bows is redeemed in this new association). The courtly compliment now turns out to be central moral vision: the only *paradiso terrestre* or Earthly Paradise is to be found in beautiful sexual attainment, in the plucking of cherries that are no forbidden apples, and just for that reason, such attainment isn't always easy. Campion's stanzaic development has served the imaginative purpose of taking seriously what might be, in a weaker song by a less serious and joyful singer, a bit of lyrical rhetoric.

In his musical setting of the poem in his *Fourth Booke of Ayres*, Campion cannot help but work in the melodic phrase of the street cry itself into his refrain. Imitative and referential bits of musical setting like this abound in later Elizabethan and Jacobean musical practice, and Campion employs them occasionally with a certain amount of delight. Thus

> When to her lute Corinna sings,
> Her voice revives the leaden stringes,
> And doth in highest noates appeare,
> As any challeng'd echo cleere;
> But when she doth of sorrow speake,
> Ev'n from my hart the strings do breake.

and there is an expressive downward turn of the vocal line underlined by a chordal sweep on the lute to suggest the breaking strings.[2] The second strophe, incidentally, moralises the anecdote in conventional fashion, applying it to the poet's own feelings, and concluding with a familiar Elizabethan invocation of 'heartstrings' (the term's literary popularity resulted from a Latin pun on *cor, cordis*, 'heart', and *chorda*, 'string'). But the musical setting of the first stanza must remain effective for the second, and the heartstrings must 'break' as well, the figurative heartbreak echoing the anecdotal damage to the instrument:

> And as her lute doth live or die,
> Led by her passion, so must I,
> For when of pleasure she doth sing,
> My thoughts enjoy a sodaine spring,
> But if she doth of sorrow speake,
> E'vn from my hart the strings doe breake.

Many of Campion's songs concern, or involve imagery about, music and its effects as celebrated in mythology, for example: 'Follow Your Saint'; 'To Musicke Bent Is My Retyred Minde'; 'Tune Thy Musicke to Thy Hart'; 'To His Sweet Lute Apollo Sung the Motions of the Spheres'; and much in the masques and court entertainments celebrate music and thereby, given Campion's personal and learned Neo-classical association of the two, of poetry as well. Even in his metrical version of the 137th Psalm ('By the waters of Babylon'), Campion pays special attention to the musical possibilities of 'We hanged our harps upon the willows in the midst thereof', and gives us

> Aloft the trees, that sprung up there,
> Our silent Harps wee pensive hung

playing deliciously on the etymological connection of 'pensive' and the Latin *'pendere'*: 'to hang'.

Even, too, the metrical example, 'Rose-cheekt Lawra' – surely the most successful 'exercise' qua poem, in our tradition – affirms a Platonistic correspondence between actual and ideal, based on an avowed relation between heavenly harmony and human music:

> Rose-cheekt *Lawra*, come
> Sing thou smoothly with thy beawties
> Silent musick, either other
>   Sweetely gracing.
>
> Lovely formes do flowe
> From concent divinely framed;
> Heav'n is musick, and thy beawties
>   Birth is heavenly.
>
> These dull notes we sing
> Discordes neede for helps to grace them;
> Only beawty purely loving
>   Knowes no discord:
>
> But still mooves delight,
> Like cleare springs renu'd by flowing,
> Ever perfect, ever in them-
>   selves eternall.

This beautiful little poem occurs in Campion's cranky *Observations in the Art of English Poesie*, a treatise on poetic metre whose attack on rhyme and championing of Classical prosody over native English verse structure seems pointless to us today. The Elizabethans are, after all, our poetic Greek and Latin poets – the English past is our linguistic and imaginative antiquity, the iambic pentameter is our Classical verse. But at the end of the sixteenth century, the desire to legitimise a national English literature by giving it good Classical credentials still led some poets and critics to espouse a literal adoption of the quantitative metres of Greek and Latin poetry. . . .

*

Campion was a loyal Neo-classical ideologue in the controversies about metrics. In his preface, To the Reader, in his 1601 book of airs, he speaks slightingly of the normal English accentual-syllabic verse in which all his airs but one are composed; they are, he says, 'after the fascion of the time, eare-pleasing rimes without Arte'. Fortunately, he never rode his hobbyhorse over the living bodies of his songs. Even in his treatise, he adapts the prevailing sort of quantitative written coding of English so that his 'long' syllables are always the ones bearing the stress accent of the word. 'Rose-cheekt Lawra' is therefore merely an unrhymed English trochaic poem, perfectly plain to the ear. Campion's one song in Classical metres which concludes his first book of airs, 'Come let us sound with melody the praises' is set for voice and lute, with note values corresponding to syllable length, in a fashion followed in Byrd's setting mentioned above, perhaps derived from a French tradition. But his unerring sense of iambic rhythm and its controlled rhetorical possibilities prevailed over his schematic beliefs.

That rhythmic sense is everywhere paralleled by other modes of stylistic tactfulness – of degree and depth of allusion to Classical models and themes; of length to which a conceit is drawn out; of the subjugation of wit and literary ambition to the limits of the song form he could make his own. His conventional Petrarchan vocabulary and imagery of love are never used mechanically, and his wit never allows empty gesture to depose verbal act. I can think of no better example of Campion's lyrical good humor than his ability to undercut even his own conventional delicacy with an equally graceful anti-Petrarchan move in the self-parodying 'Beawty, since you so much desire' from the fourth book. With its chaste original, 'Mistris, since you so much desire' from the 1601 book, the one idealising, the other faintly bawdy, we are shown two sides of the same Elizabethan coin.[3] To have been unable to toss it and cope with head or tail at equal ease would have evidenced a want of invention and a false decorum from which Campion, in all the limitations of his poetic chamber music,[4] can never be said to suffer.

SOURCE: extract from *Vision and Resonance: Two Senses of Poetic Form* (New York and London, 1975), pp. 73–81, 89–90.

NOTES

[Reorganised and renumbered from the original – Ed.]

1. It will be observed that Campion's poems, largely because they were published in songbooks, do not have titles, as do Donne's *Songs and Sonets*.
2. See the discussion of these lines in Rosemund Tuve, *Elizabethan and Metaphysical Imagery* (Chicago, 1947), p. 15.
3. [*Ed.*] The opening stanzas of the two poems are:

> Mistris, since you so much desire
> To know the place of Cupids fire,
> In your faire shrine that flame doth rest,
> Yet never harbourd in your brest;
> It bides not in your lips so sweete,
> Nor where the rose and lillies meete,
> But a little higher, but a little higher:
> There, there, O there lies Cupids fire.

> Beauty, since you so much desire
> To know the place of Cupids fire:
> About you somewhere it doth rest,
> Yet never harbour'd in your brest,
> Nor gout-like in youre heele or toe;
> What foole would seeke Loves flame so low?
> But a little higher, but a little higher,
> There, there, o there lyes Cupids fire.

4. I do not mean hereby to slight the beautiful rhythmic textures of Campion's verse, nor its internal 'music' of assonance and alliteration. These patterns have been analysed in an excellent article by John T. Irwin in *Studies in English Literature*, x (1970), 121–41.

204

Philip Hobsbaum   'Elizabethan Poetry: A Revaluation'   (1979)

Elizabethan poetry has remained under a cloud for generations. There can be few who have not opened their Palgrave and experienced a familiar sinking of the spirits on encountering this:

> Spring, the sweet spring, is the year's pleasant king;
> Then blows each thing, then maids dance in a ring,
> Cold doth not sting, the pretty birds do sing,
> Cuckoo, jug-jug, pu-we, to-witta-woo! . . .
>
> [from *Summer's Last Will and Testament*, c. 1592]

That, in little, represents the traditional view of Elizabethan poetry. It also presents us with a summary of its defects: a forced jollity, a conscientious simplesse, a conventionalised view of nature. The very imitation of the nightingale – 'jug-jug' – seems to us ludicrous now. This is a sophisticated writer pretending to rustic simplicity.

One's feelings about Elizabethan sophistication are confirmed on going through the first book of Palgrave's *Golden Treasury* (1861). There is the aureate diction of 'Phoebus, arise' by William Drummond of Hawthornden (1616), and Thomas Lodge's conventionalised portrait of Rosalynde (1590) with sapphire eyes and rosebud lips. Nor will the reader be reassured by this:

> Diaphenia like the daffadowndilly,
> White as the sun, fair as the lily,
> Heigh ho, how I do love thee!
> I do love thee as my lambs
> Are belovéd of their dams;
> How blest were I if thou would'st prove me. . . .
>
> [from *England's Helicon*, 1600]

This is attributed to Henry Constable, and he was the nineteenth-century's idea of an Elizabethan poet, if one can judge by his representation in anthologies of the period. The melting diction, the pretty-pretty images would appeal to a taste which regarded women as legless angels. There is an area in which Petrarch and Dante Gabriel Rossetti meet; but there is no need for us to inhabit it now.

This kind of poetry has, for the most part, been rejected by the educated reader; but with it, tacitly, has gone the entire corpus of Elizabethan verse. The usual account would term it aureate, accomplished, conventionalised, pastoral – very much in the line of

> Or, che'l ciel e la terra e'l vento tace,
> E le fere e gli augelli il sonno affrena,
> Notte'l carro stellato in giro mena,
> E nel suo letto il mar senz' onda giace;
> Veggio, penso, ardo, piango; e chi mi sface,
> Sempre m'è innanzi per mia dolce pena
>
> [Petrarch, c. 1340s]

which appears in one of Drummond's sonnets as

> While sleep, in triumph, closed hath all eyes,
> And birds and beasts a silence sweet do keep,
> And Proteus' monstrous people in the deep,
> The winds and waves, hushed up, to rest entice;
> I wake, muse, weep, and who my heart hath slain
> See still before me to augment my pain.
>
> [from *Poems*, 1616]

What is sweet in Petrarch becomes, in Drummond, saccharine. This form of polished elegance has never sat easily on English verse, and may be regarded as an excrescence, and not only in the sixteenth century. One sees Wyatt struggle against it, Surrey succumb to it, Sidney make it popular, and Spenser bring it to a climax in the purple passages of *The Faerie Queene*. And yet the Petrarchan convention is a by-line in Elizabethan verse. Behind the major poetry of the period is the earthy force of the great alliterative poems of the Middle Ages – *Piers Plowman* and *Sir Gawain and the Green Knight*.

This may seem a surprising point to make, in view of the usual account of medieval poetry: that it came to a halt with the Wars of the Roses and that therefore it was necessary for English poets to look abroad for their technique. There was no need for Wyatt to tether his genius to the Italianate school of Petrarch, and in fact he is at his best when he departs most sharply from his master. Few admirers of 'Whoso list to hunt' know that it is an adaptation from 'Una candida cerva sopra l'erba'; and why should they? Wyatt is at his best when he aggregates Petrarch and Alamanni to his proverbial and earthy Englishness. And this is occasionally true, also, of his much lesser contemporary Surrey – who is a poet only in his all-too-few glimpses of a personal past.

But Surrey proved to be the more popular of the two, and his lack of confidence in the native tradition affected later poets adversely. And so we find the bulk of verse in this period betraying a certain instability, between native speech and Italianate polish. That which tends towards the latter is far inferior. No doubt modern anthologists would disagree with me here: the *Oxford Book of Sixteenth Century Verse* (1932) showed remarkably little advance upon the Victorian taste of Palgrave. Like Palgrave, Sir Edmund Chambers favoured lyric at the expense of satire and translation; even though these were forms at least as central to the Elizabethan temperament. There was all the more reason, then, to welcome Edward Lucie-Smith's *Penguin Book of Elizabethan Verse* (1965), which represented Constable and Nashe very sparingly, showed a totally unexpected side of Lodge, and left out Drummond of Hawthornden altogether.

Clearly Lucie-Smith was not interested in the Petrarchan line of aureate diction, any more than the quasi-Petrarchan mock-simplesse. What did he put in its place? Well, with all his percipience, he was to some extent under the spell of another heresy – that of the scholars, who now are almost alone in reading Elizabethan poetry. They talk about the 'plain style' and Elizabethan 'classicism', without in either case appearing to know what they are committing themselves to. Classicism is a word without reference to the context of English literature, and the plain style is bearable only if it is not dull. But Daniel, Drayton and Davies – poets whom Lucie-Smith seemed to admire – are frequently dull; and it was poets such as these that F. R. Leavis deprecated when, in the first chapter of *Revaluation* (1936), he spoke of 'respectable figures who . . . serve at any rate to set up a critically useful background'. As against these, Leavis applauds Donne, whom we read 'as we read the living'.

Unfortunately this, and the fact that Leavis begins his book at the seventeenth rather than the sixteenth century, has been taken as a general condemnation of all that went before Donne. Students have been left with the idea that Donne set up a welcome revolution against large, heavy, critically respectable figures; who need no longer be read, because they have been superseded.

Certainly the Elizabethans had few other poets of Donne's stature – has any period? – but those they had were impressive: Shakespeare and Jonson are as much the last great poets of the sixteenth century as the initiating forces behind the seventeenth. And though Donne himself was characteristically forward-looking, and can hardly be called an Elizabethan without some qualifications, his restless intellect brought to a fine focus much that was troubling other poets of this transition period.

One could make a rough division between those Elizabethans who died before the new century and those who survived it. Sidney and Spenser spent their lives mastering the Petrarchan convention; but, in comparison with these, Chapman and Greville seem grown-up, disillusioned, grave – in a good sense of the word, serious poets. It is, therefore, a pity that Leavis lumped these two together with Drayton et al. as 'critically respectable figures'; and that Lucie-Smith, in his anthology, represented them all in much the same way. The fact is that Daniel, Drayton and Davies are dull sticks that sometimes rub up against a few sparks of poetry, while Chapman and Greville, together with Marston and Ralegh, are major poets by any reckoning; and their work is neglected.

One reason for this is certainly the nineteenth-century anthologists' fixation upon the sweet and conventionalised treatment of love. Another is the twentieth-century academics' respect for the dull. Chapman, Marston, Ralegh and Greville get caught in the cross-fire. And yet a third reason is the curiously British reluctance to consider any but watertight categories of literature as being acceptable.

Chapman, for example, was one of the great playwrights of his time, itself the crux of our drama, and perhaps its greatest translator. His finest poetry is found in these two connections; much of his 'original' work is digressive, rhetorical and obscure. A case for Chapman's political tragedies can hardly be made from extracts; it is rather to the translations that we must turn for an idea of his poetic texture. The *Odyssey* (1611–16) is far superior to the *Iliad* (1598–1611), which would not now attract so much attention if Keats had not praised it; but both are thoroughly English poems – far more so than *The Faerie Queene*, for instance. Translation acted upon Chapman as a discipline; and it was a discipline that he thoroughly understood. Perhaps his greatest single poem is the explanation of his methods which he prefixed to his version of the *Iliad*. Here the poetic interest comes in the numerous similes, rammed with life, which act out his meaning. This sample from it is aimed savagely at the stupid public that hankers after rubbish. The whole section, in fact, is the working out of a double pun upon the meanings of 'ass' and 'taste':

> But as an ass, that in a field of weeds
>   Affects a thistle, and falls fiercely to it;
> That pricks, and galls him; yet he feeds, and bleeds;
>   Forbears a while, and licks; but cannot woo it
> To leave the sharpness; when (to wreak his smart)
>   He beats it with his foot; then backward kicks,
> Because the thistle galled his forward part:
>   Nor leaves till all be ate, for all the pricks
>   . . .
>   So, in this world of weeds, you wordlings taste
> Your most-loved dainties; with such war, buy peace;
>   Hunger for torments; virtue kick for vice;
> Cares, for your states, do with your states increase:
>   And though you dream you feast in Paradise,
> Yet Reason's daylight shows ye at your meat,
>   Asses at thistles, bleeding as ye eat.

This is hardly a 'respectable' attitude, nor is it 'classical'; but it is certainly very considerable poetry. The subject-matter does not seem, in the abstract, rewarding – the translation of poetry is hardly an obvious theme for poetry itself. Yet the truth is that Chapman feels the theme so powerfully that all kinds of telling metaphors rush into his mind; and there can be no doubt that, in his poetry, the life is in the metaphor. Here, for example, the ass is observed with lifelike realism: 'Affects a thistle, and falls fiercely to it'. That word 'fiercely' gives us at once the savagery of the beast and of its appetite. Without reaching out of the context, the ass nevertheless takes on a life of its own. Its agonies and temptations are felt sharply: so richly understood that it gives the poet the authority to condemn, from the inside so to speak, an ass's tastes.

This poetic realism is the chief weapon of a number of poets who can be loosely associated with Chapman: in particular Jonson and Marston. After Eliot and Leavis and, more recently, Mr Johnston's edition (1954) and Mr Trimpi's study (1962), it may be taken that a cultivated reader would regard Jonson as a great non-dramatic poet, as well as the greatest English writer of comedies. But it is still worth saying that Jonson's vein of savagery was always controlled; and that, when he, like Chapman, castigated his audience, he knew exactly what he was doing:

> Say that thou pour'st 'hem wheat,
> And they would acorns eat:

> 'Twere simple fury still thy self to waste
>   On such as have no taste:
> To offer them a surfeit of pure bread
>   Whose appetites are dead:
>   No, give them grains their fill,
>   Husks, draff to drink and swill:
> If they love lees, and leave the lusty wine,
> Envy them not, their palate's with the swine.

This is from Jonson's 'Ode to Himself' (1629). And it proves that great learning in the Elizabethan period went along with a racy and idiomatic command of English. The alliterative clusters – 'grains', 'fill', 'husks', 'draff', 'drink', 'swill' – show Jonson within hailing distance of the medieval morality. This vein is never more manifest in Jonson than when he is reviling the unlearned masses. And here we may remember that Jonson, like Chapman, was an Elizabethan who lived on into another, and less appreciative, age.

This didn't prevent their friend and collaborator, John Marston, from doing the same sort of thing in his earlier years. Marston has some claim to be the most neglected major figure of the period, mainly because he is persistently regarded primarily as a playwright. He was, indeed, a most original dramatist, and Shakespeare found *The Malcontent* (c. 1600) worth study, as the many echoes of Marston in *Hamlet* go to show. But Marston's best poetry comes only as flashes in his tragedies, which will never again be read as wholes. For more sustained work we must turn to his satires.

The Scourge of Villainy (1598) has an unfortunate reputation for being coarse and savage: Hall's satires are rated far higher. May I say here that Marston's satires are not unworthy of comparison with those of Donne; and both these poets, racy and idiomatic, leave Hall standing sententiously on the sidelines? Marston knows no restraint, not even that of Chapman, and he speaks of satire not as a task but as a joyful duty:

> Fie, Satire, fie! shall each mechanic slave,
> Each dunghill peasant, free perusal have
> Of thy well-laboured lines? Each satin suit,
> Each quaint fashion-monger, whose sole repute
> Rests in his trim gay clothes, lie slavering,
> Tainting thy lines with his lewd censuring?
> . . .
> Fie! wilt thou make thy wit a courtesan

> For every broken handcraft's artisan?
> Shall brainless cithern-heads, each jobbernoll,
> Pocket the very genius of thy soul?

This associates itself with John Donne's account of the broken-down adventurer in his Satire IV (1597):

> Sleeveless his jerkin was, and it had been
> Velvet, but 'twas now, so much ground was seen,
> Become tufftaffatie   . . .

It has also something in common with the medieval Scots poet William Dunbar describing the courtiers in his 'Complaint to the King' (c. 1500): 'foul jow-jowrdane-hedit jevellis, / cowkin kenseis and culroun kevellis . . .'. One is reminded of Swift denouncing the Irish Parliament in his 'Legion Club' (1736), or Joyce Cary in *The Horse's Mouth* (1944) on the subject of the British government: 'the belly ripping abortionist, the batter-brained, cak-handed, wall-eyed welsher, the club-foot trampler, the block-eared raper that would sell its sister for a cheer . . .'. To be in the ambience of Dunbar, Swift and Cary is to be in a central tradition of satire. Marston exhibits the dual quality we saw in Jonson, and in Chapman, too: a keen knowledge of society and a violent revulsion from it – both characteristics of Elizabethan satirists at their best. Notice the detail in the passage from Marston. It is so vivid as to seem fascinated by what it denounces. The 'dunghill peasant' is attacked along with the gay suit, the courtier known only by his clothes, themselves subject to meaningless changes of fashion. And notice, too, the earthiness of the language – 'cithern-heads', 'jobbernolls'. The people are reduced to caricatures by the very vehemence with which they are described.

But it would be a mistake to regard Marston as being merely negative. There is a positive force even in the ingenuity and vividness of his condemnation; and the concept of the soul, merely stated here, finds realisation in other poems. In his eighth satire, for instance, Marston represents the stupidity that he hates in people as a natural characteristic of the body. Reason, a superior being, naturally flies from so vile a tenement:

> Our adverse body, being earthly, cold,
> Heavy, dull, mortal, would not long enfold
> A stranger inmate, that was backward still
> To all his dungy, brutish, sensual will:
> Now hereupon our intellectual,

Compact of fire all celestial,
Invisible, immortal, and divine,
Grew straight to scorn his landlord's muddy slime;
And therefore now is closely slunk away
Leaving his smoky house of mortal clay,
Adorned with all his beauty's lineaments
And brightest gems of shining ornaments,
His parts divine, sacred, spiritual,
Attending on him. . . .

The denunciation here is sharpened and particularised by means of Marston's fictional invention: soul identified with reason, reason as tenant of the dungy body. The poetry arises out of this conflict; and it is not too far-fetched to say that Marston felt himself an unwanted inmate of a foul society, as the 'reason' which he describes fights against the 'adverse body' which constricts it.

Easiness, directness, pithiness, then, are characteristics of the best Elizabethan poetry; and in such a context Donne and Jonson seem at home. This is a native English tradition; and, because of that, it can afford to assimilate a good deal of foreign material, as the great translations of the period show. But there is a distinction to be made here. Sidney, Spenser, Constable and Drummond, imitating Marino, Guarini, Petrarch and the rest, sought to Italianise their subject-matter. The great translators, on the other hand, assimilated foreign material into their English, essentially medieval and alliterative, tradition.

The first, and nearly the best, of these translators was Wyatt. One has only to consider his famous version of Seneca's attack on public life, 'stet quicunque volet potens', to see how he racks the dignified Latin into the urgency of personal statement – 'Stand whoso list upon the slipper top . . .' (c. 1530s). And H. A. Mason, in his excellent study of early Tudor poetry (1959), has pointed out how the received and conventional 'ignotus moritur sibi' is replaced with what seems to be an eye-witness account of a hanging:

himself, alas,
Doth die unknown, dazed, with dreadful face.

There is a great distinction between this and Surrey's glacial version of Virgil. Wyatt's major translation, however, is that of the Penitential Psalms (c. 1530s). This has the same dramatic felicity as the poem just quoted, even though it comes after Alamanni and Aretino:

> O Lord I dread, and that I did not dread
> I me repent and evermore desire
> Thee, thee to dread . . .

This, in its obsessively involuted rhythms, looks forward to Donne's 'Hymn to God the Father' (1623):

> When thou hast done, thou hast not done
> For I have more.

And, between these two great poems, there is a body of incomparable work, technically translation, but in fact the most inventive writing of the period.

Some of it has proved a little too inventive for the critics. Richard Stanyhurst's version of the *Aeneid* (1582), for example, was treated as a joke even by so discerning a reader of Elizabethan verse as W. A. Edwards (*Scrutiny*, 1933). [And see Saintsbury's comments, in Part Two, above – Ed.] I suppose one might say that Stanyhurst's accounts of battle are inclined to melodrama –

> In person Pyrrhus with fast-wrought twi-bill in handling
> Down beats with pealing the doors, and post-metal heaveth
> . . .

– though even here there is a dramatic appropriateness in the onomatopoeia and inversion. But Stanyhurst is probably at his best in country scenes, such as Aeneas's first sight of the fertile terrain of Carthage, with its 'clustrous herd-flock . . . in green frith browsing'. Another example is the Royal Hunt in Book iv. After contrasting the 'rustical hoblobs' with the 'Lucifer-heavenly-in-beauty Aeneas', Stanyhurst goes on:

> Then lo, behold ye, breaking, the goats do trip from the rock-tops
> Near to the plain; the herd deer doth stray from mountain unharboured,
> The chase is ensued with passage dusty bepowdered.
> But the lad Ascanius, with prancing courser high-mounted,
> Doth manage in valley, now them, now these over-ambling.
> He scorns these rascal tame games, but a sounder of hogsters
> Or the browny lion to stalk fro mountain he wisheth.
> . . .

The freshness and authenticity of this annoyed Stanyhurst's Dutch editor, who apologised for his tendency to dress Trojan subjects in an English garb. And Professor Van Der Haar (1933 edition) went on to say that Stanyhurst added over 400 words to the language. This alone would be a striking achievement; but what impresses me, however, is the great translator's pithiness and proverbial quality of speech – 'a sounder of hogsters', 'seams up the bedmatch', 'stand ye to your tacklings'. For all his coinage of new words and coupling of old ones, Stanyhurst's English is, at its best, as vivid as that of Hopkins. And, like Hopkins, he demonstrates that one need not be static in order to write within a tradition.

But most readers will find the translations of Arthur Golding more easy and direct. And, indeed, Ezra Pound praised Golding sixty years ago ('Notes on Elizabethan Classicists', 1917) for his freshness and felicity, although for the greater part of its existence Golding's Ovid (1565–67) has remained inaccessible to the general reader. This freshness is perhaps best seen in his numerous rural descriptions. For example:

> . . . country carles were gathering there these osier twigs that grow
> So thick upon a shrubby stalk, and of these rushes green,
> And flags that in these moorish plots so rife of growing been.
> . . .

There is surely no need to apologise for the English setting of these poems? Golding does not Latinise his diction into pseudo-Ovid; rather he regards it as his task to supply a local referent for Ovid's Latin. He does not translate his original so much as give him an English equivalent. Here, for example, Golding fully lives up to the Roman poet in providing us with a startling example of metamorphosis – Thracian women turned into trees:

> But everyone was stayed
> With winding root which held her down: her frisking could not boot.
> And while she looked what was become of toe, of nail, and foot,
> She saw her legs grow round in one, and turning into wood.
> And, as her thighs with violent hand she sadly striking stood,
> She felt them tree; her breast was tree; her shoulders eke were tree,
> Her arms long boughs ye might have thought, and not deceived be.
> . . .

Possibly the reader may feel that Golding is a little circumscribed, as Chapman was in his *Iliad*, by his chosen metre and rhyme. But this is certainly not a charge that could be brought against John Harington, the author of several pithy epigrams, but primarily the translator (*ante* 1591) of the sixteenth-century Italian poet Ariosto. This, far more than Fairfax's Tasso (1600), stands in urgent need of dissemination;

for it is an English classic. Unlike Fairfax, Harington absorbs his Italian masters and has no need for Spenser as an intermediary:

> For at the chink was plainly to be seen
>   A chamber hanged with fair and rich array
>   Where none might come but such as trusty been.
>   The Princess here in part doth spend the day,
>   And here he saw a dwarf embrace the Queen
>   And strive awhile, and, after homely play,
>   His skill was such that ere they went asunder
>   The dwarf was got aloft, and she lay under.

This is a more urbane poetry than that of Stanyhurst and Golding; urban, too – it serves to remind us how constant the colloquial mode of satire was from this English version of Italian mock-heroic to Byron:

> And Julia's voice was lost, except in sighs,
>   Until too late for useful conversation.
>   The tears were gushing from her gentle eyes;
>   I wish indeed they had not had occasion,
>   But who, alas, can love and then be wise?
>   Not that remorse did not oppose temptation;
>   A little while she strove and much repented,
>   And whispering, 'I will ne'er consent' – consented.
>   [*Don Juan*, Canto I (1818–20)]

As with Byron, there is a kind of mocking irreverence about Harington's work, both 'original' and 'translated'. He may begin with a gesture in the direction of Spenser; but, whereas Fairfax would have carried it on as elaborate simile, in Harington it is included only to be debunked:

> Astolfo, whilom King of Lombardy,
>   To whom his elder brother left his reign,
>   Was in his youth so fresh and fair to see
>   As few to such perfection could attain.
>   Apelles' match or Zeuxis' he might be,
>   That such a shape could paint without much pain.
>   Great was his grace, and all the world so deemed it,
>   But yet himself of all men most esteemed it.

This mocking quality carries on, too, into Harington's epigrams (*ante* 1618). I have said that Harington is urbane, but it would be a mistake to think that he is therefore uprooted from his country of origin:

'Clowns, and not courtiers, use to go by clocks.'
'Courtiers by clocks', said I, 'and clowns by cocks.'

And it is remarkable how close the Court was to the country: London in those days still retained traces of the market town and was surrounded by fields and farms. So one can say that the courtliest verse of the period is that which retains something of a proverbial pithiness. Here, for example, is Harington's epigram directed at his wife, who claimed that she was too old to dance:

Well, Mall, if needs thou wilt be matron-like,
Then trust to this, I will a matron like.

But the wit gravitates to a moving treatment of married love:

Be in my house as busy as a bee,
Having a sting for everyone but me,
Buzzing in every corner, gathering honey,
Let nothing waste, that costs or yieldeth money.
And when thou seest my heart to mirth incline,
The tongue, wit, blood, warm with good cheer and wine,
Then of sweet sports let no occasion 'scape,
But be as wanton, toying as an ape.

Though smaller in scale, this is the same world as that of Jonson's 'Penshurst' and 'Inviting a Friend to Supper': the tone is witty and judicial, but the country is never far away. . . .

SOURCE: extract from ch. 3, 'Elizabethan Poetry', in *Tradition and Experiment in English Poetry* (London and Basingstoke, 1979), pp. 68–81.

SELECT BIBLIOGRAPHY

This bibliography does not include works from which extracts have been taken, nor those referred to in the notes. Works of individual authors are not difficult to locate, so under TEXTS I have listed useful collections and anthologies of Elizabethan verse. Under CRITICISM some works, marked with an asterisk, are introductory and general, others more specialised. For detailed information about studies of writers and topics the student should consult *The New Cambridge Bibliography of English Literature*, vol. I (Cambridge, 1974), the series of bibliographies which appear in the journal *English Literary Renaissance*, and the annual guides prepared by the journals *Publications of the Modern Language Association* (*PMLAA*) and *Studies in English Literature 1500–1900*.

TEXTS

N. Ault (ed.), *Elizabethan Lyrics* (London, 1925).

E. Doughtie (ed.), *Lyrics From English Airs 1596–1622* (Cambridge, Mass., 1970).

M. Evans (ed.) *Elizabethan Sonnets* (London, 1977).

E. H. Fellowes (ed.), *English Madrigal Verse 1588–1632*, revised and enlarged by F. W. Sternfeld and D. Greer (Oxford, 1967).

J. W. Hebel and H. Hudson (eds.), *Poetry of the English Renaissance* (New York, 1929).

G. G. Hiller (ed.), *Poems of the Elizabethan Age* (London, 1977).

E. Lucie-Smith (ed.), *The Penguin Book of Elizabethan Verse* (Harmondsworth, 1965).

S. Minta (ed.), *Petrarch and Petrarchism: The English and French Traditions* (Manchester, 1980).

H. E. Rollins (ed.), *Tottel's Miscellany (1557–1587)*, revised edition (Cambridge, Mass., 1966).

CRITICISM

* P. J. Alpers (ed.), *Elizabethan Poetry: Modern Essays in Criticism* (Oxford, 1967).

G. Braden, *The Classics and English Renaissance Poetry* (New Haven, Conn., 1978).

* D. Bush, *Mythology and the Renaissance Tradition in English Poetry* (Minneapolis, 1932).

J. Buxton, *Sir Philip Sidney and the English Renaissance* (London, 1954).

D. J. Gordon, *The Renaissance Imagination*, ed. S. Orgel (Berkeley, Cal., 1975).

S. J. Greenblatt, *Sir Walter Ralegh: The Renaissance Man and his Roles* (New Haven, Conn., 1973).

* C. Ing, *Elizabethan Lyrics* (London, 1951).

D. Kalstone, *Sidney's Poetry: Contexts and Interpretations* (Cambridge, Mass., 1965).

J. Kerman, *The Elizabethan Madrigal: A Comparative Study* (New York, 1962).

G. F. Little and S. Orgel (eds.), *Patronage in the Renaissance* (Princeton, N. J., 1981).

J. Mazzeo, *Transformations in the Renaissance English Lyric* (Ithaca, N.Y., 1970).

W. Nelson (ed.), *Form and Convention in the Poetry of Edmund Spenser* (New York, 1961).

* D. L. Peterson, *The English Lyric From Wyatt to Donne* (Princeton, N.J., 1967).

* C. Ricks (ed.), *English Poetry and Prose 1540–1674* (London, 1970).

* I. Rivers, *Classical and Christian Ideas in English Renaissance Poetry* (London, 1979).

L. Zocca, *Elizabethan Narrative Poetry* (New Brunswick, N.J., 1950).

NOTES ON CONTRIBUTORS

JOSEPH ADDISON (1672–1719): periodical essayist, poet and dramatist; he had a strong influence on eighteenth-century taste in literature.

WILLIAM BALDWIN (fl. 1547): Oxford scholar, co-deviser with George Ferrers (Henry VIII's 'Master of the King's Pastimes') of *A Mirror for Magistrates*, an anthology by various authors on historical-tragical subjects.

ARTHUR E. BARKER: formerly Professor of Renaissance Literature, University of Western Ontario; his books include *Milton and the Puritan Dilemma, 1641–1660* (1942).

EDMUND BOLTON (?1575–?1633): historian and poet, who contributed poems to *England's Helicon* (1600). His grand idea, supported by James I, was for the establishment of a royal academy, but this collapsed because of Charles I's lack of interest.

THOMAS CAMPION (1567–1620): Cambridge graduate, poet, composer and physician; as well as his celebrated poems and 'Airs', he also wrote masques for court and aristocratic occasions.

SAMUEL TAYLOR COLERIDGE (1772–1834): poet and critic, co-doyen with Wordsworth of the Romantic movement in English poetry.

SAMUEL DANIEL (1562–1619): Oxford graduate, poet and playwright, diplomat and courtier.

DONALD DAVIE: poet and critic; previously Professor of English, University of Essex, and (since 1978) Andrew W. Mellon Professor of the Humanities, Vanderbilt University. His *Collected Poems* appeared in 1972. His critical works include *Purity of Diction in English Verse* (1952) and *Thomas Hardy and British Poetry* (1972); a collection of his essays, *The Poet in the Imaginary Museum*, was published in 1977, and a volume of autobiography, *These the Companions*, in 1982.

T. S. ELIOT (1888–1965): poet, dramatist and critic.

SIR WILLIAM EMPSON: poet and critic. Emeritus Professor of English, University of Sheffield; he earlier taught at Cambridge and held chairs in

Pastoral (1935) and *Milton's God* (1961); and his *Collected Poems* appeared in 1955.

ALASTAIR FOWLER: Regius Professor of Rhetoric and English Literature, University of Edinburgh, since 1972. Editor of *Paradise Lost* in the 'Longman Annotated English Poets' series (1968), among his critical works are *Spenser and the Numbers of Time* (1964) and *Triumphal Forms: Structural Patterns in Elizabethan Poetry* (1970).

GEORGE GASCOIGNE (1539–77): Cambridge undergraduate (not graduating); poet and playwright, soldier, courtier and member of parliament.

SIR JOHN HARINGTON (1560–1612): Cambridge graduate; poet and courtier; translator and satirist in verse and prose, he wrote with wit and penetration on a wide range of subjects (including sanitary appliances and contemporary public affairs).

WILLIAM HAZLITT (1778–1836): essayist, critic and political publicist; his critical writings on the Elizabethans (especially Shakespeare) had an important influence on literary appreciation in the nineteenth century.

PHILIP HOBSBAUM: poet and critic; Reader in English, University of Glasgow. His poetry includes *Coming Out Fighting* (1969) and *Women and Animals* (1972). He is the editor of *Ten Elizabethan Poets* in the 'Longmans English' series (1969).

JOHN HOLLANDER: poet and critic; Professor of English at Yale University, and co-editor of the *Oxford Anthology of English Literature* (1973). His poetry includes *Movie Going and Other Poems* (1962) and *The Figure of Echo* (1981).

G. K. HUNTER: formerly Professor of English, University of Warwick, and now Professor of English at Yale. He edited the Casebook on *Henry IV, 1 & 2*, and his editions of Shakespeare plays include *All's Well That Ends Well* in the New Arden series, and *King Lear* and *Macbeth* for the Penguin Shakespeare series.

BEN JONSON (1572–1637): dramatist and poet; he was also influential as a critic and as a counsellor of younger writers ('the tribe of Ben').

JOHN KEATS (1795–1821): poet, with a particular admiration for the Elizabethan achievement in literature.

JAMES MCPEEK: formerly Professor of English, University of Connecticut. He is the author of *Catullus in Strange and Distant Britain* (1939) and *The Black Book of Knaves and Unthrifts in Shakespeare and Other Authors* (1959).

LEONARD NATHAN: poet and critic; Professor of Rhetoric, University of California at Berkeley, since 1968. His poetic works include *Glad and Sorry Seasons* (1963), and among his critical writings is *The Tragic Drama of W. B. Yeats* (1965).

EDWARD PHILLIPS (1630–?96): elder nephew of Milton (not to be confused with John Phillips, the poet's younger nephew); tutor to children of upper-class families – including John Evelyn's – his philological dictionary, *New World of Words* (1658), was celebrated in his day.

EZRA POUND (1885–1972): poet and critic; a leading figure, with T. S. Eliot, in the modern movement of the first half of the twentieth century.

GEORGE PUTTENHAM (d. 1590): a pioneer of literary criticism in England, though *The Arte of English Poesie* (1589) is ascribed by some to his elder brother, Richard.

I. A. RICHARDS (1893–1979): poet and critic; he taught at Cambridge and Harvard; in 1964 he was made a Companion of Honour, and Honorary Fellow of Magdalene College, Cambridge (where in earlier years he had been a colleague of C. K. Ogden, helping in the development of 'Basic English'). His *New and Selected Poems* appeared in 1978, and his critical writings include *Principles of Literary Criticism* (1924) and *Practical Criticism* (1929).

GEORGE SAINTSBURY (1845–1933): literary critic and historian; Professor of Rhetoric and English Literature, University of Edinburgh (1895–1915). His many works include *A Short History of English Literature* (1887), *A History of Criticism* (1900–4), *A History of English Prosody* (1906–10), and writings on wine which are still highly regarded.

SIR PHILIP SIDNEY (1554–86): Oxford undergraduate (not graduating); poet, soldier and courtier.

BARBARA HERRNSTEIN SMITH: Professor of English and Communications, University of Pennsylvania. Her critical works include *On the Margins of Discourse* (1978).

HALLETT SMITH: Professor of English (1949–75), California Institute of Technology. His books include *Shakespeare's Romances* (1972) and *The Tension of the Lyre* (1982).

RAYMOND SOUTHALL: formerly teaching in the University of Sheffield, he is now Professor of English, University of Wollongong, Australia. His publications include *Literature and the Rise of Capitalism* (1973).

ALGERNON CHARLES SWINBURNE (1837–1909): poet and critic; his writings in criticism include *Essays and Studies* (1875), *Miscellanies* (1886), monographs on Shakespeare and other dramatists, and articles on poets and playwrights in contemporary editions of the *Encyclopaedia Britannica*.

WYLIE SYPHER: formerly Professor of English, Simmons College, Boston, Massachusetts. His publications include *Rococo to Cubism in Art and Literature* (1960).

RICHARD TOTTEL (d. 1594): publisher, best-known for his compilation (with Nicholas Grimald) of *Songes and Sonnettes* (1557), more generally known as Tottel's *Miscellany*.

ROSEMOND TUVE (1903–64): was Professor of English, University of Pennsylvania. Her critical writings include *Elizabethan and Metaphysical Imagery: Renaissance Poetic and Twentieth-Century Critics* (1947), *A Reading of George Herbert* (1952) and *Images and Themes in Five Poems by Milton* (1957).

THOMAS WARTON (1728–90): poet and critic; Professor of Poetry, Oxford (1757–67) and Poet Laureate; in addition to his *History of English Poetry*, his critical works include *Observations on the 'Faerie Queene' of Spenser* (1754).

YVOR WINTERS (1900–68): poet and critic, was Professor of English, Stanford University. His works include *In Defense of Reason* (1947), *The Function of Criticism* (1957), *Forms of Discovery: Critical and Historical Essays on the Forms of the Short Poem in English* (1967) and *Collected Poems* (1952, revised and enlarged 1960).

ACKNOWLEDGEMENTS

The editor and publishers wish to thank the following who have given permission for the use of copyright material: Arthur E. Barker, extract from essay 'An Apology for the Study of Renaissance Poetry' in *Literary Views* (1964), editor Carroll Camden, by permission of The University of Chicago Press; Donald Davie, 'Syntax as Music in the Poetry of Thomas Sackville' from *Articulate Energy* (1955), by permission of Routledge & Kegan Paul Ltd; T. S. Eliot, extracts from *The Use of Poetry and the Use of Criticism* (1933), by permission of Faber & Faber Ltd, and from *The Sacred Wood* by permission of Methuen & Co. Ltd; William Empson, extract from *Seven Types of Ambiguity* (1953), by permission of Chatto and Windus Ltd; Alastair Fowler, extract from *Conceitful Thought* (1975), by permission of the author and Edinburgh University Press; Philip Hobsbaum, extract from *Tradition and Experiment in English Poetry*, by permission of the author; John Hollander, extracts from *Vision and Resonance: Two Senses of Poetic Form*, copyright © 1975 by Oxford University Press Inc., reprinted by permission of the publishers; G. K. Hunter, extract from essay 'Drab and Golden Lyrics of the Renaissance' from *Forms of Lyric: Selected Papers from the English Institute* (1970), by permission of The English Institute, Inc., Columbia University Press, and the author; James A. S. McPeek, extract from *Catullus in Strange and Distant Britain* (1939), by permission of the author and Harvard University Press, copyright 1939 by the President and Fellows of Harvard College, copyright © 1967 by James A. S. McPeek; Leonard Nathan, essay 'Gascoigne's "Lullabie" and Structures in the Tudor Lyric' in *The Rhetoric of Renaissance Poetry* (1974) by permission of University of California Press; Ezra Pound, extract from *Make it New: Essays by Ezra Pound* (1934), by permission of Faber and Faber Ltd; I. A. Richards, extract from 'The Sense of Poetry: Shakespeare's "The Phoenix and the Turtle"' in *Poetries: Their Medias and Ends*, by permission of Mouton Publishers; Hallett Smith, extract from *Elizabethan Poetry* (1966), by permission of Harvard University Press, copyright © 1952 by the President and Fellows of Harvard College, © 1980 by Hallett Smith; Barbara Herrnstein Smith, extract from *Poetic Closure* (1968), by permission of the author and The University of Chicago Press; Raymond Southall, 'The Decline of Court Poetry' from *The Courtly Maker*, by permission of Basil Blackwell Publisher Ltd; Wylie Sypher, extract from *Four Stages of Renaissance Style*, copyright 1955 by Wylie Sypher, by permission of Doubleday & Company Inc.; Rosemund Tuve, extract from *Elizabethan and Metaphysical Imagery* (1947), by permission of The University of Chicago Press; Yvor Winters, extracts from essay 'The Sixteenth Century Lyric in England: A Critical and Historical Reinterpretation' in *Poetry*, vol. III (1939), by permission of Mrs Janet Lewis Winters and The Modern Poetry Association.

INDEX

Figures in **bold** typography denote material in this Casebook.

FOR READERS' NOTES

FOR READERS' NOTES

FOR READERS' NOTES